LOVE, WAGES, SLAVERY

BARBARA RYAN

Love, Wages, Slavery

THE LITERATURE OF SERVITUDE

IN THE UNITED STATES

UNIVERSITY OF ILLINOIS PRESS

URBANA AND CHICAGO

#631082917

A book subvention for this project was provided by
University Scholars Programme, National University of
Singapore.

Library of Congress Cataloging-in-Publication Data

Ryan, Barbara, 1958–
   Love, wages, slavery : the literature of servitude in the
United States / Barbara Ryan.
   p.   cm.
Includes bibliographical references and index.
ISBN-13: 978-0-252-03071-0 (cloth : alk. paper)
ISBN-10: 0-252-03071-0 (cloth : alk. paper)
   1. Domestics—United States—History.   2. Master and
servant—United States—History.   3. Domestics in
literature.   I. Title.
HD6072.2.U5R94   2006
331.7'61640460973   2006000321

Contents

Introduction

. . . as to the idea of a faithful servant, it is all a fiction.
—Catherine Anne Devereux Edmondston, diary entry
(1863)

Historians of the nineteenth-century United States have long recognized that Northern homemakers complained about "free" servitors. Many were the wage payers, then, concurring with the New England mistress who judged that "there is none good, no not one." More recently, scholars have noted that Southern mistresses voiced grievances, too: "I believe my servants are going to craze me," an Alabama woman reported of attendants who were enslaved.[1] Though the conditions of "free" and chattel attendance were distinct enough that these assertions may seem unequally yoked, comparable gripes reveal tension about in-house staff that was not restricted to either side of the Mason-Dixon Line. Responding to the tension, from the 1820s on, sentimental didacts taught that service relationships could and ought to be family-like. Histories of U.S. manners have masked the prevalence of such counsel by emphasizing instructions to consider servants understood to be "essential actors of the household" as "nonetheless . . . not members of the family, figures to be relied upon but 'nonpersons' to be socially ignored." When, however, the source of information is not etiquette guides but advice about household government that might be read in the North or South, the ideal was quite different. The ideal, in this counterdiscourse, was an attendance remarkable for "the strong bond existing between faithful servants and the families with whom they are connected."[2]

Today, this standard is likely to be associated with proslavery prop-
aganda. Yet it was promoted quite fervently, for much of the nineteenth
century, by sentimental writers who decried that subset of servitude.
Thus, nearly all who tackled the so-called servant problem shared the
notion that family-*like* labor was the right model for in-house staff.
This espousal may seem to rest on assumptions too obvious to require
explanation. Yet probing work by Jeanne Boydston suggests that early
U.S. gestures toward "that most endearing union of interest and affections—called a *family*"—helped assuage concern about women's civic
role and men's economic agency.[3] While there was precedent for speaking of servants as "family," there was nothing inevitable about continued use of this term, as thoughts on householding, productive and
"free" labor, as well as rank, race, and gender roles altered over the
course of the nineteenth century. Nor was there anything ultimately
stable about what the term "family" connoted, even among those who
promoted this standard most assiduously.

It was never settled, for instance, what family-likeness had to do
with race or ethnicity: "Oh these white servants!" groans a letter of
1847. "But there is trouble with all."[4] Nor was the balance between parentlike discipline and parentlike nurturing of a dependant's potential
ever calibrated decisively, any more than consensus was reached about
the family-likeness of immigrants in need of nonkin homes, relative to
that of native-born attendants. In vagueness, it is fair to infer, lay the
roots of sentimental counsel's nationwide and long-lived appeal. "Let
us, as masters, not be hindered from rendering to our slaves that which
is just and equal," a Mississippi minister taught in 1836. "They are 'our
households.'"[5] Twenty years later, a mistress in Michigan agreed.
Though Elizabeth Sullivan Stuart found her own servants annoying
(and frequently complained about them, with no trace of shame), she
counseled her grown daughter to "remember, *abidingly* remember,"
that mistresses stood in loco parentis to nonkin staff. Problematic—and
not only to today's eyes—is the implication offered by *Scribner's
Monthly Magazine* in 1873 that "in manners and social training servants are as children" in the homes of those whose leisure, comfort, and
cleanliness they supplied.[6] More was at stake, though, than the matura-
bility of service workers in visions of the family-likeness of coresidential cooks and maids. Most obviously, variant conceptualizations of
"family" life were being folded into U.S. thought even as incommensu-
rable understandings of slavery—as well as "free" and "bound" labor—
were affirmed along with a span of gender, race/ethnic, and status roles.
Last but not least, ideas about advice literature and its practitioners

were broached and challenged, first by male writers but later by the first generation of U.S. women to earn college degrees.

Certainly, complaints about servants had been recorded in the British North American colonies, too. But complaints signified differently once U.S. legislators voted to permit some laborers to leave their posts, pro rata wages in hand, on their own say-so.[7] This innovation was odd enough to warrant notice from a visiting Briton. "There is no power given you, as a master," he reported in 1805, "to confine a hired servant by law: that is one part of their liberty and equality."[8] Three years later, a Scot expressed nostalgia for the immobilized attendance of her childhood in the colony of New York. "These negroe-women," she recalled, "piqued themselves on teaching their children to be excellent servants, well knowing servitude to be their lot for life, and that it could only be sweetened by making themselves particularly useful, and excelling in their department."[9] This vision could have raised grim smiles among the delegation of Virginia mistresses who drafted a legislative appeal in 1831 in which they asked to be released "from servitude to their quondam slaves." Yet as long as slaveholders muted laments about "uppish" chattel and visitors such as Alexis de Tocqueville found U.S. "free" service so unfettered as to threaten social destabilization, Southern domesticity could be portrayed as a homemaker's idyll. "In the slave states," a disseminator of this fantasy sighed in 1843, "the affairs of the household are generally conducted with more regularity and order than they possibly can be where there is a continual change of domestics."[10] Challenging this claim was the prayer of a North Carolina mistress: "may the Lord deliver me," she wrote in 1855, "from any more such property."[11] Its charm nonetheless endured. "I have heard more than one lady declare," Harriet Beecher Stowe testified in print in 1866, "that she didn't care if it was unjust, she should like to have slaves rather than be plagued with servants who had so much liberty."[12]

Envy of the supposed beauties of chattel-dependent domesticity was, to say the least, overdetermined. Recent work by Carole Shammas suggests, however, that an underappreciated aspect of wage payers' wishfulness was anxiety about a management system that seemed to be more respected in the South. This system, the rise and fall of which Shammas charts in *A History of Household Government in America* (2002), lumped together wives, children, and servants—the legal status of the last irrelevant—as "dependants." Tributes to "family-like" service did not challenge that lumping; central, however, to the sentimental program was stress on the idea that mistresses were responsible when the polity in need of regulation was the home. Pitiable, under this affective rubric, was the servant who "had never had one employer who had regarded it as a duty to attempt to reform the faults, and enlighten the moral sense, and strengthen the feeble virtue of her inferior and dependant." Admirable, in contrast, was the worker who repaid motherlike care with daughterlike warmth. "Do not work merely for money," taught an anonymous guide for servants in 1839, "but seek to gain the affections of your employers, and thus enjoy the happiness which this relation affords."[13] Advice of this kind is redolent of what Mary Louise Kete calls "sentimentality's obvious threats." It nonetheless suggests the extent to which women of relative privilege were encouraged to take up responsibilities previously allotted to masters while highlighting the efficacy servants might find in charging that "family" was a job site properly held to a behavioral standard higher than that expected of, say, a factory owner toward the mill girls in his employ. Agreeing, then, with Lora Romero's assertion that "the politics of culture reside in local formulations" rather than generic mandates, but guided too by the Civil War-era perception that "[t]he household is the scene of a perpetual revolution," this book probes the literature of nineteenth-century U.S. service to chart developments in a body of print that promoted powerful "truths" about class, age, natal provenance, gender, race, rank, and advice literature as such things related to the best sort of home and "family" life.[14]

To grasp the politics of the culture in which the literature of U.S. service flourished, we must begin with recognition that domestic labor lost prestige, especially but not exclusively in the "free" states, during the antebellum years. "As households became homes," Catherine Kelly demonstrates in *In the New England Fashion: Reshaping Women's Lives in the Nineteenth Century* (1999), "housework became something other than work."[15] This development had huge consequences for laborers whose efforts were homebound. Probing the ubiquity of workers who were not kin, Faye E. Dudden calculated that servants were the norm in 15–30 percent of homes in the industrializing Northeast, while David E. Schob found reliance on nonkin even more common in rural parts of the North and West (though there, seasonal "help" likely outnumbered attendants utilized year-round). Figures are harder to come by for the slaveholding states. Yet Eugene Genovese offers "guesswork honored by time and repetition" that estimates the number of U.S. slaves who worked primarily within owners' homes at about one-quarter of the total number of bondsmen and bondswomen.[16] After emancipation, the demand for servants rose markedly, and complaints of scarcity were heard.[17] "The housekeeper's great want of today is servants," *Lippincott's Magazine* asserted in 1869; "not simply good servants, but in many instances servants at all." This view of the matter cannot be dismissed, since many of the people who might once have served had begun to pursue other lines of work. Yet Catharine Beecher was sure there was no shortfall: "We abound in domestic helpers," she avowed the same year that *Lippincott's* pointed to a dearth.[18] Taking cries of scarcity as evidence of privilege imperiled rather than clear or mere demographic truth, this study emphasizes the familial standard that sanctioned a sense of grievance against attendants who, being free to go, all too often went.

Scrutinizing strife between the serving and the served some time ago, Faye Dudden explained the "servant problem" as the result of a shift from the neighborly arrangement of "hired help" to reliance on "domestics" hired through a for-profit agency, while Carol Lasser attributed midcentury aggravation with servants to an influx of female Irish immigrants who seemed ineradically foreign to their employers. This scholarship is especially valuable for enhancing comprehension of expressions of resentment toward the Irish peasant who was reviled as "Princess Biddy," such as can be found in a letter of 1853. "I think the cause of the trouble is treating [servants] with too much consideration," Elizabeth Sullivan Stuart opined. "[T]hey are not accustomed to it, & immagine themselves something when they are nothing."[19] Obscured, though, by focus on strife in wage-earning areas, is the effect that perceptions of slavery would have had on Northern homemakers' attitudes. In more recent scholarship, Amy Dru Stanley argued that Gilded Age Americans understood "free" service within parameters worked out by debates over abolition. *From Bondage to Contract: Wage Labor, Marriage, and the Market in the Age of Slave Emancipation* (1998) shows more interest in labor reformers than in literature.[20] Stanley's book nonetheless reveals how much can be learned from attempts to recover a fuller sense of problems with service than was available to (and perhaps desired by) the sorts of sources on which social historians rely. As important as diary and letter commentary to the chapters that follow are attitude-shaping efforts such as a short story published long before "Harriet Beecher Stowe" became a household name. "What shall we do?" this story had a mistress-character wail, when "free" servants' comings and goings drive her to distraction. "Shall we go for slavery, or shall we give up houses, have no furniture to take care of—keep merely a bag of meal, a porridge pot, and a pudding stick, and sit in our tent door in real patriarchal independence?" Henry Thoreau might have thought the second suggestion (which appeared in *Godey's Lady's Book* in 1839) worth pursuing. But

Harriet E. Wilson could have reminded him of a third option: "bound" servitude. Mindful of this corrective, my research brings existing scholarship on the "servant problem" into conversation with studies of slavery and postemancipation African American labor to create a more complex account than has previously been rendered. A significant gain incident on what Shammas calls "putting the elements back together" is recognition that affective visions had to be shaped and reshaped to accommodate new perceptions and realities.[21]

By scrutinizing changes in the literature of nineteenth-century U.S. service, over a span of almost nine decades, I have come to see the emptiness of the early twentieth-century gibe that it was "quite a fad with sentimentalists . . . to insist that the servant must be made a member of the family." First, this insistence was nothing so ephemeral as a fad. Second, this gloss assumes that one concept of "family" drove all affective advice, though that was not the case. I agree, then, with Elizabeth Barnes that nineteenth-century sentimentalists conceptualized "family" life according to "a New Testament ethos that sees filial relations as determined by faith rather than blood."[22] My research shows, however, that that line of thinking left room for large differences of opinion about such variables as race, age, and gender but also about the sort of hierarchies appropriate to the home. This was highly significant leeway during an era in which, as Christine Stansell has observed of antebellum New York City, "One could not really *be* a lady, if one did not have a problem with servants."[23] Much of the "humor" of the literature of nineteenth-century U.S. service affirmed this charge. "Head of fine gold, feet of iron and clay," a New England satirist had a mistress-character remark, in 1871, of a roomful of women in search of service posts. "*We* are the head of fine gold; *you* are the iron and the clay." Fueling the asperity, though, after the slaves were freed was a sense that servants had gained so much clout that mistresses and staff constituted "natural enemies" (*Godey's Lady's Book*, 1868); that intrusive or inept attendants had the capacity to foment "a state of actual, open and unceasing war" (*The Revolution*, 1869); and even, as a Philadelphia homemaker put it in 1867, that waged domestics comprised so many "strangers or enemies in the house."[24] The most interesting, because conflicted, advice of this period tried to preserve remnants of the old creed: "servants," *Harper's Bazar* waffled in 1874, "are in some measure wards intrusted to [homemakers'] care."[25] This claim does not ring with assurance. Noticeably more genial, however, than the vitriol that surged through other writers' counsel, waffling could have seemed like the only way to honor the obligations implied by the conduct book of 1830,

MISTRESS.—"Well, how do you like our Nursery?"
NURSE.—"Oh! Ingrain Carpet, I declare! I never was in a house where there wasn't at least Brussels in the Nursery."

BRIDGET.—"Indade, Misthress Smith isn't in the House. She tould me to tell you so, this very minit, when she set her eyes on you."

PEGGY.—"Please, Ma'am, Cook is dressin' for the ball to-night, and says would you lend her a brooch, and a pair of bracelets, and a scarf, and a wreath.

Servants' presumptions were a favorite theme in comedy intended for mistresses' eyes; this cartoon from Harper's New Monthly Magazine *(1857) is typical. Special Collections, University of Virginia Library.*

which taught that a good mistress was one so embracingly maternal that she "forms for herself a set of honest, respectable domestics, who, together with her children, 'look up to her, and call her blessed.'"[26]

The marked disparities among "free," chattel, and "bound" labor may seem to justify segregating advice intended to soothe "the peculiar difficulties of our southern housewives" from that which addressed what Ralph Waldo Emerson called "the uneasy relation of domestics."[27] Yet quite apart from nineteenth-century commentary that shows how attentively people in the North and South eyed each other's labor, historians of reading have made persuasive arguments about print's ability to engage previously unsuspected constituencies.[28] A case in point is Beecher's *Treatise on Domestic Economy* (1841). This text looms large in most studies of nineteenth-century U.S. home and "family" life. But it is not often recognized that slaveholders could have nodded approvingly over its certainty that masters and mistresses were to "supply the place of parents" to household staff. Slaveholders could also have liked the rationale Beecher set forth in a follow-up work, though it alluded to wages they did not pay. "God ordains that parents shall have a home of their own," taught *Letters to Persons Who Are Engaged in Domestic Service* (1842), and "one main support of this blessed institution of family and home is, those domestics who are hired to do the chief labours of the family."[29] The differences between the messages propagated in the *Treatise* and Beecher's later publications have not been carefully probed. It is time to do so, though, because examination of this kind shows how difficult it was to escape the influence of sentimental bromides. That difficulty would be significant if it only illuminated changes in counsel from one respected advisor's pen. Yet in fact, many nineteenth-century contributors to the literature of U.S. service were snagged in comparable ways, including some not widely recognized as the sort to have been influenced by affective precepts. Among the latter are essayists such as Emerson and a protomuckraker named Helen Campbell, a range of servant-writers and assorted members of the Brook Farm community, and pundits as distinct as George Fitzhugh and Melusina Fay Peirce.

While scholarship on sentimental print and culture has flourished, in recent years attention to the variegated literature of service has been sparse. Bruce Robbins helped get the conversation started with a study of British servant-characters titled *The Servant's Hand: English Fiction from Below* (1986). Yet his findings shed little light on texts produced in a republic that immobilized some attendants for life while "binding" others for a stated period and making others "free." It may be true, then, for the British writers Robbins examines, that each servant-character represents "the scandal of a figure which both stands at the confrontation of the Two Nations and refuses to represent historical and social difference at all."[30] Yet servant-characters crafted by nineteenth-century U.S. writers were often quite responsive to both these things. More attuned to the exceptionalist aspects of the literature of U.S. service, Jeffrey Robert Young recently analyzed commentary about attendants in light of ideas disseminated in print. I want to believe Young's claim in *Domesticating Slavery: The Master Class in Georgia and South Carolina, 1670–1837* (1999) that romance novels were a key part of the milieu in which slaveholders began to feel love and appreciation for chattel staff—if this means that reading materials humanized a labor arrangement that was almost unspeakably cruel. Yet I query one of his premises. "Because the slaveowners offered these sentiments in private correspondence with family members (instead of presenting them publicly to refute abolitionism)," Young contends, "we can assume some measure of sincerity on their part."[31] I disagree because I see claims of family-like affection as reflective of a rhetorical option, the relationship of which to feelings and behavior remains opaque until supported by information about the goals and anxieties in specific sentiment-espousing households. It is important, then, that a Southern mistress wrote of her slaves in familial terms: "how attached we are to these house servants," she mused; "we love them, not as servants, but as something nearer."[32] But it is equally significant that a "free" worker used the same language in 1883. "I have a good home as long as I choose to stay with them," Ann Coleman Thomas reported. "I am not treated as a servent but as one of the family."[33] I contend that this kind of self-portraiture (and other-portraiture) is proof of nothing more conclusive than adherence to a popular way of articulating service relationships—if only because Thomas did not stay at the post about which she was initially so pleased.

More evidence that the relationship between rhetoric and real-world behavior must be adduced carefully can be found in the letters of two waged antebellum servants. In the first, Adeline Brown reported that her mistress had asked to be addressed as "Mother," while in the second, Anna Smith chose to head a letter to *her* mistress "My dear mama."[34] As that hailing is not repeated in any of Smith's extant letters to her employer, there is a good chance that she had acted on her own initiative and been rebuffed. These examples seem to juxtapose neatly since Smith was a white British immigrant who worked for a white American family, while Brown was an African American serving in an African American home. Yet in fact, there is no telling how racial considerations affected the probability that where one person chose familial nomenclature, the other resigned herself to it (though not without twitting her mistress in a letter to a distant friend). If this information is taken to show that sentimental precepts pleased some service workers while leaving others cold, it additionally implies that the ways in which people articulate relationships may not reflect all of their feelings. Relevant to this implication is the paucity of attention, in any but "dark moralist" print, to the opportunities for sexual predation to which nonkin coresidence gave rise.[35]

Setting the rules for which topics would be pondered, and which ignored, were advisors whose disagreements kept the literature of service contentious. One of the most salient discords was that between Catharine Maria Sedgwick and Caroline Howard Gilman, two widely known sentimentalists who, being near-peers in age, education, and religious conviction, were recognized as "matriarchs" of U.S. literature before the Civil War. However, Sedgwick and Gilman advised differently, since Gilman defended slavery while Sedgwick thought it wrong. A Northern "transplant" to South Carolina, Gilman deplored "free" servants' mobility in a novel of 1834. "How many girls . . . have I passed months in drilling," she had a mistress-character moan, "when, just as I began to realize the effects of my care, they have taken a sudden whim and departed!" Countering this call for self-pity, in 1837 Sedgwick imagined right-minded households, however urban or genteel, as "little primary schools, over which we, in virtue of our characters as mothers and mistresses, preside."[36] Pedagogical imagery had various connotations at this time. Yet in this context, reference to a period of instruction from which servants could be expected to graduate defied those who judged chattel service the superior form of attendance because it was the most family-like. Seen from this vantage, conflict between Sedgwick and Gilman (explored at length in chapter 1) bears out the truth of Stephanie Coontz's contention that "the family is always as much a political institution as a personal one." At the same time, advice literature had cultural connotations that broaden the scope of Jeanne Boydston's charge that "industrialization, in all of its social, cultural, and economic manifestations, was not merely a specter that waited around the corner for women and men who ventured from their homes. Equally, it was a process *of* the family." I agree but would add that the process Boydston discerns was complicated by proslavery claims to the effect that chattel service was "an affair of the heart."[37]

Eager to refute this claim, Sedgwick wrote several tracts and novels that made servant-characters important or included preachy passages about right-minded household government. Most of these works won a wide following. Yet the most openly service-oriented was greeted with mixed reviews. *Live and Let Live; or, Domestic Service Illustrated* (1837) put Sedgwick at the forefront of the literature of nineteenth-century U.S. service for a time. What fans did not know is that Sedgwick's affective visions were predicated on the relationship she had enjoyed with an ex-slave, named Elizabeth Freeman, who had been a fixture in her childhood home.[38] Nell Irvin Painter recently suggested in a biography of Sojourner Truth that African Americans who had been raised to live and die as property constituted a unique group, some members of which would have carried heavy psychological baggage.[39] Yet the effect that a harsh upbringing might have had on Freeman's self-image, or values, is not what Sedgwick chose to emphasize in the epitaph she wrote for her beloved "nurse-*gouvernante.*" "She could neither read nor write," this tribute avowed, "yet in her own sphere, she had no superior nor equal. She neither wasted time nor property. She never violated a trust, nor failed to perform a duty. In every situation of domestic trial she was the most efficient helper and the tenderest friend. Good mother, farewell!"[40]

W. E. B. Du Bois, a committed "race man" who claimed kinship with Freeman, may have wondered whether she would have appreciated being memorialized in ways that resemble a letter of reference for a new post; equally, he may have had reservations about Sedgwick's request to be buried at Freeman's side in the Sedgwick family plot, since the ex-slave had raised a family of her own with whom she might have preferred to have lain.[41] Pending information on either point, the inference I draw from the sales figures of the advice Sedgwick based on memories of her relationship with Freeman is that praise of familial "free" service owed much to appreciation for the immobilized attendance emblematized, even in the twentieth century, by servants who were property.

Sedgwick would never have admitted as much. More to the point, though, than contradictions that ramify only in an individualized way is the fact that an esteemed advisor could espouse daughterlike love for Freeman (whom she knew to have been harshly abused physically) yet oppose radical antislavery activity. "I am excessively sorry to find," Sedgwick would write of a British activist, "that her mind is so much excited on the abolition question. She seems to me to see everything in as exaggerated and false a light as if she looked at objects by a conflagration." Sedgwick's politics were no secret, and after her death, Lydia Maria Child would judge her "very deficient in moral *courage.*"[42] This is how the case would have looked to any abolitionist. What Child failed to see, however, is that by setting out new tenets for "free" service, Sedgwick redrew the contours of household government and thus in-home labor as a whole. Indeed, it is not too much to say that this one writer contributed so powerfully to the literature of nineteenth-century U.S. service that all subsequent advisors had to negotiate her legacy. That legacy—traversed, as it was, by specific racial assumptions and half-admitted emotional dependency—would have long-term consequences, many of which persisted even after the slaves were freed.

Historians as alert as Drew Gilpin Faust, Tera W. Hunter, Jacqueline Jones, and Marli F. Weiner have already pondered freed attendance in terms of standards of behavior that circulated while human bondage was the law. My survey of the literature of nineteenth-century U.S. service draws on this work but adds to it, too, by delineating postemancipation attempts to revise ideals that lay at the root of many people's sense of self-worth and personal identity. These attempts have not intrigued historians of sentimental culture. Yet they are a matter of considerable interest insofar as advisors with national readerships responded in different ways to the news that freedpersons were leaving their erstwhile homes in droves. Some recirculated familial bromides—"You are the girl's God-ordained guardian while she is with you," taught a manual of 1879—while others dismissed those claims: for example, in 1883 the *Popular Science Monthly* ran an article titled "The Legal Status of Servant-Girls," which explained that employers were not responsible for providing chambermaids with medical care.[43] Most representative, though, of Reconstruction-era counsel are *post*sentimental propositions such as the allegation that when servants fail to achieve the goal of family-likeness, "there is always something foreign in the household, and there is disintegration at the very foundation of home."[44] This ugly accusation, which ran in *Harper's Bazar* in 1877, may not look very affective. Yet it was much closer to Sedgwick's position than was the prize-winning essay of 1900 that announced that the "relation between mistress and maid is before anything else a money relation," one in which "not poetic sentiment, nor Christian charity, but straight business principles are to govern."[45] What had changed? After the 1820s, the sort of person willing to serve nonkin shifted significantly as job opportunities for native-born white women expanded throughout New England and the mid-Atlantic states.[46] Following hard on that innovation was one even more shocking: a slew of "kitchen witnesses," most of whom had been enslaved, found ways to testify about nonkin attendance from an attendant's point of view. This dramatic irruption in the literature of nineteenth-century U.S. service exposed grievous flaws in sentimental bromides, even though some of the things kitchen witnesses chose to say could have been interpreted as upholding affective ideals. Less ambiguous was the *coupure* that a Georgia minister called "the dark, dissolving, disquieting wave of emancipation."[47] The product of all these forces and more, later nineteenth-century advice literature interlaced intricately with changing notions of served and serving roles but also with turmoil over what, exactly, it meant for labor to be "free."

According to the later nineteenth-century reformers who were styled "New Women," what it meant, in the context of service, was an end to advice disseminated in the form of novels, stories, and fireside chats. The revocation of authority from such venues was a large part of the agenda behind the "rationalist" call to turn discussions of "the horrors of the servant question," such as were found in "ladies' clubs and comic papers," into a field of dispassionate research. Though not a belletristic wrangle, this was a literary tussle inasmuch as dismissal of "comic papers" was central to the contention that trouble with service was not just "a little personal row among women" but, rightly understood, "an integral part of the great labor question" of the day.[48] Having begun, then, with the era in which advisors adopted warmly affective tones, this study ends when the literature of U.S. service moved into the realm of home economic textbooks. Characteristic of that era was the purposefully stark proposition that familial precepts were nonsense. "The domestic employee is not, and cannot be, a part of the family," Professor Lucy M. Salmon declaimed in 1898; "she never in all her history had had more than a semblance of such a relationship and even that semblance has long since disappeared. The presence of the domestic employee in the family is not essential to the existence of the family; the domestic employee comes and goes, but the family remains." Indeed, Salmon concluded, "the presence of the domestic employee does something to destroy the integrity of family life."[49] This was a direct attack on those whose authority to advise had been based implicitly on claims of special access to knowledge of the truth of the human heart.

To initiate discussion of developments in the literature of nineteenth-century U.S. service, chapter 1 outlines the ideals of attendance and mistress-ship that sentimentalists put into play. Chapters 2 and 3 show that certain New Englanders tested affective ideals by setting up alternative domesticities. None of these alternative domesticities proved successful in the long run. Probed carefully, they nonetheless show that though sentimental precepts had impact, they had been challenged well before fugitive and former bondspeople collaborated with never-enslaved editors to mount incisive critiques of the idea that America's "peculiar institution" could be justified by reference to a plantation "family." The rise of waged, "bound," and chattel servants' voices—some of which were ventriloquized—is the subject of chapter 4. Chapter 5 surveys the confused and contradictory nature of advice published after emancipation, while the Epilogue explores modernizers' determination to drain authority from sentimentalists by ridiculing all who took affective counsel to heart.

This book's emphasis on change over time should alert scholars that gripes about U.S. servants have never been a static field. More fundamentally, though, my work draws attention to a body of print not previously seen as a whole to shed new light on texts as familiar as Henry David Thoreau's *Walden* (1854) and as neglected as a novel titled *The Greatest Blessing in Life* (1850) but also on authors as forgotten as Marion Harland and as emergent as Elizabeth Keckley. New findings in this realm will intrigue historians of U.S. labor and sentimental culture. Yet they have at least as much to tell students of feminine authority, male householding, and the promotion—often through contestation—of powerful truisms about the ever-shifting meaning of home and "family" life.

1 The Family Work

Every slave is a servant but every servant is not a slave.
—*An American Dictionary of the English Language*
(1828)

Sentimental advice literature structured nineteenth-century complaints about nonkin service by setting up criteria for judging attendants as good or bad. However, proponents of the affective standard did not work in harmony, since some disliked slavery while others defended it vigorously. Looking, in this chapter, at advice written for the first generation of U.S. citizens to grapple with the fact that some household staff were free, at a moment's notice, to go, the key point to bear in mind is the envy a wealthy Philadelphian expressed, in 1837, for a friend's "most excellent servants, such as are to be found only in the slave holding states." It is impossible to know now how many wage-paying masters and mistresses would have expressed themselves as bluntly. Yet considering the energy put into lauding the ministrations of fictive servants who, though legally free to quit a job, attended nonkin with family-like love and loyalty, it is fair to infer wishfulness for the service thought characteristic of house chattel. All but admitting as much is Sedgwick's recollection of "the transitive state—when the old well-trained slaves had disappeared"—leaving homemakers at a loss. "I rode the country round," she recalled of this period decades later, "to get, for love and money, girls to do the family work."[1]

What this memory occludes is, of course, the disappearability of servants who were property. Runaways were one source of concern; pertinent too, though, were acts of resistance such as one woman's decision to set the drapes on fire because she preferred to work in the field. This arsonist served in the South. Yet similar acts of resistance must have erupted among enslaved servants in those parts of the North in which slavery was permitted, making stories about such things widely available to wage-paying homemakers. If envy of house slaves persisted under these conditions, that was partly because information did not flow evenly to all parts of the United States. Influential too, however, were protestations of "mutual affection between the white and the colored members of the same family," resulting in a "relation more like that of parent and child, than like any other with which it can be compared, and . . . altogether stronger than that which binds the northern employer and his hired domestic." If attracted by such claims, wage payers were likely to attribute to the South "many of the things which they felt the North lacked: the vestiges of an old-world aristocracy, a promise of stability and an assurance that gentility—a high sense of honor, a belief in public service and a maintenance of domestic decorum—could be preserved under republican institutions."[2] The sense that domestic decorum was on the wane in the "free" states kept early U.S. homemakers focused on deference. Expressions of anger at servants who did not "know their place" are pertinent here. But so is a Northern traveler's admiration for the home in which his Southern hostess had "nothing to do with setting the table" since "an old family servant, who for 50 years has superintended that matter, does all that."[3]

Reports of this kind were not so much defenses of slavery as affirmations of a taste for in-house hierarchies that, many antebellum Americans believed, was more readily available from chattel. Trying to portray deference in a different way so that it seemed like a quality wage payers might be able to secure, Sedgwick's first novel praised a particularly family-like servant as so conformable to "the virtues of her station" that she "never presumed formally to offer her advice," though "she had a way of suggesting hints."[4] This passage from *A New-England Tale* (1822) reveals adherence, in the mind of one widely read sentimentalist, to the charge that "free" servants had been spoiled by notions of social equality. So does a review of Sedgwick's work that was probably written by Sarah Josepha Hale: "She affects no indifference to the accidental advantages of condition," it noted, approvingly.[5] And so does, finally, a householder's remark from the same year in which *A New-England Tale* was published: "In these United States," one man reported, "nothing would be wanting to make life perfectly happy (humanly speaking) had we good servants."[6]

Agreeing, early antebellum manners-mavens equated nonkin staff with intrusion and instability. "Gone," says C. Dallett Hemphill, in

Bowing to Necessities: A History of Manners in America, 1620–1860 (1999), "was the revolutionary-era impulse to 'soften'" the master-servant relationship.[7] This assessment is sound when the topic is guides to genteel etiquette. Over in the realm of conduct fiction, however, Sedgwick was one of several conscious republicans who tried to keep alive a version of the idea that in the kind of "free" service that enhanced "family" life, masters and mistresses had obligations to servants that, in turn, indebted laborers. The most marked distinction between Sedgwick and most of her contemporaries, in this respect, was that she wrote as though mistresses needed affective instruction as much as servants did. To address both the serving and the served, with special interest in women, she eventually worked out a genre that I think of as "didactic novellas." Typical of this genre is *Home* (1835), a story that praised a married couple as the sort of employers who "did not regard their servant as a hireling, but as a member of the family, who, from her humble position in it, was entitled to their protection and care." This was, significantly enough, a claim about sentimental outreach rather than egalitarian politics. "I have no fanciful expectations of a perfect equality, a dead level," Mr. Barclay clarifies; "this can only exist among such savages as the Hottentots."[8] That this was the correct attitude, in Sedgwick's view, is ratified by the long-term loyalty of Mrs. Barclay's cook; though legally free to go, the scripturally named Martha grows old in this good woman's household.

Later in this chapter I will have more to say about the vision of family-like service Sedgwick propagated in a didactic novella that enjoyed considerable popular success. Yet to see what was exceptional about early U.S. writings on servitude, it is necessary to know what sort of counsel was being rejected. An overview of the British guides available in the young United States provides this background.

A long-term favorite before the "invention of free labor," Jonas Hanway's *Advice from Farmer Trueman, to His Daughter Mary*, first published in London in 1770 and Boston in 1774, taught servants to be clean, thrifty, and honest; follow orders cheerfully; and honor God. Yet Hanway also insisted on deference, in no uncertain terms. In one such passage, the farmer advises a daughter who is heading off to service to keep in mind "thy particular situation as a servant" and the "superior standing of thy mistress" since both, he taught, "will naturally lead her to expect a degree of homage from thee." To the sort of U.S. citizens who refused to accommodate mistresses who "rode the country round" in search of in-house staff, the word "homage" would have been harsh. Worse, though, was Hanway's view of the proper service relationship.

"If her regard for thee should incline her sometimes to speak familiarly, never forget she is thy mistress," the farmer cautions his daughter. "If she should occasionally consider thee as her humble friend, and companion, thy task will become the more difficult."[9] Though this was, and would continue to be, good advice for domestic workers dependent on a mistress's favor, it was not a note repeated in advice literature such as *A Friendly Gift for Servants and Apprentices*, a guide originally published in Dublin and London but printed in New York and Baltimore in 1821. Instead, this manual taught that the good servant "becomes attached to her master and mistress, and their children, and serves them faithfully and attentively, from love, as well as from duty."[10]

Another British guide that did not suit republicans was Ann Martin Taylor's *Present of a Mistress to a Young Servant* (1816). Taylor's suggestion that in-house laborers think of nonkin service as "your *trade*, that by which you are to obtain your livelihood," was apt.[11] Nor would many Americans have queried Taylor's idea that homemakers should provide servants with "a comfortable home, a plentiful table, and good wages" or failed to esteem a servant-character said to have been so "greatly attached" to those she serves that "their interest was as dear to her as her own." Taylor's directive that servants should use up candle ends and dine on table scraps could explain why *The Present of a Mistress to a Young Servant* was not reprinted in the United States after its first appearance.[12] More pertinent, though, for our purposes is the fact that no sentimentalist could have approved praise of a servant so "faithful" that, in two decades of service, she visits her aged parents just two times. This lapse would be bad enough if it were only a matter of daughterly responsibility. But it was worse than that, because, this servant having been introduced as a poor relation of those she served, fault could be found with the master and mistress who failed to respect parental claims. Sedgwick would mount a similar criticism in *A New-England Tale*, as if to discourage the practice of turning impoverished relatives into drudges.[13]

All the while, evangelical tracts originating in Great Britain included messages about servitude; representing this faction, Hannah More's *Onesimus; or, The Run-away Servant Converted* (18??) equated nonkin service with the expiation of sin. More readily available, though, in the young United States were *The African Servant* (ca. 1813) and *Fidelity and Filial Affection* (ca. 1816); both were reprinted in the thousands before the Civil War.[14] Though the "popularity" of both texts depended on sponsorship from tract societies, *Fidelity and Filial Affection* must have charmed servant-readers who sought expressions of respect for their kinship ties, since its servant-heroine uses her savings to help kin. The reason Elizabeth L**** is able to pay her parents' medical expenses and buy them a cow is that she works hard and saves her earnings; helpful too, however, is the appreciative master who makes her a legatee. The maxim here implied—that loyal attendance merits recompense but never supersedes obligations to one's kin—would recur in Sedgwick's *Live and Let Live; or, Domestic Service Illustrated* (1837). In contrast, none of Sedgwick's advice literature picked up on the moral that Legh Richmond made central to *The African Servant*, a tract that foregrounds race and directs servants' eyes toward God. Kidnapped from his homeland but eventually freed, William never mentions parents, siblings, a wife, or offspring.[15] Instead, he ruminates about how to serve faithfully, the better to live as a Christian. "Me sorry to think," he rues in a climactic speech, "how bad servant me was before the good things of Jesus Christ come to my heart. Me wish to do well to my massa, when he see me, and when he not see me, for me know God always see me."[16] Sedgwick admired Richmond's work.[17] Yet when she crafted servant-characters of explicitly African descent in *Redwood* (1824), *Clarence* (1830), and *The Linwoods; or, "Sixty Years Since"* (1835), she ignored piety to focus on such attendants' willingness to serve like family.

Advisory material imported from Great Britain had impact. But what of the literature of U.S. service, in all its uniqueness? Early republican belletrists who tackled attendance chose a comic tone; one thinks, for instance, of Hugh Henry Brackenridge's *Modern Chivalry* (1792) and Washington Irving's "Salmagundi" stories about an African American manservant who manipulates his master to a nicety. By the 1820s, though, James Fenimore Cooper was ready to make serious allegations in romances such as *The Spy* (1821) and *The Pioneers* (1823). Chief among these was a sharp (and, to today's eyes, gratuitous) attack on the "vagrant class" of servants who "roam through the country, unfettered by principles, or uninfluenced by attachments."[18] Concern about "attachments" reveals that Cooper, though not usually classified as a sentimental writer, played a part in advancing the idea that affect was the standard by which service should be judged.

Pairing servant-characters so as to contrast deferential, yet affectionate, chattel to obstreperous non-African servitors, *The Spy* fomented distaste for attendants who were assertively "free." The enslaved Caesar is not one of Nature's elite; still, he is a more pleasant person in the household than is the nosey Celt whose conditions of employment are not specified. Fuzziness on this topic makes the main contrast between Katy and Caesar neither job mobility nor, arguably, whiteness but rather that he "identified himself with the welfare" of those whom it was his lot to serve, while she likes to poke and pry.[19] Neither servant-character plays a major role in *The Spy*. Yet precisely as if this kind of pairing intrigued Cooper (or as if he thought it would interest readers), *The Pioneers* revived it. Again, the slave-character is self-subordinating, while his "free" counterpart is obtrusive. But in the later novel, Cooper put an ugly epithet in the assertive menial's mouth as part of a speech in which she claims that democracy obviates deference. "Mistress!" snorts Remarkable Pettibone when asked to address her employer's daughter by that title; "don't make one out to be a nigger. . . . I don't crave to live in a house where a body musn't call a young woman by her given name to her face. I *will* call her Betsy as much as I please; it's a free country, and nobody can stop me."[20]

A male correspondent noticed this character with delight. "Miss Remarkable," he enthused, constituted a "most happy instance of one of the thousands of those beings to be found anywhere amongst us, who let themselves out to make themselves and the family as uncomfortable as possible."[21] Tellingly enough, Cooper did not let Remarkable Pettibone get the upper hand (she subsides upon "contemplation of the ease and comforts of her situation"); at least as important, though, is the finding that he limited the degree of characterization, and the number of lines, given her slave-counterpart. Thanks to the research efforts of Alan Taylor, we know that Cooper owned slaves and complained bitterly about property who ran away.[22] He had his favorites, though, one of whom was included in a formal portrait of Cooper's mother; "Governor" Joseph Stewart attended the Coopers as chattel and then as a freedman until his death in 1823.[23]

I do not say that Cooper was a sentimental writer comparable to, say, Susan Warner. Yet he did not have to be a sentimentalist of that stripe to characterize and plot in ways that advance the idea that servants should be family-like, since that ideal meant so little, in concrete terms, to readers who differed markedly over such things as the degree and rigidity of the hierarchies appropriate to family life; the nature and justification of parental discipline, as well as of filial duty; and the precise meaning of nurture, love, and obligation among members of a household. Indeed, ambiguity was crucial to the widespread and long-lived appeal of the idea that nonkin service should be family-like. Yet to my mind, the more illuminating finding is that the proximate coexistence of "free" and chattel service made it impolitic to inquire closely into the specifics of other people's "family" lives. A few bold agitators did so inquire, even early on; one thinks, for instance, of George Tucker's

"I GUESS, MA'AM, YOU WANT A HELP?"

Though U.S. cartoonists lagged behind belletrists in mocking "uppish" white servants who were native-born, "Yankee Doodle" took on the topic in 1847. Courtesy, American Antiquarian Society.

Letters from Virginia (1816), a homegrown indictment of Southern slavery. Taking a less confrontational approach just a few years later, Catharine Sedgwick won laurels on both sides of the Mason-Dixon Line.

To see how Sedgwick's novels and tracts contributed to sentimental visions of servitude, a few plot synopses from her earliest publications will be helpful. Focusing on servant-characters, these overviews show how little she cared to be guided by Cooper's visions and views, except insofar as he evaluated attendance in terms of affect.

1. A New-England Tale *(1822)*

Begun as a disquisition on religious fanaticism, this debut novel revised the story of Cinderella. The heroine is a teenaged orphan forced to serve a grasping aunt. Though raised for better things, Jane serves faithfully until she marries. At one low point, she is comforted by an older woman whose concern for the girl grows out of loyalty to the memory of a beloved mistress, Jane's dead mother. Loyalty is crucial because Mary Hull owes Jane nothing: never the girl's employee and indeed no longer an attendant, Mary is nonetheless more loving and supportive than Jane's exploitative kin.

2. Mary Hollis *(1822)*

Published under Unitarian auspices and targeting the impoverished, this tract teaches that service is a good job for a poor, fatherless girl. Yet it implies that family-like servants are raised, not born. The story focuses on a virtuous but struggling widow who agrees to send her daughter to nonkin service when she realizes that the right kind of mistress will give the girl a family-like home. As if to reward Mary's wisdom, this tract ends with Sally Hollis laboring happily, "respected by all who know her, and beloved by her mistress."[24]

3. Redwood *(1824)*

Imitating Cooper, Sedgwick's second novel contrasts kin service among rural New Englanders to Southern slavery. The most fully characterized kin servant is the shrewd but good-hearted Deb, while the most impressive slave is Africk, a noble bondsman tamed by kindness. *Redwood*'s other notable slave-character is a flatterer who tricks her Southern mistress out of a money-filled purse to fund a flight for freedom. As if to mitigate such turpitude, Sedgwick has already shown that the belle is lazy: "there is no living without slaves," she sighs, complacently. Her wise father replies, "I fear, my child, that we shall find there is no living with them."[25]

Sedgwick's reuse of Cooper's tactic—contrast—suggests a literary duel. She joined him, nonetheless, in judging nonkin attendance in terms of warm feelings between the serving and the served.

To unpack these synopses further, it is salient that the virtues of the "free" servant-characters in Sedgwick's first two novels demonstrate the criteria of service found in Elizabeth Freeman's epitaph: trustworthiness, efficiency, and loving concern. This point is worth making, because Sedgwick's first tract advances a vision of admirable service in which faithful attendance is less a matter of a worker's character than it is a reflection of a mistress's motherlike nurturing. There is food for thought, particularly about intended audiences, in this finding. Yet the more broadly suggestive finding, among students of the literature of nineteenth-century U.S. service, is the implication that Sedgwick's ideals of good service were based on her experiences with a worker whose values and attitudes had been inculcated in slavery. Sedgwick never made racist imputations like the nonsense J. H. Ingraham promoted in *The Sunny South* (1860). "It is not in training," a white character in that romance protests, as he extols the service of house slaves. "They seem born to it!"[26] On the contrary, Sedgwick seems to have tried to forestall that attitude by maintaining silence about the race or ethnicity of *A New-England Tale*'s Mary Hull and by noticing in *Redwood* that "help" on a "Vermontese" farm may be black or white.[27] Nevertheless, in the tract that encouraged poor women to send their daughters out to serve, Sedgwick made a point of clarifying that young Sally was "not negro." This clarification probably enlarged the audience for *Mary Hollis;* it clashed, however, with the color-blind visions of good service in Sedgwick's early novels. Here then, as elsewhere, this advisor failed to take a position on the conditions of labor appropriate for African Americans who were free.

How free, we must ask, was Elizabeth Freeman? In an essay published in 1853 that tried to present New England slavery as mild compared to conditions in the South, Sedgwick painted a rosy portrait of the freedwoman's role in an elite household. Thus, as Sedgwick told it, on winning her manumission with help from Theodore Sedgwick, Freeman "immediately transferred herself to the service of her champion, if service that could be called, which was quite as much rule as service."[28] This representation of what was, in fact, a state of servitude recalls the "Salmagundi" farces; what it does not do is reveal how Freeman felt about the Sedgwicks, how free she felt to leave their household (and under what sorts of rationales), or even how she was recompensed for laboring in their home. Pertinent to this inquiry is the fact that one elite antebellum family, the Francis Cabot Lowells of Boston, did not pay their "free" servants on a regular basis but instead settled accounts sporadically.[29] Sedgwick would challenge that system in the novel *Clarence; or, A Tale of Our Own Times* (1830) by showing that a bad mistress (and unloving mother) is poorly served because she is so lax about paying wages to her staff. The message seems clear enough: "free" servants must be paid, and on time. Here is the snag: this same novel extols an extraordinarily loyal "free" servant-character who refuses to leave a bankrupt mother and grown son. "When I asked him," his bemused ex-employer reports, "where he meant to go when we left the house, he drew up with the greatest dignity, and said, 'With *the family*, to be sure.'" Since this vignette was supposed to depict heartfelt loyalty, it is crucial that Agrippa is of African descent. Knowledge of the freedman called "Grippy," who served in Sedgwick's childhood home, is salient here; so, perhaps, is the fact that Freeman died while *Clarence* was in manuscript.[30] Still, fictional Agrippa's loyalty does not clear up the question of how "free" Freeman really was. Instead, it rather disturbingly implies that if Sedgwick thought African American laborers had a place in the wage-earning world, that place was not equivalent to that of other attendants'.

Returning to the period in which "free" service was still new, a New Englander named Sarah Savage wrote a guide for U.S. servants that addressed wages and deference. Yet *Advice to a Young Woman at Service in a Letter from a Friend* (1823) also preached affect: "the longer you live in a family the more you will feel interested in its concerns," Savage taught; in addition, "you will probably love the family better, and will consequently be more happy." This was not what Farmer Trueman had told his daughter as she prepared to serve in a nonkin home. Hanway's guide turns out, nevertheless, to be Savage's most obvious model, in that *Advice* counseled in the voice of a manual laborer related to the young-girl addressee. The major difference between *Farmer Trueman* and *Advice* is that the latter feminized, sentimentalized, and republicanized ideas about servitude. The feminization is patent, since Savage's counselor-character is a loving aunt; the sentimentalization is clear, considering what she says about coresidential attendance. "Let it be your ambition and your happiness to send the dishes up to the table in a manner that will gratify the family," the aunt teaches. "Enter into their feelings." Efforts to please are not debasing, she adds, to the right-minded republican. "Do not suppose," the aunt instructs her niece, "because I have recommended a plain dress, that I would have you feel as if you were in a low, degraded state. Far otherwise. We are all in some respects," she asserts, "upon an equality. We have the same country, the same religion, the same virtues to exercise." If hierarchies still obtain, she elucidates, that is because youth and gratitude foster a ranking that is family-like and therefore natural. Thus, Savage's narrator recalls that her feelings for the woman she had served included a dash of fear. The aunt adds, though, that she had "loved" her mistress "far more" and "was distressed that she should be troubled and perplexed." This avowal would have been congenial to Sedgwick. Yet it would be years before she would be as explicit about personal budgets, savings accounts, and the benefits of a nest egg. "How pleasant it would be," Savage's *Advice* imagines, "to have it in your power to furnish a room, to have one of your sisters or nieces live with you, and together with yourself take in work amongst your own people, and in the neighborhood of your relations and earliest friends."[31] Equally important, Sedgwick showed little to no interest, after *A New-England Tale*, in what happened to servitors after they left a nonkin home.

Down South, where the audience for advice to "free" servants was minuscule, Sedgwick's fiction was esteemed.[32] Yet, of course, bookish

Southerners read other authors, too, and when the topic was U.S. serv-ice, opinions in print ran the gamut. One traveler, who published his views in 1824, expressed disgust at plantation housekeeping. "[O]ne need not to be over-fastidious," he reported, "since, however neat the mistress, good luck is it if the kitchen is not lined with little half-naked smutchy implings, rolling and clawing about."[33] With equal candor, a conduct book for Southern mistresses admitted that slave management was a headache. Worse yet, Virginia Cary acknowledged immoral behav-ior—"The seeds of vice are scattered secretly with the very aliment that sustains life"—and cruelty. "It is not very long," *Letters on Female Character* admitted, "since I detected a young and *beautiful* female in inflicting corporal chastisement *with her own hands*, and in severe measure, upon a woman older by many years than herself. 'Tell it not in Gath!' lest it give our maligners just occasion to cast further and more direful aspersions upon us. But I trust these instances are rare."[34]

Few belletrists pursued this revelation in the 1820s; more common were Cooperesque juxtapositions of cranky "help" and loving, con-tented slaves. Reuses of this formula include Sarah Hale's novel *North-wood* (1827), which claimed that slaves were satisfied with "love as a recompense," and James E. Heath's forgotten *Edge-Hill, or, The Family of the Fitz-royals* (1828).[35] It may be coincidence that the name of Heath's clownish Irish housekeeper—Katy Waddle—is phonologically comparable to "Barbara Winkle," the name of John Pendleton Ken-nedy's comic English housekeeper in *Swallow Barn* (1832).[36] If, how-ever, a proud Southern riposte is indicated, it matters that the family-like slave in *Edge-Hill* is manumitted after a gesture of selfless loyalty, while *Swallow Barn* praised masters who accepted responsibil-ity for workers who were so childlike they could not survive on their own. Divergences of this sort are telling. Yet the crucial point is that for all their differences, each of these novels affirmed the idea that good service was family-like.

Sedgwick returned to the construction, maintenance, and market-ing of ideas of faithful attendance in *Hope Leslie; or, Early Times in the Massachusetts* (1827). There is no question about the appeal this romance had for antebellum Americans. *Hope Leslie* was "the most decided favourite of all [Sedgwick's] novels," according to John S. Hart's *Female Prose Writers of America* (1852), and "has continued," Sarah Hale attested, "to be her most popular tale."[37] This novel has much to recommend it: assured scene painting, dynamic action, a large cast of engaging characters, and spurts of elegant irony. In addition, the puta-tive heroine, Hope Leslie, has won admirers in the manner of spunky protagonists such as Capitola and Nancy Drew. More magisterial, though, is the grave and wise Magawisca, a Pequot girl taken into a white Puritan household and put to service chores. Over time, this stint of service brings her so close to a young Puritan man that she sacrifices an arm to save him from execution at her own father's hands. The fact that Elizabeth Freeman told a story of her days in slavery about a bloody attack on her upper arm cannot be incidental here.[38] But of course, few nineteenth-century readers of *Hope Leslie* could have known what Freeman endured. What most were likely to notice, then, was yet another juxtaposition, this one between noble Magawisca and gossipy Jennet, an English servant who is extremely annoying.

The contrast between these two servant-characters is important enough for Sedgwick to draw it several times. Thus, Magawisca repulses Jennet, who greets the Pequot girl with a gratuitous racist slur at their first meeting; thus, Magawisca could no more be Jennet's colleague than one "might . . . yoke a deer with an ox"; thus, Magawisca is somber and watchful, while Jennet's loose lips cause her undoing; thus, Hope considers Magawisca "neither a stranger, nor a servant," but finds Jennet a thorough nuisance.[39] Called "faithless," "our evil genius," and "an obstinate self-willed fool," Jennet offers only the burrlike brand of permanence that is fidelity's evil twin. "Long possession" had given free rein, Sedgwick writes, to Jennet's "tyrannical humours, which were naturally most freely exercised on those members of the family, who had grown from youth to maturity under her eye. In nothing was the sweetness of Hope Leslie's temper more conspicuous, than in the perfect good nature with which she bore the teasing impertinencies of this menial, who, like a cross cur, was ready to bark at every passer by." Nor was there any reason to see the barking as hiding a heart of gold, for Sedgwick, as omniscient narrator, explains that though Jennet displays "a sort of attachment to the family she had long served," it is only "that of an old cat for its accustomed haunts."[40] The obvious question—why would a homemaker allow such an obtrusion into the home?—is answered in terms of a necessary evil: Jennet's household skills are said to be "invaluable" to those she serves.

The "lamentable dependance of housekeepers on servants" that bothered so many nineteenth-century U.S. didacts rested on new concepts of gender and in-house labor as much as on gentility. Yet it was presented as a privilege in advice designed for wealthier women's leisure reading: the trials of domestic management, taught an 1836 article in *American Ladies' Magazine*, were "a tax which the rich must pay for their exemption from labor." Knowledge of this line of argument makes it all the more noticeable that the high point of *Hope Leslie*'s action-packed plot comes when Jennet dies in an explosion. I cannot be certain how odd this piece of plotting appeared in 1827. Yet its violence should give pause, especially when compared with the rest of Sedgwick's fiction. Perhaps it is overreading to suggest that this death intimated boons to a labor arrangement that allowed the privileged to dismiss a servant before he or she had accrued enough power to harm those the servant was supposed to attend. Yet in fact, scant sympathy is expressed for Jennet's "awful destiny," since it is seen as one she "herself indirectly prepared" by tattling on those whose affairs she should have protected. Pertinent here too is Sedgwick's decision to have *Hope Leslie*'s two admirable servant-characters, Magawisca and a British man named Digby, leave service to live with kin or, as intended readers might have put it, "their own kinds." This is, of course, what Freeman had chosen to do when she left the Sedgwicks to marry an African American man. In contrast, Jennet had looked set to stay on forever, to act as an irritant comparable to the discomfort of "pinching shoes, and smoky rooms."[41]

Such sustained attention to servants' mobility is striking, since the topic had last been raised, in Sedgwick's oeuvre, with regard to the slave-character in *Redwood* who runs off to be free. Magawisca does not run off or otherwise contest the rules of engagement that leave her serving white Puritans. If she is nonetheless out of place in that setting, since the labor does not suit her and her fellow workers are hostile, there are different ways to interpret that authorial strategy. The bottom line, for our purposes, is that her eventual departure has the feeling of order being restored. As this message is a bit surprising from a sentimental didact, it is fair to ask what Sedgwick accomplished by the removal. The answer is that she removed the threat of cross-race intimacy between Magawisca and a young white gentleman while making it possible for her heroine to meet the Pequot woman as something other than a servitor.

Exactly where rank distinctions fit into the Magawisca-Hope relationship is a matter of some interest, since despite the former's years as a servant, the latter is never her mistress; instead, the two meet as adults, long after nonkin attendance has come to an end. The Puritans with whom Magawisca was interned have ties to Hope, because they are the people with whom she would have lived if all had gone according to plan. Since, however, plans went awry, Hope and Magawisca are able to establish a cross-race friendship in which rank seems to play no role—a pretty picture, to some eyes. Yet service hides at its heart insofar as the two could not converse if Magawisca had not learned English while serving as, in effect, a prisoner of war. Historically, the composition of *Hope Leslie* precedes, by a considerable span of time, the "tender violence" Laura Wexler has discerned in the real-world interactions of whites and Native Americans in mission schools; there too, though, a favored form of training was domestic. Like other recent critics of sentimentality, Wexler focuses—quite rightly—on the "aggressive potential" embedded in deployments of affect across kinship and community lines.[42] Back in the antebellum period, though, a different objection to portraiture such as Sedgwick's was raised: the utter impossibility of enforcing sentimental precepts.

Two African American advisors of Sedgwick's era understood this aspect of affective counsel and tackled it in print. Neither Robert Roberts nor Maria W. Stewart referenced Sedgwick. Yet both were explicit about wages, and Stewart in particular spotlighted unequal job opportunities. Roberts acknowledged racism, too. Having amassed considerable wealth, however, as a butler in several elite U.S. homes, he was more ready to affirm aspects of the sentimental program while trying to give nonkin service something like professional dignity.

A man of standing in Boston's free black community, Roberts became wealthy enough, through hard work and thrift, to own several homes.[43] This fact helps to explain why he presented nonkin service in a positive light in *The House Servant's Directory* (1827) but also how he was able to craft what is thought to be the first book by an African American to be published on U.S. soil. *The House Servant's Directory* displays formidable expertise in the arcane field of fashionable practices concerning precedence, conversation, table service, and the order of dishes, napery, and a dizzying array of tableware. Knowledge of such things grounded Roberts's attempt to advance a race-marked model of "free" service in which cooks, maids, and footmen are laborers who deserve to be fed, housed, nursed, clothed, and paid. This is a good deal more than the benevolent nurture that slaveholders claimed to take as a religious duty, since Roberts's model employer pays for his manservants' several suits and various pairs of shoes. That, however, is not a point that *The House Servant's Directory* chose to raise; instead, as might be expected, Roberts mounted his campaign with *politesse:* "It would be presumption in me, a servant, to urge aught . . . to my superiors," one passage bows. More delicacy is seen in a rebuke of bad servitors that appears to be designed to flatter mistresses. "There are many young men who live out in families," Roberts scolds, "who, I am sorry to say, do not know how to begin their work in proper order unless being drove by the lady of the family, from one thing to another, which keeps

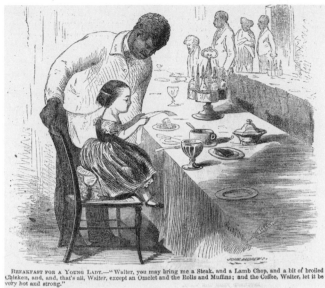

BREAKFAST FOR A YOUNG LADY.—" Waiter, you may bring me a Steak, and a Lamb Chop, and a bit of broiled Chicken, and, and, that's all, Waiter, except an Omelet and the Rolls and Muffins; and the Coffee, Waiter, let it be very hot and strong."

In 1856, Harper's New Monthly Magazine *acknowledged the truism that African Americans made the best attendants—so good, in this case, as to bow solicitously to a precocious young miss. Special Collections, University of Virginia Library.*

them continually in a bustle and their work is never done. . . . [H]ow disagreeable it must be for the lady, who has to tell them every thing that she wants to be done."[44]

Another example of Roberts's tact is his penchant for quoting sources as irreproachable as Scripture and *The Cook's Oracle* (London, 1822). His samplings are instructive, for from Luke 10:7 he drew the passage "the labourer is worthy of his hire," while from the British work he took the idea that "Mere money is a very inadequate compensation to a complete cook."[45] The implied QED was that nonkin service, a unique form of work, had to be organized in a special way.

The House Servant's Directory differs from sentimental fiction about service in three important ways. First, it counsels (as Farmer Trueman and Sarah Savage had only pretended to do) in the tones of one who has obeyed an employer's rule. Second, Roberts does not deplore lazy mistresses; instead, he takes on the tricky task of teaching employers to regard nonkin service as a job rather than a demonstration of kinlike fealty. Third, *The House Servant's Directory* puts an African

American man in an authoritative role. Ministers such as Richard Allen and poet-essayists such as Jupiter Hammond had written as teachers already. Yet in Roberts's case, the fact that the people most likely to buy his book were wealthier whites meant that the temerity of his teaching had to be excused by a pretense that his intended audience was young black servants, especially men—that is, readers much like Roberts himself, except in terms of age. Who better, *The House Servant's Directory* murmurs, than a head servant trained in genteel ways to teach young workers how to attend other people's homes? What Roberts does not say is that the same head servant is also the right man to teach homemakers (whose money could have been recently acquired) what is currently correct. Instead, as if to deprecate his own speech, Roberts notes how prudent it is for servants to watch how they speak and what they say. Servants "should never be pert," *The House Servant's Directory* advises, "or strive to enter into conversation with their employers or any visitant that may come to the house, unless they speak to you or ask you a question"; should that happen, Roberts counseled, "you should answer them in a polite manner, and in as few words as possible."[46] As *The House Servant's Directory* is polite and far from pert, there could be no objection that Roberts had overstepped his "place." But that, Maria W. Stewart indicated in 1832, was precisely what was wrong with advice of this kind.

A brave and committed activist, Stewart deemed wages for nonkin service a given yet judged the work itself a bad proposition. Like Roberts, she spoke from personal experience; however, as a former "bound" girl, she had toiled through years of nonkin labor that had little in common with his supervisory role. "I have heard much," Stewart told a Boston audience in 1832, "respecting the horrors of slavery; but may Heaven forbid that the generality of my color throughout these United States should experience any more of its horrors than to be a servant of servants, or hewers of wood and drawers of water! Tell me no more of southern slavery; for with few exceptions . . . I consider our condition but little better than that."[47]

Hopes of emulating the extraordinary financial rise of the fortunate few among U.S. servants were vain, in Stewart's eyes. "Neither do I know of any," she commented, "who have enriched themselves by spending their lives as house-domestics, washing windows, shaking carpets, brushing boots, or tending upon gentlemen's tables."[48] Quite apart from this job description (which distinguished between the job of butlering and that of the average maid-of-all-work), Stewart insisted on the primacy of issues that Roberts chose to mute. One was that free black

Americans were forced into service work because access to better jobs was restricted. Another, which Stewart knew from painful personal experience, was that even if the provision of room and board helped domestic servants save a percentage of their wages, it could be hard for black Americans to hold on to what they had earned.[49] For these reasons, as much as race pride and personal dignity, she told black parents not to send their children to service posts under the delusion that a few years of nonkin attendance would pave the way to better things. Not only was this result uncertain, but far more troubling overall was black Americans' inability to enforce either sentimental tenets *or* Roberts's correctives. For a writer as politically astute as Stewart, this last point made all well-intentioned, but practically impotent, advice a stumbling block.

The fact that domestic advice was little more than a clutch of suggestions (as opposed to, say, a reform bill or even a clear-cut example of agitprop) may seem to imply that didactic fiction was a waste of time. But antebellum Americans did not think so, since Mary Kelley has found a Southern girl writing home from boarding school in 1839 with an urgent request for her copy of *Home,* while Marli Weiner has described a plantation mistress who "filled a combined diary and commonplace book" with material quoted and clipped from contemporary print, including Sedgwick's work.[50] Fellow advisors were impressed, too, for Catharine Beecher commended *Live and Let Live* in her *Treatise on Domestic Economy* (1841), and Caroline Howard Gilman passed critical judgment on *The Linwoods.* The South Carolina resident showed respect: "We have no existing American female writer quite equal to Miss Sedgwick," Gilman avowed. But even a writer of stature could be wrong, for Sedgwick "misunderstands [slaves'] character," Gilman remarked, "if she means Rose as a specimen" since Southern slaves "are the most careless, light-hearted creatures in the world."[51] As Rosa is not the heroine of *The Linwoods* and does little to advance the plot, this comment reveals extraordinary attention to servant characterization. Gilman may have felt irked to learn that Nathaniel Hawthorne would name Sedgwick "our most truthful novelist."[52] But she would certainly have recognized Marie St. Claire, the lazy Southern mistress in *Uncle Tom's Cabin,* as a near-copy of *Redwood's* pettish belle. Returning to Roberts and Stewart, the timing of their remarks suggests desire to respond to something current. If that interpretation holds, then their work should be understood as (among other things) a measure of the clout that literary representations of service were seen as having well before Alexis de Tocqueville opined about service relations in a democracy and radical abolitionists chose to allege that waged service was a form of slavery.

Predating those interventions, and shaping the opinions of didacts such as Sedgwick and Gilman, were texts as different as David Walker's *Appeal* (1829) and Thomas R. Dew's "positive good" arguments for slavery. For a sentimentalist attentive to nonkin service, Walker's manifesto could seem tangential. There was direct relevance, in contrast, to Dew's assertion that *"homes and firesides"* alone "can change the wandering character of the savage, and make it his interest to cultivate peace instead of war." Though some antebellum Americans found Dew's theses compelling, the strong antislavery convictions of Sedgwick's family gave her reason to doubt. So did a trip to Virginia in 1833, during which she recorded the sight of "two slaves who stood on the outside and planting their ears against a broken pane of glass listen'd intently" to guests' celebrations of the Fourth of July, as if they thought the "declar'ns as applicable to them as us. One had a lowering brow," Sedgwick remembered, "and if I mistake not made his own deductions." After this trip, she made it a point to admit that the "horrid blight of slavery . . . seems to me far worse since I have seen it."[53] The plot of *Redwood* shows how strongly Sedgwick had always resisted assertions, such as Frances Trollope's in *Domestic Manners of the Americans* (1832), that "the state of a domestic slave in a gentleman's family was preferable to that of a hired American 'help.'" Only in the 1830s, though, did she make discussions of servants' wages explicit and clarify that family-like service did not mean the abjuring of kinship ties. A more radical commentator was right to say that her service-labor theory was "not truly democratic."[54] Yet this onlooker almost certainly failed to realize how decidedly Sedgwick had amended assumptions and predilections that she had come to see as wrong. The one glaring blind spot left in her vision of "free" service, after the amendments of the 1830s, was that she did not insist her rules for the payment of wages be applied to attendants of African descent.

To explicate this argument, it is helpful to recognize that one of *Clarence*'s many subplots has an Irish manservant accept a bribe to secure the money needed to rescue his father and siblings from poverty. Readers of *Hope Leslie* already knew that members of heterogeneous households could go on feeling attached to "their own people." There, though, Sedgwick had had to deal with the fact that she could not let her Anglo hero marry Magawisca, and, from this vantage, it was handy to have a home to send her off to. In contrast, *Clarence* has a Celt agree to perjure himself against the novel's heroine, a good mistress-character who has never done him wrong, because he wants to help kin emigrate. "Conolly," says the shyster who hopes to suborn a few lies, "this is a hard case and we must try every expedient—every way to get justice done; now if you will stand by us—my client is generous, and he has authorized me to spare neither pains nor money to get witnesses for him—name a particular sum, my good fellow, . . . three or four hundred dollars?" . . .

"Three, or four! *four!* I have one hundred already, and that would just make up the sum, and fetch them all over; the old man, and Peggy, and Roy, and Davy, and Pat, and just set them down gentalely in New York. . . . It would be heaven's mercy to the poor souls that's starving at home. What is it ye'll have me forget?"[55]

The plainest sign that Sedgwick wanted readers to sympathize with this servant's plight is his joy when the perjured testimony is disproved. Equally striking, though, is the fact that the only attendant more faithful (in this novel) than Conolly is Agrippa, the black servant who refuses to leave employers who can no longer pay. This refusal looks designed to warm sentimental hearts. It would have been more compelling, though, if Agrippa had been characterized enough for readers to know what his options were, that is, if he had kin anywhere or alternate ways of finding a home.

A similar criticism arises with regard to *The Linwoods*'s "happy ending" for Rosa, a mixed-race lady's maid who longs to be free. Rosa's love and trust for her mistress suggest a politicization of advice disseminated in *Godey's* in 1833. "Look at the mode," this snippet exclaims, "in which the French treat their servants! If a French maid-servant has a love affair, she consults her mistress about it, and debates all the pro's and con's with her; the natural emotions of the heart are not stifled; the mistress feels interested in the welfare of her dependent; she advises her, and promotes her happiness, because she feels that she is part of her own family."[56]

Rosa's mistress does try to promote the happiness of her beloved maid. Yet because she is not this slave's owner, there is little she can do to bring her manumission about. I appreciate this novel's argument that women of all ranks and races were entrapped in variant versions of an overarching patriarchy.[57] There is a real shortfall, though, in the way Sedgwick wraps up the story of the freedwoman who, having been granted the boon she seeks, goes on serving happily. "Rosa's outward condition was in no wise changed," *The Linwoods* beams, to dispense with this character, yet because "her mind was freed from galling shackles . . . she now enjoyed the voluntary service she rendered."[58] This was one way to handle the question of what to do with freedpersons—put them to the same jobs they had held in slavery—and it would be offered repeatedly in nineteenth-century U.S. print. It was incomplete, however, since Sedgwick could easily have devoted a sentence or two to explaining the basis on which Rosa went on working: where she slept, who paid for her clothes, and so on. This she did not do until she left the world of novels to write about servants who earned wages in a format Mary Kelley has named the "tale cum tract."[59]

This classification is basically sound. But considering the length, plot complexity, and sentimental purpose of the advisory texts Sedgwick developed after her trip to Virginia, the word "tract" may mislead. It is true that *Home, The Poor Rich Man and the Rich Poor Man* (1837), and *Live and Let Live; or, Domestic Service Illustrated* were published in a size suited to a pocket, or smaller hands, and that the diction in all three is less elevated than that found in *Hope Leslie* and *The Linwoods*. Pertinent, too, is Sedgwick's decision not to write short, simple texts like *The African Servant* or indeed her own *Mary Hollis*, especially since the format shift resulted in what would be hailed as "one of the most popular series of works ever published."[60] To keep Sedgwick's nonevangelical agenda and narratological decisions in view while avoiding the pejorative connotations of the word "novelette," I categorize her best-loved work of the 1830s as "didactic novellas" similar in tone and complexity to the boys' and girls' books by Horatio Alger Jr. This format appealed to working-class readers well before Alger's day, however, for Sedgwick was thrilled to hear, in 1835, that a Lowell mill-girl approved of *Home* and was proud to report, almost twenty years later, that a "carman" had been seen "reading in the crowded street, and [was] apparently absorbed" in *Live and Let Live*.[61]

What did these didactic novellas teach? Starting with *Home*, the book is a plotted and characterized primer on nurturing home and "family" life. Parenting, care for the elderly, and responsibility to the local poor are among the topics woven into the story of a respectable but not wealthy family. However, the topic of most interest to students of service literature will be Sedgwick's treatment of Martha, an attendant so embracing and embraced that "the family joys and sorrows were part and parcel with hers, hers with theirs." Martha is explicitly free to go, and her formal recompense is emphasized. "As her qualifications increased with her years, and her labors with the growth of the family, [her employers] had augmented her wages."[62] This directive is all the more striking in that it appeared the same year that *The Linwoods* had had nothing to say about how a freed servant was recompensed.

A point of interest: same-year publishing was something Sedgwick had done before, since *Mary Hollis* and *A New-England Tale* both appeared in 1822. Quite apart from productivity, however, same-year publication reveals a pattern, which is that in both 1822 and 1835 Sedgwick discussed the conditions of family-like service in one novel and one non-novel but put considerably more detail about this topic into the didactic texts. Equally suggestive is the fact that the two novels end up releasing gently bred girls from service responsibilities, while the two shorter texts conclude with girls from poor homes contentedly serving agreeable nonkin, with no marital prospects in sight. Race is not the key variable here, for if Jane in *A New-England Tale* was white, Sally Hollis is "not negro," and while Rosa in *The Linwoods* is a lighter-skinned slave, Martha in *Home* seems to have been purposefully unraced. Ambiguity here is easy to miss, for while Sedgwick clarifies on page 7 that Martha is a "young girl whom [Mrs. Barclay] had 'taken to bring up,'" she only notes in passing, on page 114, that "the poor laborers" of the area in which the Barclays grew to adulthood were both "black and white." Since Sedgwick could easily have been more explicit here (by, for example, mentioning Martha's "red face" or "ebon hue"), the inference has to be that she chose to direct attention to the importance of making *any* nonkin coresidential menial feel like "a member of their family" and "their friend." Perhaps no antebellum reader wondered, in the face of meager characterization, whether Martha was black, white, or other. Yet it is well to be cautious about assuming much on this score, since Sedgwick may have expected readers to know that a modest urban household in the North, which relied on one "maid of all work," was a likely place to find a servant of African descent.[63] If she left the matter open to give *Home* greater identificatory potential, indeterminacy may explain why she found this didactic novella "more generally acceptable than anything I have before written."[64]

Of course, the character of Martha is not the only reason *Home* sold widely and well. Yet if served Americans approved of a character who is glad to cook and clean with affect and for decades, Americans who might have to serve (or consider that line of work for their children) could have been as pleased to meet employer-characters who treat a "free" laborer lovingly. "[T]here would not be half so much complaining of help," *Home*'s mistress-character teaches, "if the master and mistress had a religious sense of their duties to them, and took proper pains to promote their happiness."[65] This ecumenical gesture is not incidental, since *Home* was published in the same Unitarian series that had hosted *Mary Hollis*. There are nonetheless marked differences between what *Home* had to say and the vision of good service relationships offered by stories such as Sarah Savage's *Trial and Self-Discipline* (1835) and the anonymous *Ann Connover* (1835), and these differences help demonstrate why Sedgwick would work out a new storytelling format for efforts such as *Live and Let Live*. Neither *Trial and Self-Discipline*, which appeared in the same Unitarian series that hosted *Home*, nor *Ann Connover*, a text printed under the auspices of the American Sunday-School Union, enjoyed anything close to the tremendous sales of Sedgwick's didactic novellas; nor did either call on employers to extend themselves to make coresidential attendants feel familial. If servants do come to feel that way, both *Trial and Self-Discipline* and *Ann Connover* indicate, it will be due to their own efforts rather than any obligation masters and mistresses are bound to recognize.

Looking first at *Ann Connover*, kin-training is shown to be the recourse through which poor immigrant girls are inducted into a right-minded view of their serving lot. Ann's story begins with her mother's death, after which the teenaged girl must find a job and home. The obvious answer, "free" service, is approved by her Aunt Jane, the family-like inmate of a nonkin home. Jane teaches Ann that popular notions of service work are wrongheaded: "Servants," she admonishes, "are not slaves." To bolster this argument, Jane insists on the willed nature of "free" service and says that it protects workers in that if a mistress "requires more than is proper, or reasonable, you know the girl may leave her. So where is the hardship? It is a fair bargain between them."[66] As this explanation recalls one of the most popular defenses of "free" labor, it is telling that *Ann Connover* is at pains to demonstrate that kinship ties are not negated by coresidence with employers; indeed, kinship claims may enhance wage earners' loyalty. If a related insinuation is that the Irish are clannish, *Ann Connover* does not hold that attribute against them; instead, it makes clan responsibilities a good substitute for the family-like warmth mistresses may fail to provide. Significantly, then, while Ann's first employer is pleased with her, there is no suggestion that she feels responsible for the teenager living in her home. Silence on this topic may have been a backhanded stab at slaves' mistresses, since this Southern-bred mistress-character spoils a black servant boy until he cannot be made to work. *Home* deplored the evils of slavery more directly. Targeted there, though, are the failings of Northern homemakers who do not treat waged attendants like family.

Turning now to *Trial and Self-Discipline*, Savage's central servant-character is not a young Celt but a grown black woman so family-like that she offers to share her life savings with an erstwhile employer who goes bankrupt. Race was crucial enough to the lesson Savage hoped to teach that *Trial and Self-Discipline* remarks on Phillis's "jet complexion"; acknowledged here, then, is African Americans' presence in the "free" service labor pool. Perhaps Savage hoped to rebut Maria W. Stewart's charge that nonkin service was not African Americans' best bet for financial security or to find African Americans decent, loyal, and religious. There were drawbacks, though, to the decision to make nonkin affection these workers' leading quality: "it is so unusual," Savage's mistress-character chirps, "to be . . . beloved by our domestics." In this respect, little differentiates Phillis from Sedgwick's Agrippa. "I cannot leave you," Phillis tells the mistress who can no longer pay. "Where you go, I must go."[67] The idea that a "free" black servant might stay and serve without wages was not as absurd as may be supposed, considering the psychological effects of racism and restricted job opportunities. Yet as long as sentimental advisors failed to advance similar tributes to servant-characters of all races and ethnicities, they embroiled affect in the never-ending task of crafting notions of whiteness, class/gender, and gentility.

By leaving Martha's race and ethnicity vague, *Home* evaded this pitfall. The question is, did silence redress the damage done by making Agrippa and Rosa so blithe about recompense? The novelist who responded most directly to Sedgwick's efforts did not say whether "free" black servants were or were not worthy of their hire for the simple reason that she did not identify any of her "free" servant-characters as of African descent. Caroline Gilman nonetheless reported having "received thanks and congratulations from every quarter" for *Recollections of a Housekeeper* (1834). This memory is borne out, to some extent, by the review in *The New-England Magazine* that praised this novel as "full of truth, and liveliness."[68] However, "every quarter" has to have meant geography rather than an array of social and class designations, since servant-readers could not have found much to like about this story of a Northern mistress driven near mad by untrained farm girls, Irish drunks, and petty thieves. Thus, one attendant breaks china and dresses showily, while another claims to be pious but turns out to be "the mere child of excitement. She attended every denomination," mistress-character Clarissa recalls, so that she was "out every evening." Nor is the hiring of a gently raised servant the answer since, even though she shows "no affectation of better days" and "went through her work with precision and fidelity," her speedy death suggests that ladies cannot handle heavy chores. If, however, gentility and hard labor do not mix, neither do nonkin service and personhood, since the worker Clarissa describes as "'the perfectest pattern of excelling' housekeepers"—so efficient that her household "affairs went on like clockwork"—does not stay long enough in her employment to merit a name.[69] The point of all this is the tacit proposition that waged servants obtrude on "family" life.

In contrast, there is clear merit to "bound" service, in Gilman's eyes, as long as mistresses accept motherlike responsibilities. Clarissa's failure to do so, at a certain point, took me by surprise, since she had struck me as that pitiable figure, a devoted homemaker forced to hire from an abysmally deficient labor pool. More is revealed about her, though, when Gilman deems it time to teach that, the shortcomings of the Northern situation being understood as a given, a good woman makes the best of the situation by working out a form of home management in which servitors feel like family. Such a system is most likely to develop, *Recollections of a Housekeeper* suggests, in the case of workers such as Polly, "an orphan from the Female Asylum, bound to me," Clarissa recalls, "until the age of eighteen." Things go agley, however, when she leaves Polly—a worker initially "so docile and innocent" that "could I always have sheltered her under my own wing, she would have been pure as a bird, and might have plumed her flight from me to Heaven"—under the direction of one of those "unprincipled wretches [who] may be brought into the very heart of our domestic circles" by the vagaries of "free" service. The prospect of one's home harboring a villain had to cause alarm. Yet the real culprit, Gilman intimates, is the mistress foolish enough to relinquish control of the household after noticing that her *"little girl"* has begun to wear cheap finery and curl her hair. Clarissa's excuse for letting a blowsy cook become Polly's new surrogate mother is the claim of a closer tie. "My whole soul was absorbed," she recalls, in her infant son, "or perhaps I should have noticed the under-current that was hurrying Polly to destruction. To see his intelligent smile . . . to kiss his rounded limbs . . . to feel his dimpled hand on my cheek . . . to sing him lullabies . . . was not this occupation enough for a young mother?"[70] *Recollections of a Housekeeper*'s implied answer is "No, not enough," for Clarissa's assertion that "I had loved Polly like a younger sister" is weakened by her confession of absorption with kin. Readers were to conclude, then, that good women "mother" all coresidents, not just those related by blood.

As a work of sentimental advice, *Recollections of a Housekeeper* had much in common with Sedgwick's output. It diverged significantly, though, in teaching that "free" service is bad and "bound" service better (note that Polly returns, humbled and newly grateful for a home). This finding hinted that a still more immobilized form of in-house service would be best of all. Building on this premise, Gilman's second (and final) novel insisted on the impossibility of relying on a white servant in the South. Like *Recollections of a Housekeeper*, *Recollections of a Southern Matron* (1838) must have evoked chuckles in some homes. There was nevertheless strong didactic intent to a story packed full of episodes showing that when slaves need supervision, their mistresses provide it without self-pity. At times, indeed, it appears that *Recollections of a Southern Matron* was written to expose Clarissa's failings. Where, for example, the Northern mistress admits having been influenced by a cook who is hard of hearing—"I often forgot," she notes, "that others were not deaf, and caught Edward [i.e., her husband] smiling at my trumpet-tongued style"—the Southern homemaker denies that slaveholders' children pick up chattels' pidgin. "I have never felt any more apprehension," the Matron avows, "at having my children associate with negroes, lest their dialect should be permanently injured, than I should have at their listening to the broken English of a foreigner." In slaveholding states, this remark shows, social boundaries are maintained. The one place confusion may arise, the Matron adds, is if any try to transport Northern labor arrangements to the South. Not only is this caring mistress bemused at the innovation of directing a "free servant" who reads Walter Scott's romances: "how could I think," she dithers, "of ordering such a person? I was really embarrassed, said *ma'am* to her in my incertitude, and used as much form, and perhaps more, than I should to a distinguished stranger." More disturbing, to the tenderhearted, is her discovery that the white girl does not like to hear herself labeled "*servant!* Poor Lucilla, a dark cloud rested for several days on her countenance."[71] The name "Lucilla" may have been chosen randomly. But maybe not, since Sedgwick had won plaudits, a year before the Matron's recollections appeared, for a didactic novella about a "free" white servant named Lucy Lee.

I will discuss *Live and Let Live* presently. It is worth saying first, though, that one review of *Recollections of a Southern Matron* brought up the idea of rivalry: "Miss Sedgwick must look to her laurels," this piece purred.[72] Evidence that Sedgwick took up the gauntlet is slender. Yet the book she wrote after *Live and Let Live* includes what may be a tweak. "The condition of our country calls for more enlarged powers in our women," *Means and Ends* (1838) opined. "The northern mother and housewife need them," Sedgwick continued, adding that, "The southern matron eminently needs them."[73] While it would be rash to assume a poke at Gilman, "eminently" does seem designed to provoke. Perhaps Sedgwick was vexed by the review that deemed the two *Recollections* books "finely adapted to the promotion of social intercourse and kindly feelings between the different parts of the United States."[74]

If so, she would not have been best pleased, decades later, to find Sarah Hale attesting that Gilman "never parades fictitious woes."[75] Hale made this statement in 1855, three years after Gilman had republished her two servant-oriented novels in a single volume and renamed the first *Recollections of a New England Bride*.[76] The implication that antiabolitionists felt the heat generated by *Uncle Tom's Cabin* is supported by the return of *Swallow Barn* and *Northwood*, in revised form, in 1852. At this point, Kennedy added remarks about "contentment and good humor and kind family attachment" among the black and white members of a plantation household, while Hale added chapters on slavery and changed the subtitle of *Northwood* (which had been "A Tale of New England") to "Life North and South: Showing the True Character of Both."[77] Here is more evidence that sentimental didacts read each other's work with an eye on discussions of servitude.

Returning, though, to *Recollections of a Housekeeper*'s allegation that every new "free" servant comprised "a forlorn hope—one of those experiments that New-England ladies are so constantly obliged to make of the morals and dispositions of strangers," the distinct differences between Sedgwick's and Gilman's advice merit scrutiny. Perhaps it is incidental that both women spent most of their childhoods in Massachusetts and that, as adults, both would proudly recall their families' distinguished New England lineages. More might be made of the fact that both chose to write professionally in a day when that career was unusual for a lady and that both were Unitarians with responsibility for managing nonkin staff.[78] Yet I would stress that both had been exposed to chattel service at an early age, since Sedgwick grew up near the people who abused Freeman, while Gilman "passed four winters" on her brother's plantation near Savannah. Gilman's views may have been formed in childhood, with or without the influence of that slave-owning brother. Yet plainly enough, it would have become prudent to affirm a proslavery stand once she and her husband moved to Charleston, South Carolina, a city she would come to call "my dear home, the home of my choice."[79] That being said, prudence may not have been the only or main consideration, given Gilman's incredulity at the idea that two other Charlestonians had freed (rather than sold) their human chattel.[80] It is hard to be sure, since one early twentieth-century source says that Samuel and Caroline Gilman hired other people's slaves, while another says that the couple bought domestic workers in order to train and free them.[81] Back in her own day, Gilman herself seems to have maintained that she could live with whatever social arrangements Providence might, in its wisdom, mandate. Thus, according to Harriet Martineau, Gilman professed a "doctrine . . . that the one race must be subordinate to the other, and that if the blacks should ever have the upper hand, she would not object to standing on [the block] with her children, and being sold to the highest bidder."[82]

It is impossible to imagine Sedgwick saying anything of this kind. Yet she could and did ponder deference. "If the servants become wiser than their mistresses," she opined in 1828, "and the ladies have their own labor to perform at last, it will but fall into the hands of the inferior class. But this is horrible democracy . . . treason against my caste."[83] As if to justify her "caste," Sedgwick expended more energy than any other U.S. writer trying to help Americans adjust to "free" attendance. Feeling her way in and around innovation, she sometimes had to rethink her counsel. Thus *Home* asked mistresses to abjure a term to which "free" service workers had been known to object. "Servant!" exclaims the narrator of this didactic novella, "we beg Martha's pardon, *help*. Serving most assiduously, she had an antipathy to the word *servant*. Was she not right? . . . *Help* may have a ludicrous and perhaps an alarming sound to unaccustomed ears; but is there a word in the English language more descriptive of the service rendered by a New-England domestic?"[84] This effort was doomed, at least for urban readers, since it flouted the dictates of gentility. So *Live and Let Live* taught something new. "How can a person," its good mistress-character asks,

> "who contracts to perform a certain labour under your roof, who makes her own stipulations, and may leave you with impunity at any moment, any more be called your servant, in the *old sense*, than the builder who builds your house, or the engineer who constructs your roads?"
>
> "How can they? Why they always have been called servants—my servants do the same work my grandmother's did, who were slaves—the same work that servants do in other countries."
>
> "Yes, but is not their condition changed, and does not that change the relation? Rely upon it, we make a fatal mistake, not so much in retaining old terms as in not fitting ourselves for the new relation—"
>
> "But stay, Sara, don't you call your servants servants?"
>
> "No, I call them domestics."[85]

This exchange precedes, by nearly three years, de Tocqueville's interest in the way in which democracy altered the "mutual relations" of master and servant, a finding that cannot be incidental to the fact that in so much of her oeuvre, Sedgwick countered the Tocquevillian contention that "free" service precluded "warm and deep-seated affections" between attendants and attendees.[86] Gender was central to this campaign insofar as where writers such as de Tocqueville routinely figured masters and servitors as men, sentimentalists had much more to say about mistresses and maids. This principle reached its fullest expression in *Live and Let Live,* the story of an intelligent and native-born white girl who, having fallen on hard times, needs to work in nonkin homes.

Enter Lucy Lee, a far cry from the rough-hewn Martha of *Home.* Designed as a servant for a new day and a specifically urban setting, Lucy was a gentrification of Sally Hollis, another girl forced into nonkin service because her father drank. More to the point, she was a *de*-gentrification of the Cinderella in *A New-England Tale* who has to serve until a gentleman offers her the haven of marriage; in stark contrast, Lucy leaves service to marry a baker's son. Lucy's clearest literary forebear, Elizabeth L****, does not marry at all. Yet like Lucy, Elizabeth serves faithfully because she wants to support her parents. This motivational decision permits *Live and Let Live* to affirm the importance of kinship ties while making a case for "free" servants' job mobility: needing to care, that is, for unemployable blood relatives, Lucy is shown to be willing to stay at a post yet to have cause to leave if higher wages can be found. Ann Connover and the faithful Phillis were also free to go. Yet since the writers who crafted Ann and Phillis did not choose to *have* them go—while Lucy does change jobs several times in *Live and Let Live*—Sedgwick must be seen as more purposefully working out what "free" attendance entailed.

Family-like affect was so central to *Live and Let Live*'s message that Lucy approves of her favorite employer by exclaiming: "How like mother she does talk!" The idea that mistresses who are not motherlike create their own domestic trials had been mooted in most of Sedgwick's previous publications. Yet it was pushed much more forcibly in *Live and Let Live.* Thus, one lazy homemaker "made it a rule never to take girls that had not lived out—they required too much teaching!" Another scoffs at the idea of "turn[ing] a gentleman's house into a school" for servant girls, while a third rejects Lucy when she finds that Mrs. Lee has already taught her daughter in-house skills. "I shall have to unlearn her the ways of such sort of people as you," she tells Lucy's mother, because "those of a gentleman's family are so different!"[87] Aware that Lucy is gently bred, readers were to see this snob as missing out on a girl who would have been an asset to her household.

Fortunately for Lucy, she has a wise mother to guide her toward motherlike mistresses. In the home of the first (who eventually becomes Lucy's mother-in-law), she is "reminded by nothing but the regular receipt of her wages that she was at service." This was a clear directive about the importance of paying live-in servants on a fixed schedule. Yet since it would seem to describe the epitome of family-like attendance, it is telling that Sedgwick plucks Lucy out of this home and sends her off to one that is more genteel. The genteel home can be called family-like. But it is not family-like in the warm and fuzzy way of the baker's household; instead, it is family-like in the sense that Lucy's new mistress accepts "untransferable duties" toward her live-in staff. Elegant and fashionable, then, but still maternal (since this is the mistress whose conversation reminds Lucy of her own mother's), Mrs. Hyde teaches her live-in staff about cleanliness and hygiene, budgets and accounting, plain sewing and child care. This was a stern view of mistress-ship, and Sedgwick knew it. "Just put the last word to my first draught of 'Live and Let Live,'" she noted in a diary. "It will offend some and shock many, but I am satisfied that it is in the main right."[88]

Friends concurred with the intimation that *Live and Let Live* was bold. "I can not," William Henry Channing told Sedgwick, "without violence to my feelings, refrain from expressing to you the great gratification with which I have read your 'Live and Let Live.' Thousands will be the better and happier for it; thousands, as they read it, will feel their deficiencies, and resolve to do better. No relation is so little understood among us as that of head of family and domestic. . . . No relation needs reform so much." Though this prominent minister (and frequent visitor to Brook Farm) did not say which "thousands" he had in mind, *Godey's* was more explicit. Finding *Live and Let Live* "a work which we can hardly praise too highly," it recommended the story of Lucy Lee to "every lady who wishes to learn how to do good."[89] This was the tone of most of the commentary in print. "We cannot doubt," proclaimed the *Knickerbocker Magazine*, "that the warmest hopes of the benevolent writer, in relation to her work, may be realized; that it *will* rouse female minds to reflection upon the duties and capabilities of mistresses of families, making them feel their obligations to 'inferiors in position,' and quickening their sleeping consciences."[90]

More praise emanated from some who thought servants the intended audience. "Miss Sedgwick pursues her design of instructing and entertaining the humbler classes of our citizens," the *American Quarterly Notice* enthused, "and her aim and execution are both to be commended." If the *New-York Review* disagreed, calling *Live and Let Live* "precisely the book we should wish to keep out of the hands of a numerous class of servants," a male homemaker thought that the real issue was practicability. "How we glow over these novels!" Ralph Waldo Emerson wrote of Sedgwick's most servant-centered story, but "How we drivel & calculate & shuffle & lie & skulk, in life!"[91]

Emerson's perception of a gap between literature and life may not change anybody's mind about whether sentimental precepts were, or were not, pernicious. Yet the larger point here is that sentimental tenets were advanced by pro- and antislavery writers, with and without identifications of "good" servants' race and ethnicity, and carrying burdens distinct enough that, for instance, *Ann Connover* asked more of maids whereas *Live and Let Live* asked more of mistresses. Divergence of this kind raises questions as to what Sedgwick might have accomplished if she had written one last piece of domestic advice literature that depicted a specifically African American worker as family-like as Agrippa yet with the majesty of Magawisca, the wages of Martha, and the job mobility—extending to marriage mobility—of Lucy Lee. Yet Sedgwick had already gone as far as she could, for her next book emphasized "heart-services" performed for kin-in-need rather than nonkin attendance.

In this respect, *Means and Ends* delighted diet-and-hygiene lecturer William Andrus Alcott. "I hate the practice," he had written, "of having domestics in the family." No sentimentalist would have agreed with Alcott that nonkin service was "rotten to the very core." More crucial, though, to the literature of nineteenth-century U.S. service, is the fact that writers of this ilk bracketed a question he raised in 1837. "By what right," Alcott inquired, "can one family claim part of the services of another? And why should A. be entitled to the services of a member of B.'s family, any more than B. is entitled to those of one of the members of the family of A. In other words, if a family is to be broken in upon, who is to decide whose it shall be?"[92]

The fact that affect-oriented advisors never grappled with this challenge is one measure of their efforts' theoretical shortfall. But Alcott was not the only antebellum American to note a dubious premise, for the reformers surveyed in chapters 2 and 3 saw tangles in sentimental advice, too. Affective ideals nonetheless proved quite difficult to revise, and not only because they were more suggestive than rigorous. Equally important, the ideal of family-like service implied an orderliness and stability that were vitally attractive to "privileged" Americans uncomfortable with the exigencies of a rank/gender status most would not have relinquished for the world.

2 Domestic and Social Experiments

He is not yet a man if he have not learned the Household Laws. . . .

—Ralph Waldo Emerson, "Home" (1838)

The fact that Emerson dismissed *Live and Let Live* may seem to require no explanation. Yet his decision to pick up a slender volume of advice literature—which, we recall, some reviewers thought was directed toward servants—is rather odd. Not only did Emerson generally mock sentimental nostrums; equally important, this devoutly intellectual man spent most of his time with weightier tomes. The best explanation of this oddity is that, as a tyro homemaker, Emerson had come face-to-face with what he would call "the woes of 'help.'" When he commented on Sedgwick's didactic novella, he had not yet initiated the reformist experiments that this chapter explores. But he *had* started to think about "the social position of domestics" and, not incidentally, to twit the conceit of those who opposed slavery.[1] "I hope," notes a journal entry of 1837, "New England will come to boast itself in being a nation of servants & leave to the planters the misery of being a nation of served."[2] Emerson ignored *Live and Let Live*'s claim that tension between homemakers and "free" attendants originated in attitudes passed down from the days in which household staff had been property. But he showed considerable interest in, and anxiety about, how to master. Lessons in maternal mistress-ship did nothing to dispel this anxiety.

Many aspects of Emerson's life and thought have been canvassed. Yet he is rarely classified as a producer of domestic counsel even though he had much to say about service and mastery after buying his first house and moving there with his second wife. This oversight is understandable, since reports on the "domestic & social experiments" conducted at "Bush" are not prominent in the lectures and essays Emerson published during his lifetime. They crop up repeatedly, however, in the Emerson Family Papers, an archive that includes letters written by Lidian Jackson Emerson and some of the staff on whom she relied.[3] Material of this kind makes it possible to draw inferences about the different ways in which members of one antebellum household regarded nonkin service during the period between the publication of *Live and Let Live* and 1844, the year in which Emerson publicly denounced the slave trade.

The Emerson who had the most to say about "struggling toward better household arrangements" during this period was not Lidian but Waldo. "It is more elegant to answer one's own needs," he wrote in his journal in 1840, "than to be richly served; inelegant, perhaps it may look, today & to a few, but elegant forever, and to all."[4] This aphorism is obviously congruent with proclamations about self-reliance and working with our own hands. Where, however, some Transcendentalists turned such avowals toward communitarian ends, Emerson devoted himself to managing his own household. While chapter 3 probes domestic service reform at Fruitlands and Brook Farm, worth mentioning here is the reason Emerson gave for declining George and Sophia Ripley's invitation to join the "New Family" they began organizing in 1840. "I think," he explained, "that my present position has even greater advantages than yours would offer me for testing my improvements in those small private parties into which men are all set off already throughout the world." Home ownership did not mandate reactionary attitudes or practices, he avowed. "The principal particulars in which I wish to mend my domestic life," this letter continues, "are in acquiring habits of regular manual labor, and in ameliorating or abolishing in my house the condition of hired menial service. . . . But surely I need not sell my house & remove my family to Newton in order to make the experiment of labor & self help. I am already in the act of trying some domestic & social experiments which my present position favors."[5]

This assertion presumably expresses Emerson's view of his situation. Yet hindsight suggests that, in fact, his specific rank/gender "position" went a long way toward *creating* the conditions of the experiments mentioned as well as a taste for such things. So did agitation about human bondage, since Emerson substituted "ameliorating or abolishing" for his first thought, "discontinuing," as if to nudge his reforms into conversation with antislavery activities. More evidence that slavery was on Emerson's mind, as he pondered "hired menial service," is the lecture of 1840 that praises those who work "for the freedom of the servant and the slave."[6] This phrasing supports the premise of this study: that complaints about waged service signified in relation to concerns about workers in fetters. More helpful, though, to those who would know why Emerson experimented when and as he did is recognition that he affirmed householding just as this component of masculine identity was beginning to erode.

The idea that the 1840s marked the onset of what Carole Shammas calls "the household's civil war" could be contested by those who respect the pressure that literature can bring to bear on ideologies in flux. Patent, though, from the research Shammas collects in *A History of Household Government in America* is a reduction of men's power over wives, children, and dependants, which followed hard on challenges to the idea of mastery in the world of "productive" labor that loomed so large in nineteenth-century notions of gender. In a study of these challenges, David R. Roediger has shown that manual and menial laborers made known their resentment of "masters" who could not demonstrate the skills relevant to their trades. What Shammas's study adds to this finding (as well as to Jeanne's Boydston's work on the devaluation of domestic labor on the grounds of its "nonproductivity") is evidence that mastery of the home was in crisis, too. Emerson was unusual, then, but quite right in seeing that a number of near-tectonic shifts and pressures converged at conceptualizations of mastery over "free" in-house staff. Recognizing this convergence, he spent years trying to establish a form of domestic management that could be called family-like, in a sense superior to the claims and protestations of those who exploited slaves.[7]

This argument leagues me alongside Len Gougeon, the historian who emphasizes the evolution of Emerson's thought between 1837 and 1844, rather than with Robert D. Richardson Jr., the biographer who asserts that Emerson was "firmly antislavery" in 1837 "and had been so for many years."[8] The significance of the year 1837 is that this was when Emerson first spoke in public about Southern labor practices, while 1844 marks the point at which his "Address on Emancipation in the British West Indies" identified him with the antislavery cause. I agree with Gougeon that the "Address" differs so markedly from the talk of 1837 that it reveals new attitudes on Emerson's part. I think nonetheless that Gougeon reifies a distinction so patent to us now that we forget that it once had to be worked out and naturalized—that is, the distinction between service that is "free" and that which is immobilized. Some sentimentalists dismissed this distinction as they tried to build a feeling of unity along the lines of wealth and privilege. Thus, Sarah Josepha Hale, in a short story of 1828, had a wage payer find that whereas slaves' mistresses "complain of their *servants,*" Northerners lament "our *help*. They talk of selling the *blacks* because of bad behaviour, and we of turning away our *whites* for similar faults."[9] Emerson did not leave any comment in his journals, lectures, or letters about Hale's sketch. He challenged its willed blindness, though, with every reference—high-minded *or* griping—to his own servants' mobility.

This "take" on antebellum discussions of U.S. labor nuances Gougeon's idea that the period between 1837 and 1844 comprised Emerson's "silent years" by revealing that, in fact, this was the period in which his papers show most interest in servitude, serviceability, and the meaning of "family" life. His public was granted a glimpse of this concern in a lecture of 1840 which promised that "in a community where labor was the point of honor . . . a mountain of chagrins, inconveniences, diseases, and sins would sink into the sea. . . . Domestic hired service would go over the dam. Slavery would fall into the pit. Shoals of maladies would be exterminated, and the Saturnian Age revive." This declamation manifests the "whimsy of manual labor which," Emerson noted in 1841, "infects us all like an influenza."[10] Yet its greater significance, for the purposes of this chapter, is its inference that "free" service was to be wiped away completely as a form of labor that ripped through kinship groups and virtually ensured sexual victimization while depriving millions of native-born Americans of essential legal rights. Such an inference could be taken at face value. Yet calls for banishment and eradication reveal more if viewed as symptoms of half-confessed dis-ease about the authority of householders whose residuals were legally free to go.

Feeding Emerson's dis-ease, in all likelihood, were sentimental visions of how lovingly Southern masters governed their human property. Widely available, then, was the claim William Alexander Caruthers staked in *The Kentuckian in New-York; or, The Adventures of Three Southerns* (1834). "I have known masters in Virginia to exhibit the most intense sorrow and affliction," a character in this novel states, "at the death of an old venerable household servant, who was quite valueless in a pecuniary point of view."[11] This was a charming image, in some eyes, if only because of the grim alternatives. The question was, what (if anything) did it say about mastery of servants who were "free"? That puzzler hovered over the homes of Northerners who recompensed nonkin staff as their parents had: that is, not as wage earners, in the modern sense, but as participants in a household economy. Thus, many antebellum servants were given credit with local merchants or paid a lump sum after a season of labor, credit or sum being determined by the state of the finances in the household they attended.[12] Sedgwick campaigned against this system by mentioning Martha's pay raises in *Home* and noting Lucy's "regular receipt of her wages" in *Live and Let Live.* Counteracting this aspect of her work, though, was the energy she (and others) put into lauding service that was family-like. Familial plaudits may have made life easier for some U.S. servants, sometimes. Yet they can only have made it more difficult to think of "free" servants as laborers in the sense of cobblers at their lasts or threshers in the fields; fostered, instead, was the idea that servants labored as add-on children or as spouse supplements.

In this respect, sentimental advice encouraged employers to feel aggrieved when attendants asserted themselves in any number of ways, including those that were permitted by law. Then, some masters fell as ornately wroth as Emerson when, on a bad day in 1839, he told his journal that "my wife has come to church in hope of being soothed & strengthened after being wounded by the sharp tongue of a slut in her house."[13] Nomenclature as Elizabethan as "slut" may seem far from sentimental effusions. Yet aggravation with waged attendants can only have been fueled by comparisons between waged and chattel service that found the latter superior. One such comparison was offered by a Louisiana writer whom Emerson had met before marrying Lidian, and thus before he knew much about what householding really meant. "The northern States are jealous of our slaves," Achille Murat boasted in *The United States of North America* (1833); "we envy them nothing." Aggravating, too, could have been Alexis de Tocqueville's contention that "equality of conditions turns servants and masters into new beings, and places them in new relative positions."[14] No one can gauge, now, how clamorously these voices sounded in Emerson's head when he first became a householder, considering the antislavery convictions of Lidian, many of his friends, and some of his closest kin. Unembarrassed, though (at least in 1840), was his hope that just as waged service was going "to go over the dam," slavery would "fall into the pit" too. Here was an abolition more sweeping than anything advocated in the *Liberator*, advocacy of which must have been exhilarating to a greenhorn householder unsure how—and even, perhaps, whether—to achieve mastery.

Exhilaration would have been welcome during Emerson's supposedly "silent years" due to tense uncertainty over household management. Marriage was not the irritant, since he was a widower when he brought Lidian to Concord in 1835. However, during his brief first marriage,

Emerson and his first wife had "boarded out," which meant that some-one else had supervised the servants who attended to their comfort. When the situation changed and the supervisor was his own wife, he veered between feeling protective and hard done by: "my housekeeping should be clean & sweet," rasps a journal entry of 1839, and "should not shame or annoy me." Emerson drew a strict line of demarcation, never-theless, between house*hold*ing, and house*keep*ing; thus, a journal entry of 1841 found him grousing that "literary men" ought to take "a shrew for a wife, a sharp-tongued notable dame who can & will assume the total economy of the house, and having some sense that her philosopher is best in his study suffers him not to intermeddle with her thrift."[15] This was, of course, the tenor of the times. *The American Lady* (1836) taught that "a husband who should personally direct the proceedings of the housekeeper and the cook, and intrude into the petty arrangements of daily economy, would appear in all eyes, except his own, nearly as ridiculous as if he were to assume to himself the habiliments of his wife, or to occupy his mornings with her needles and work-bags."[16] A hint that counsel of this kind may have increased Emerson's perplexi-ties about his own domestic authority appears in those journal entries that have a defensive ring. "He shall be master but not mistress," notes an entry of 1837; "Let a man behave in his own house as a guest," teaches another from the same year.[17]

So much for Waldo's hesitancies and delimitations during the first few years of his second marriage. But what of Lidian's? This pious and bookish woman never became a hectoring shrew. Yet she did not need to in order to win tributes for exceptional homemaking skills or to inspire admiring remembrances of teaching at least one of the "Bush" staff to read, nursing any servitor who fell ill, and arranging a funeral for the child of an Irish cook whom she barely knew while raising four lively children *and* keeping the home fires burning despite her husband's hectic travel schedule and the demands of his growing fame. The ability to handle such a workload was not equipment Lidian brought with her to "Bush." On the contrary, according to a memoir written by her elder daughter, she had hesitated to accept Waldo's marriage proposal, fearful that "wholly aside from housekeeping she should not be a skillful mistress of a house and that it would be a load of care and labour from which she shrank and a giving up of an existence she thoroughly enjoyed and to which she had become exactly fitted, and she could not undertake it unless he was sure he loved her and needed her enough to justify her in doing it."[18]

Inevitably, Emerson replied that he *was* sure and so put a novice at the helm of his first independent household. Lidian found her new role

*Lidian Emerson. By
permission of the
Concord Free Public
Library.*

daunting. "I have not divided the work for the girls," she told her sister
two weeks after arriving in Concord. "I don't know that I can when all
the things are here unless I have you to tell me how." Though Lidian's
sister was generous with advice, young Mrs. Emerson (like Caroline
Gilman's Clarissa) had to learn mistress-ship for herself. It was a slow
process, for, after three years of marriage, her husband recorded the perception that "when she gives any new direction in the kitchen she feels
like a boy who throws a stone and runs."[19]

Decades later, Lidian would say that she had been slow to pick up
the household's reins. "My mind was so full, so occupied," she recalled,
"with the greatness, the solemnity, of marriage that all other things, the
housekeeping & c., were as nothing."[20] During this phase, she was gratified by a "free" cook's use of familial rhetoric: Nancy Colesworthy
"says she has lived with the Emersons first & last 10 years," she reported,

"and she loves them as her own." Almost a year into married life, Lidian recurred to this sentimental standard. "I *love* N.," Lidian told her husband, "for the heartiness of her love to your family—and to me all human beings are equal." Though this was a lofty claim, it is revealing that Lidian found Colesworthy "a lady in her heart and mind" and thus "a very . . . [illegible] contrast to the common run of people in her station."[21]

As it happens, relations with Colesworthy were never smooth. Yet more complaints are found in Waldo's papers than in Lidian's. That is partly because young Mrs. Emerson was determined to find all things in her new home good. "This Nancy of the Emerson's is indeed a treasure," she observed of the cook she "inherited," as a bride, from her coresidential mother-in-law. "I will when I have time write you particulars concerning her—such a rare blessing as wise and faithful *help*, is worth writing about."[22] Later, though, when the gloss wore off, Lidian had learned enough about homemaking to see how much she owed in-house staff. The issue here was not the naivete she had exhibited back in 1822 when she wondered, to a married sister, "how you can get along with so many 'to make & mend for' and bad help. I see but one remedy against being hurried all the time out of your wits, and that is to hire work enough done to enable you to get along easy. What is expense in comparison with the comfort of one's life and the improvement of ones mind."[23]

Instead, the key discovery was the daily exigencies to which Catherine Kelly alludes when she contends that "the relatively high status of provincial help was embedded" not in community ties (as, for instance, when one's "hired girl" was a neighbor's daughter) but "in women's appreciation of [the] demands of housework itself." Mistresses in places such as Concord "valued 'help,'" Kelly concludes, "not because they identified with the women they hired but because they understood the value of the labor these women performed—understood it personally, immediately, and physically."[24] Evidence to support this thesis is found in the letter in which an Ohio mistress decided, in the mid-1840s, that "it was better to have [a servant] and be mad than to have to work hard, and be mad."[25] But it is not found in lectures such as "Man the Reformer" (1841) in which Emerson disparaged male attendants with an expression of hope "that each person whom I address has felt his own call to cast aside all evil customs, timidities, and limitations, and to be in his place a free and helpful man, a reformer . . . not content to slip along through the world like a footman or a spy."[26] Nor was it admitted in his journals, for there he liked to contrast low figures such as "the cook . . . & the self despised" to icons such as "the generous and abstemious self commander."[27]

Prejudice aside—since cooks and footmen were valued laborers who earned good wages—unrealistic expectations explain the disappointment that characterizes Waldo's writings on servitude. "The common household tasks are agreeable to the imagination," he rhapsodized in 1839; "they are the subjects of all the Greek gems."[28] Some of the disappointment consequent on trying to believe such goop was admitted in public; thus, a lecture called "Home" expressed consternation that "in the family in which he had supposed a perfect understanding and intimate bonds subsisted he finds with surprise that . . . all are in a degree strangers to and mutually observant of each other's acts."[29] This comment does not clarify whether Emerson included nonkin servants in the "family" he had in mind. Yet it is hard to imagine Lidian feeling surprise at strangeness, considering how many of her letters from this period make reference to workers—Hannah, Lucy, Hitty, Abby, James, Annie, Margaret, and Hepzibah, to name some but not all—who are never referenced again. Telling, too, is the fact that she learned to manage staff in such a motherlike way that a former "Bush" servant asked to name a child after her one-time mistress. "I . . . feel," Louisa Snow Jacobs would tell Lidian, "that your nursery was a school, educating me, that I might be better enabled to take charge of the little treasure that is intrusted to my care."[30] Here is realization of a vision Sedgwick had proffered in *Live and Let Live.* "The condition of servant-girls," Lucy's mother explains, "is no longer what it once was. They are not servants in the old sense of the word. Their relation to their employers is one of mutual advantage and mutual dependance. In a well-ordered family, a girl is fitting herself for the duties that belong to her sex. She is learning to fill honourably the station of a wife, mistress, and mother of a family."[31]

Though often enervated by the demands of housekeeping, Lidian seems to have implemented this ideal as Sedgwick intended it. If her husband did not, that is at least partly because no body of literature set out guidelines for mastery of servants who were "free."

Offered instead, as Emerson may well have known, was a notion that ministers had a special call on nonkin staff. This idea was adduced, for instance, in *Ann Connover* as part of Aunt Jane's attempt to persuade her niece to serve nonkin for pay. As there is no evidence that Emerson ever read the tract that bears Ann's name, he may not have known about her worry that a servant is "a low and a mean thing to be" or realized that Aunt Jane justified domestic chores with the reminder that "if there were no mechanics and no servants, then preachers and writers, and all such as have gained a good education, would have to get their own food and clothes, and do housework for themselves. And that would keep them busy all day long, and every day; so that they would not have time to preach and write books, and spread knowledge and religion, however fit and able they might be to do it; so there would be little or no good done." If, however, Emerson did happen to have seen these lines, he knew how comforting Ann found her aunt's ideas: "I see," she concludes happily, "that servants help to get the gospel taught." This argument was winning enough—to certain audiences—to reappear in William Alcott's *The Young Woman's Guide to Excellence.* This guide was not published until 1847. But it was written in 1836, at which point its ideas could have reached Emerson through Alcott's cousin Bronson or by circulation amongst "Newness" reformers. One of those ideas was a version of the preceding story that extends the idea that ministers deserved good service to the assertion that teachers could make the same claim. "She is an ordinary domestic," Alcott wrote, of a jewel of a servant who labors in a teacher's home, but "if ninety millions, or even one tenth that number should, in the course of the next two centuries, reap the benefit of his labors, and become lights in the world, is it too much to say that she has been an important aid in accomplishing the work?"[32]

If, however, Emerson had any sense that the Transcendental ministry to which he devoted so much time and thought ratified his own household mastery, he must have felt nonplussed when Nancy Colesworthy threatened, during a period in which "Bush" hosted a slew of visitors (many of whom had not been invited), to post a sign reading: "This House is not a Hotel."[33]

Though antebellum advice literature was most commonly the work of those who had never had to keel a nonkin pot, mention of Colesworthy reminds us how strange it was for Emerson to take an isolationist position when passing up the opportunity to join Brook Farm. Personal reserve may have been a factor here, since he was not an outgoing man. However, in a passage so hyperbolic that it begs a demurral, he emphasized his own "sloth & cowardice," claiming to be "so ignorant & uncertain in my improvements that I would fain hide my attempts & failures in solitude where they shall perplex none or very few besides myself."[34] More moderately, in a letter to another friend, Emerson deprecated schematized domesticity. "[D]o you think George & Sophia Ripley can by any arithmetic or combination give anything to me," he inquired, "which with a little resolution & perseverance I cannot procure for myself?" Considering how many other people would necessarily become implicated in such procuring, this pose looks exaggerated. Yet this was emphatically his stance. "I think that all I shall solidly do,"

Emerson told the Ripleys, "I must do alone."[35] This singular self-portraiture recalls David Leverenz's contention, in *Manhood and the American Renaissance* (1989), that gender anxiety led men such as Emerson to conceive of their social obligations in terms of a "patrician" paradigm that required them to uphold "property ownership, patriarchy, and republican ideals of citizenship."[36] At the same time, this self-portrait denies Lidian any role in the experiments that were about to get under way. This is a noteworthy denial, since it exemplifies the householder's sine qua non: to take full and final responsibility for subordinated coresidents' activities.

As intriguing as self-presentation is the timing of the "domestic & social experiments." They did not begin, as might be assumed, when Waldo and Lidian moved to "Bush." In fact, it was not until two years later that his journals begin to record complaints about servants and a year after that to list the topics agitating U.S. society as "War, Slavery, Alcohol, animal food, Domestic hired service, Colleges, Creeds, & now at last Money."[37] On a more personal level, Waldo was chagrined when, in May 1837, Nancy Colesworthy requested permission to use the front door of "Bush" to go to church.[38] In 1839, he handled his anxiety by accusing Northerners who decried slavery as so many whited sepulchers. "We swell the cry of horror at the slaveholder," he charged, yet simultaneously "treat our laborer . . . as a thing; women, children, the poor; and so do hold slaves."[39] Use of the first-person plural in this avowal can be seen as candid or disingenuous, since "family" life at "Bush" relied on laborers who were women, children, and the (at least relatively) poor; more noteworthy, though, is the implication that there was little to choose between "free" laborers and chattel. Emerson would take this position—in the privacy of his journals—as late as 1844, in a pose of moral superiority that other liberals deployed more boldly. "Let those who proclaim themselves Abolitionists begin," Horace Greeley demanded in 1845, "by thoroughly abolishing Slavery where they can abolish it; so that . . . no household servant exist in a state of ignorance, drudgery, terror and heathenism."[40] Though this stand looks wrongheaded now, it measures how far Emerson's thought had to travel before he could deliver the antislavery "Address." In the process, it helps to gauge the state of confusion in which other served and serving Americans lived and worked, before it had been figured out—and then drummed home—what "free" labor engendered.

As significant as confusion, though, to this study of the literature of nineteenth-century U.S. service is the sentimentality of the "experiments" attempted at "Bush." This categorization may be unexpected, since Emerson distanced himself from the affective appeals on which antislavery activists relied. Writing, for example, of Lidian's sympathy for bondsmen and -women, he told his journal in October 1837 that "to such as she, these crucifixions do not come. They come to the obtuse & barbarous to whom they are not horrid but only a little worse than the old sufferings." This remark is of a piece with his sense that abolitionists comprised "an altogether odious set of people, whom one would be sure to shun as the worst of bores & canters," and with the passage in "Self-Reliance" that scoffs at those who express "incredible tenderness for black folk a thousand miles off."[41] All echoes of Emerson's criticism of *Live and Let Live* are pertinent here. Pertinent too, though, is the finding that when the "domestic & social experiments" got under way, they seemed designed to realize the visions of service disseminated by the sentimental literature discussed in chapter 1.

It is fair to ask, under these circumstances, whether Waldo or Lidian Emerson did more to impel the "experiments" that will be examined presently. The fact is, the record does not say. True, he made claims of doing solidly what he did alone. More compelling, though, to an informed sense of the situation is the improbability of Lidian investing time or thought in domestic innovations after having spent five years establishing herself as a housekeeper. Putting this thought another way, my research indicates that though observant and caring (if acerbic, at times), she had fewer domestic anxieties to resolve than her husband had. Support for this position can be found in one of the franker assessments in the Emerson Family Papers: Lidian's conviction that the idea of inviting Bronson and Abby Alcott, along with their four daughters, to coreside at "Bush," was a "wild scheme." It is not clear whether this "scheme" fizzled because Lidian disapproved, because Abby refused charity—"It is this dependence on others," she fretted, "which is the worm gnawing at the vitals of my tranquillity"—or because a husband developed qualms.[42] What *is* clear is that Lidian judged this idea wrongheaded after enough experience with what she would call the "Martha-like care of wine & custards" to give her the confidence to speak her mind.[43] This was not always the case, for late in life Lidian would laugh at how biddable she had been at first; wifely submission was not required, she would decide, when a husband talked nonsense about domestic arrangements. Perhaps she remembered, as she laughed, the experiments of the early 1840s, each of which failed in some important way. This rendering of the case is admittedly conjectural.[44] Ultimately, though, there would have been little Lidian could have done to stop a householder with reform on his Transcendental mind.

This point being noted, it is not incidental that Experiment #1 consisted of finding a male child to supplement the household staff at "Bush." Waldo announced Alexander McCaffery's arrival from New York gingerly. "If we find that he is not good help for us," he told his brother William, "we can let him come back." Hesitancy did not spring from anything untoward about the new coresident, for Lidian described Alex as "my idea of what we should desire in a servant-boy, being quick & skilful as well as pleasant and orderly."[45] Nor could it have been a matter of the lad's antecedents, since an older McCaffery was already serving in William Emerson's home, and it was standard practice to recruit servants from among one's relatives' staff.[46] (This was, we recall, how Nancy Colesworthy came to be Lidian's cook.) What, then, explains Emerson's sense of engaging in experimentation? It is unlikely to have been discomfort about McCaffery's Roman Catholicism since he overrode that detail: "he is to go to Church with us, & to Sunday School." More likely, discomfort stemmed from recognition that, male servants being a master's responsibility, Waldo himself was on trial. Nor was his reluctance to govern McCaffery a secret, since, a full month after the lad's arrival in March 1840, Emerson admitted that "I have still left him to the women, & have not summoned him to my side."[47] Inexperience probably explains why Emerson did not "bind" the boy legally or make provision for his wages. "I have made no other bargain with his sister," he noted, "than that I will board & clothe him at present."[48] Yet this turned out to be inept management, since Waldo expressed himself crossly when Alexander's mother took the boy away. Irritated that his household was disturbed, he portrayed his servant's mobility as excessive: "boys must not be expected to come & go like sheets of lightning," America's most famous philosopher complained. Sounding very much like James Fenimore Cooper when one of his teenaged slaves ran away—and apparently unimpressed that McCaffery had already lived at "Bush" for a year—this impotent master ended Experiment #1 in a huff: "we had intended to keep the boy."[49]

Whence such intentions? Obviously, poor children and orphans were being taken into nonkin households all over the United States at this time to exchange service for lodging or, with luck, a caring home. As important as that social reality, however, is advisors' agreement that this form of charity could benefit homemakers in search of staff. Sedgwick had implied as much, we recall, when *Mary Hollis* taught poor mothers that nonkin service was a good recourse; more recently, Gilman (whose husband had been one of Emerson's college classmates) made the argument explicit in *Recollections of a Housekeeper*, after which Sedgwick pushed the idea again in *Live and Let Live.* "I have often wondered," the motherlike Mrs. Hyde remarks at one point, "that housekeepers in the country do not more frequently secure *help* by taking children 'to bring up.' Young children may always be obtained; and care and kindness, while they are too young to render much service, is amply paid afterward." Quite apart from the salvific vision of removing a poor child "from a vicious family, or from a shiftless, ignorant, or over-burdened mother," Sedgwick's good mistress-character explains her preference for child-workers on moral grounds: "young subjects can be remoulded and taught. You can inspire them with confidence," she concludes, "and make them zealous fellow-workers with you in their own improvement." This idea remained popular into the Gilded Age. "If the young housekeeper," Eunice B. Beecher taught in 1878, "would take a young girl, and kindly and carefully train her to do the work in the most desirable manner, when the child grows up, and the mistress's cares are steadily increasing, giving her much less time than she once had to devote to household labor, she would then begin to find her reward for all the care she gave this girl in the commencement of her married life." Though the book that proffered this rosy promise was in the Emerson family library when Waldo died in 1882, its vision is probably harsher than what he had in mind when he brought Alex McCaffery to "Bush."[50] In contrast, he may well have been guided by Sedgwick since, despite dismissing *Live and Let Live* overall, he singled out its mistress-character for special praise.

It would be interesting to know if Mrs. McCaffery retrieved her son because she had become aware of criticisms of male servants that emphasized deceit and fraud. Yet for whatever reason she decided that her son would do better elsewhere, Emerson's resistance to her judgment shows how little he approved of "free" service when it disrupted his own home. Even before Alex left, however, another disturbance rocked the master of "Bush"; this time, though, the disturber was his still-toddling, cherished son. According to a family memoirist, the howling began when Waldo Jr. was told that he would have to stay at home with a servant. The boy refused, with angry tears, wailing, "I do not want to go with Mrs. Hill! Because she has red on her face and red on her arms, and she eats at a [different] table . . . and she is not beautiful."[51] Waldo Sr.'s more immediate recollection of this same episode in December 1840 is distinct but complementary in that he has his son refusing to accompany a servant "because," the boy remarked, "you live in the kitchen."[52]

As if impelled by this charge, Experiment #2—which took place within days of McCaffery's mother-dictated exit from "family" life at

"Bush"—focused on dining arrangements. This experiment proved disappointing, too. But it was over more quickly than Experiment #1, since the invitation to dine along with the Emersons was scotched by one of Nancy Colesworthy's successors. "Lidian went out the other evening," Waldo told his brother in a description of this fiasco, "& had an explanation on the subject with the two girls. Louisa accepted the plan with great kindness & readiness, but Lydia, the cook, firmly refused—A cook was never fit to come to table, &c. The next morning Waldo [Jr.] was sent to announce to Louisa that breakfast was ready but she had eaten already with Lydia & refuses to leave her alone."[53]

Though this account is not supplemented by information about the way things looked to Louisa Snow or Lydia (surname unknown), it is safe to say that reform was stymied in this case by a wage earner's assertion. Motivation to experiment in this way can be traced back to Waldo Jr.'s outburst. Yet since it did not take place until three months later, it may be more germane that Experiment #2 followed hard on abandonment of the "wild scheme" of sharing "Bush" with the family of Bronson Alcott. A hint that concern about ownership of a large, "private" home was bothering Emerson at this time can be derived from his hopeful vision of what it would mean to open his home to the Alcotts: "Liberty, Equality, & a common table." Other concerns, however, had to be negotiated simultaneously, among them Abby Alcott's insistence that "the families and tables" be kept "seperate," even if some living-space was shared.[54] In a way, Lydia the cook made the same objection. Nor would strong-arming her acquiescence have been politic, since competent meal-preparers were servants a homemaker as capable as Lidian would do her best to keep.

Like the McCaffery experiment, the invitation to dine *en famille* can be tied to sentimental literature. On the one hand, it harks back to the evocations of rural harmony that Sedgwick had put on offer in *Redwood*; on the other, it rejects Gilman's jokes about bumptious country lasses who disrupt privileged "family" life. In *Home*, Sedgwick tried to refute such snobbery with praise of the "republican independent dependent" whose services were willingly given to those who recognize the merits of agreeing to "dispense with obsequiousness and servility, for the capability and virtue of a self-regulating and self-respecting agent." William Andrus Alcott was nearly as blithe. "How happy will be the day," he caroled in 1838, "when there will be no such thing known as two classes of persons in families, a higher and a lower—jailers and prisoners—but when all the family, however numerous and how little soever united by ties of consanguinity, will be equal and free, dwelling together, eating and drinking together, and whether of one nation or another, always united around the same domestic altar."[55]

Insofar as Alcott's vision was less gendered than Sedgwick's, it could have been attractive to a householder in search of guidance concerning mastery of "free" attendants. Yet since Emerson may never have perused the advice literature cited, it is more salient that he helped to edit a journal that printed several discussions of servitude. The piece in *The Dial* most pertinent to Experiment #2 was an essay that taught that "no one, whatever be his station, wants, attainments, or riches, has any right to receive from another any service which degrades the servant in his own eyes, or the eyes of the public, or in the eyes of him who receives the service."[56] If the invitation to dine along with the Emersons was intended as a way to de-degrade coresidential staff, then it is noteworthy that Experiment #3 rested on the decision to put a disciple of "the Newness" into the anomalous position of unhired man.

Henry David Thoreau's stay at "Bush" may not look like a continuation of the "domestic & social experiments." Yet the chores assigned to him included the gardening and child care that had been McCaffery's responsibility. Then, too, Thoreau moved into "Bush" while memories of the Irish lad were fresh and just a month after the ill-fated invitation to servants who had not had a chance to study at Harvard. Thoreau left no comment on these things in his papers. But he did report, on his first night at "Bush," that "family" life there was neither comfortable nor relaxed. "[T]he civilized man," he wrote, "has the habits of the house. His house is a prison, in which he finds himself oppressed and confined, not sheltered and protected. He walks as if he sustained the roof; he carries his arms as if the walls would fall in and crush him, and his feet remember the cellar beneath. His muscles are never relaxed. It is rare that he overcomes the house, and learns to sit at home in it." This feeling of suppression did not diminish; rather, it increased. "I want to go soon," Thoreau told his journal a full eight months later, "and live away by the pond"; a few weeks after that, he wrote again of feeling stifled.[57] "I am constrained," he reported, "to live a strangely mixed life" in which "all I hear about brooms and scouring and taxes and house keeping" reminded him that "even Valhalla might have its kitchen."[58]

These remarks clash with Emerson's jubilant announcement of Thoreau's coresidence. "[H]e is thus far a great benefactor & physician to me," the householder crowed, "for he is an indefatigable & a very skilful laborer & I work with him as I should not without him. . . . Thoreau is a scholar & a poet & as full of buds of promise as a young apple tree." Perhaps "thus far" hints at recognition that this experiment rested on a delicate balance. But if so, it was Thoreau who bore the brunt of it until he left in May 1843, not to live by the pond but to work at a job more commensurate with his academic training. In the letter that sets up the new posting, Waldo put the matter in terms of Thoreau's preference. "He says," the householder wrote, that tutoring "is such a relation as he wishes to sustain, to be the friend & educator of a boy."[59] Considering the anxiety and disorientation Thoreau had chronicled in private jottings, it is significant that he chose a gentlemanly role for his next job. It is equally significant that in addition to wages, he stipulated a room of his own, with a fire.

These stipulations may seem unexceptionable. Yet they reveal that Thoreau left the Emerson household with a new appreciation of social ranking and the perquisites that higher rank generally entails. Perhaps he never wholly abandoned belief in the Asian scripture he shared with readers of *The Dial*; Menu taught that the pure man "must avoid service for hire."[60] But he did learn to query the charge that menial work could not humble a Brahmin since people of that caste were "transcendently divine"; indeed, some five months into his stay at "Bush," he told a correspondent that "I shall hold the nobler part at least out of the service."[61] Thoreau's misery during Experiment #3 may touch some heartstrings. Yet it has its comic side as well, if only because it is hard to see how two intelligent men blinded themselves so completely to social realities.

Indeed, there is a real question to ask about why Thoreau lived at "Bush" when he could have easily walked there every day and gone home to his parents once work was through. Then, too, while it was common at this time to take in people—especially women and children—who lacked a home, it was decidedly strange to remove a college graduate from his parents' residence to put him to work in a nonkin house and yard. Twentieth-century biographers of this pair addressed the strangeness in two ways. First, Sherman Paul, citing a nineteenth-century source who said that Thoreau lived in the Emersons' home like a "younger brother or a grown-up son," explained his coresidence as comparable to that of a "poor relation." That, however, is very likely the analogy that would have bothered Thoreau most, since he was neither poor nor kin except in the metaphorical sense of feeling spiritual affinity with the Emersons. More recently, Robert D. Richardson Jr. tackled the anomaly of the situation negatively, finding the young seeker "certainly not a 'hired man' or a 'boarder'" at "Bush." This statement of the case is true, as far as it goes. Yet in a still more recent study focused not on Thoreau but on Emerson, Richardson revised this finding: Thoreau, he summarized, "occupied a special position, being neither family nor servant but closer to family than not."[62] It is no small matter that Richardson's careful wording remains negative, since Emerson would admit to some "inconveniency" in having his acolyte coreside. Nor was Thoreau everyone's idea of amiable. Wondering about that aspect of Experiment #3, a neighbor predicted strife. "It may well be," Nathaniel Hawthorne opined, "that such a sturdy and uncompromising person is fitter to meet occasionally in the open air, than to have as a permanent guest at table and fireside."[63] The best response to this observation is, I think, that a sturdy uncompromiser was precisely the sort to take seriously— and even to extremes—the line in *Nature* (1836) that teaches that "a thing is good only so far as it serves." Support for this suggestion includes Sherman Paul's observation that Thoreau's journals from this period "are full of passages on the desire to serve."[64] Quite apart, then, from the somewhat fumbling inquiry called "The Service" that Thoreau composed at this time are remarks in his journals that seem anomalous for a young bachelor with no householding responsibilities. "All those contingences [*sic*]," one such entry ponders, "which the philanthropist, statesman, and housekeeper write so many books to meet are simply and quietly settled in the intercourse of friends." More evidence that Emerson's hobbyhorse had informed some of his talks with Thoreau is found in a letter the younger man wrote to the older after leaving "Bush"; it voices concern that he was not "especially serviceable" to the William Emersons "except as inflictions are sanctified to the righteous." Quite different was a letter, on the same topic and from the same period, that Thoreau wrote to his parents, for it remarks that the people whose son he tutored "are not indeed of my kith or kin in any sense—but they are irreproachable and kind."[65] If Emerson did encourage Thoreau to consider exogamous utility a worthy aim, that lesson need not have been self-interested. That being said, there is no denying that the goal of serving could have caused tension between a disciple and a guru trying to work out an improved form of mastery.

I do not mean to accuse Emerson of callous insensitivity in this, the single most important of the "domestic & social experiments," since he does seem to have inquired about Thoreau's happiness during the coresidential stint. "I am well and happy in your house," the younger man avowed in February 1843; earlier, he had asserted that as Emerson's "pensioner," he felt "free as under the sky." This evaluation is less than candid, considering the frequency with which Thoreau referred to himself during this period in private letters as Apollo in thrall to Admetus: a god forced to serve a king. Yet insofar as this evaluation responded to an expression of concern from Emerson, it explains why he could assure a mutual friend that Thoreau "had been one of the family" while core-siding at "Bush."[66] There may have been some face-saving here. But Emerson was actually recalling in this passage the delight that his recently deceased son had taken in the "toys whistles boats popguns & all kinds of instruments" clever "Uncle Henry" was able to "make & mend"; the thrust of this epithet, then, was toward recalling a warm and loving time, an image of "family" life at its best.[67] However, there *was* a perspective that Waldo could not or did not see, which Thoreau put on view in two essays he published after leaving "Bush." Neither of the articles in the *United States Magazine and Democratic Review* came right out and attacked Emerson. Yet both took issue with over-confident assumptions about (self)-mastery, and both were available to people who would have known about Experiment #3.

The initial thrust, which was published in 1844, was a mocking review of J. A. Etzler's *The Paradise within the Reach of All Men, without Labor, by Powers of Nature and Machinery*; in this piece, Thoreau scorned those who evaded labor.[68] "We saw last summer," the essay recalls, "a dog employed to churn for a farmer's family, travelling upon a horizontal wheel, and though he had sore eyes, an alarming cough, and withal a demure aspect, yet their bread did get buttered for all that." Thoreau agreed with Etzler that the wind could be an "indefatigable and energetic servant"; the question was, why should any moral agent be relieved of labor? "[N]o work can be shirked," the ex-unhired man attested, adding that "We believe that most things will have to be accomplished still by the application of Industry."[69] Emerson would have agreed with this general statement: "He who does his own work frees a slave," he told his journal in 1844. It is not clear whether he realized that Thoreau might have been recalling his time at "Bush" as labor like that of the mindlessly circling dog. But he did acknowledge, in the same journal entry, that service could be grim. "Whilst we sit here talking & smiling," this now-experienced master noted, "some person is out there in field & shop & kitchen doing what we need, without talk or smiles."[70]

It is possible, of course, that Emerson saw nothing personal in the Etzler review. That possibility breaks down, though, in the case of Thoreau's second piece, which appeared in 1845. To the uninformed reader (which would be most of those who perused the *United States Magazine and Democratic Review*), "The Landlord" must have looked like a straightforward assertion that those who would eat should cook their own food. But to any who knew about Experiment #3, this essay dropped a broad hint that Emerson was less "a man of more open and general sympathies, who possesses a spirit of hospitality which is its own reward, and feeds and shelters men from pure love of the creatures," than one who cherished "such universal sympathies, and so broad and genial a human nature, that he would fain sacrifice the tender but narrow ties of private friendship to a broad, sunshiny, fair-weather-and-foul friendship for his race."[71] Thoreau did not add, as he might have, that "universal sympathies" could put a heavy burden on wives, children, and staff. But "The Landlord" did suggest what he might have learned in situ: that a certain type of householder might be so graceless as to consider "the farthest-traveled is in some measure kindred to him" though "he treats his nearest neighbor as a stranger." A clear implication of all this is that a proprietorial attitude makes impossible the kind of home in which a "traveler steps across the threshold, and lo! he too is master." Again, this was not the message that most readers could or would have derived from "The Landlord"; nonetheless, those aware of Thoreau's stay at "Bush" must have wondered. Waldo may have raised an eyebrow too, since, as Steven Fink has noted, "Thoreau does not seem to have mentioned 'The Landlord' at all in his correspondence with Emerson," despite the older man's interest in, and apparent support for, the younger's writing career.[72]

If either of these essays stung Emerson at all, that would not disprove Amy Schrager Lang's notice of the "characteristic, even definitive, denial of class by the nineteenth-century middle class and its concomitant unwillingness to admit the existence of the values, interests, beliefs, and ways of living embraced by those of other classes," in that there had never been any question of Thoreau being a member of the working class. Perhaps he was no patrician; certainly he worked with his own hands. But Emerson can never have considered the younger man a servant like Nancy Colesworthy or Louisa Snow—the latter probably the all-time favorite of the many nonkin who attended the Emersons at "Bush." Snow was the woman who, after working several years at "Bush," left to be married and, on becoming a mother, asked permission to name her baby "Lidian Emerson." Well before she left his home, however, Emerson had begun to see her as specially family-like: "Remember me to Louisa & all the household," he wrote in January 1843. The perception that this servant stood in a special relationship to his near and dear explains why, when Emerson heard of her plans to go, he told Lidian to hold on tight: "blessings on Louisa!" he wrote, "whom I hope you will not let go, unless for her plainest good." This articulation of the situation must be assessed carefully, since it was not Emerson's fault that the standard verb phrase for this eventuality—to "let go" of staff—had a possessive ring. By the same token, there are different ways to interpret a comparable comment. "We are heartily grieved to hear of the woman's coming whom you speak of," he told Lidian in a follow-up letter, "for the girls do not want her, nor any body else: & I mean to engage Louisa to stay, if she comes by again."[73] Some may feel that "I mean to" bespeaks dismissal of Snow's will, since it indicates reluctance to give her the chance to refuse whatever offer Emerson made. Yet because "I mean to" can be reworded as "I plan," this phrase may have been intended to show that he was ready to agree to any terms Snow might choose to set. In that case, we would see here an accommodation to "free" labor realities that recalls the evolution of Sedgwick's visions of family-like attendance.

Moving now to the more public development in Emerson's thoughts on service, we arrive at his decision to "come out" for abolition. It is too much to say that any servant employed, or unemployed, at "Bush" sufficiently explains why he agreed to commemorate the cessation of the West Indian slave trade. Yet if, as Len Gougeon has argued, Emerson's politics took a noticeable swing toward the antislavery cause in 1844, it was not because he had developed a more positive attitude toward the people in that camp. "Two tables in every house!" groaned a journal entry for that year; "Abolitionists at one & servants at the other! It is a calumny that you utter."[74] Nor was it because he had solved the "servant problem" in his own home. On the contrary, not only may the "calumny" have been self-directed in part, but equally important, the "domestic & social experiments" continued for a few more years. Quite unlike Sedgwick, then, Emerson labeled "free" service "precarious," in the "Address" that railed against the inhumanity of relying on attendants who were enslaved. This cheerless depiction— damned if you do, but also if you don't—was lightened only slightly by the assertion that mobile labor comprised the lesser of two evils: "it is cheaper," the "Address" limps, "to pay wages than to own the slave."[75]

What did this cost-benefit analysis mean? It meant that despite the "picturesque luxury" of the form of "vassalage" found in Southern homes and what Emerson imagined as the "silent obedience" of house slaves, he saw one unbeatable benefit to "free" labor.[76] Since the "Address" did not make this point and then plunge into comparative economics, it is fair to assume that the benefit he had in mind was not the sort totted up in ledgers; rather, it was a moral accounting consonant with the abolitionist position that the traffic in human beings comprised a sin or crime. This position was defensible, of course. Knowing what we do, though, about Emerson's experiences with service workers during the "silent years," it is fair to ask if a crucial component of his cost-benefit analysis was recognition that the payment of wages justified certain expectations: most centrally, that servants would be discreet about their masters' and mistresses' affairs. Antebellum advisors had much to say on this topic. "Servants," the *American Ladies' Magazine* sighed in 1836, "seldom keep the secrets of the family in which they live, be those secrets of ever so much importance; and it usually makes servants arrogant and unfaithful to be entrusted with a confidence which they can turn to the disadvantage of their employers."[77]

Assertions of this kind remind us that advice literature marked boundaries constantly, in this case between who really was family and who could only ever be family-like. "One thing I charge you to be circumspect about," Mrs. Lee tells Lucy in *Live and Let Live*, "the private circumstances of a family must be more or less exposed to the persons employed in it, and a feeling of honour should restrain them from talebearing—I am afraid there is very little of this."[78]

I will have more to say in chapter 4 about the restraints that nineteenth-century advisors tried to place around nonkin coresidents and their "tattle" because servants' ability to make known the affairs of their social "betters" posed a grave challenge to sentimental bromides. Here, though, my point is the more limited one that the experiment in unwaged service left Emerson unexpectedly vulnerable to Thoreau's willingness to expose his "private" life. Snared by this loophole in an evolving etiquette, he could do little in response except portray the practice of unhiring as carrying an exorbitant price tag.

Waldo Emerson's interest in probing the "servant problem" in relation to slavery ended with the rather gusty show of resignation in the "Address." He was not quite finished, however, with his exploration of home and "family" life, even if the decision to turn "Bush" into a boardinghouse was inspired by desire to withdraw from the responsibilities of household government and thus return, in a sense, to the unburdened state he had known in his first marriage. Thoreau too had one more shaft in his quiver that, albeit couched as humor, was intended to pierce complacency.

Starting with the more radical foray, the decision to turn "Bush" into a boardinghouse was contrary to everything sentimental advisors were saying about the perils of giving into the supposed comforts of a de-privatized form of domesticity. No one worried much, then, when circumstances forced people into heterogeneous living arrangements (e.g., travelers often had to stay at inns and settlers in multifamily homes). No excuse was thought good enough, though, in sentimental literature, for people of means to dispense with the "privacy" of kin-centered domesticity. Sedgwick did not have much to say about this topic apart from a quick reference in *Live and Let Live* to the disruption of "family" life experienced in residential hotels. In contrast, Sarah Hale took the matter of de-privatizing quite seriously, both as the editor of *Godey's Lady's Book* and in novels written during the mid-1840s, the more pointed of which was *"Boarding Out": A Tale of Domestic Life* (1846). Like other detractors of what was thought a "promiscuous" form of domicile, Hale excused husbands of wrongdoing: "whenever we find a married man at a boarding-house," one commentator sniped, "it is most frequently owing to the choice of the wife."[79] This is a debatable point, since it is not clear who decided to de-privatize "Bush." Yet in the world of sentimental literature, where gender is ceaselessly monitored, women were targeted from all angles: the privileged for being too lazy to homemake, maidservants for taking advantage of de-privatized domesticity to spread secrets, and landladies for providing the illusion of home—for a fee. Attacks of this kind comprised a large part of the arsenal assembled by those who were determined to make "privatized" patterns of home and "family" life the measure of respectability.

Looking first at the charges brought against servants, boarding-houses were reviled as unnatural on the grounds that they allowed attendants to rise to dangerous heights.[80] Thus, *"Boarding Out"* has much to say about a nursemaid who is "really more welcome than her mistress, as more information concerning family affairs was divulged by her." Three years earlier, *Godey's* had depicted a boardinghouse courtship as distastefully exposed. "All watched, and all whispered," this story mourned, "including waiters and chambermaids. Even boots had his opinion." It was ladies' duty, advisors taught, to erect barriers against such prying but also against the social instability implied by the opportunity to peer. Writers who upheld this ideal found a blessing in the long hours that training and directing servants required, because "from whatever cause" a privileged woman's "keeping at home may arise, the effect is, no doubt, of incalculable benefit to herself, to her husband, and to her children." The goal was a crafting and, in time, maintenance of the kind of "family" life that could provide a site of resistance to the dangers of the wide, wide world. Thus, for one commentator, "when the check of *home* is removed (and a Boarding-House is emphatically NOT a home) all sorts of evils are liable to rush in."[81]

More culpable than servants, then, in sentimental fiction were ladies too idle or inept to run their own homes. Charges of idleness were brought against privileged women throughout the nineteenth century.[82]

Yet in this case, the specifically sentimental focus was that such failings exposed privileged people to money-grubbers. Thus, in 1837, a *Godey's* tale presented a boardinghouse proprietor as "a hungry hawk," while another, published a year later, had an iniquitous landlady using her pretty daughter as bait.[83] "Not one of the young gentlemen in my house would stay a week at the prices I charge them, if Ellen were gone," this grasper gloats. "Beauty is a fortune to a girl—and to her mother also, if she knows how to manage."[84] The best way to avoid such harridans, advisors taught, was to shoulder the burden of homemaking. "Every married woman in good health," Hale taught, "should keep her own house: it is a sacred office, from which she has no right to shrink; it is a part of her marriage covenant—it gives dignity to her character."[85] The novel that made this claim, *Keeping House and Housekeeping* (1845), was another "Tale of Domestic Life" that lectured privileged women on the foolishness of delegating household chores. The villain of this piece is, in fact, a mistress-surrogate (portrayed as "masculine in the extreme") who eavesdrops on her employers, corrupts the servants under her command, pads the grocery account, and orders exotic viands for her own table. This would seem horrific enough. But Hale saved her best ammunition, in the two tales of domestic life she published in the 1840s, for women who chose to "board." Indeed, however much *Keeping House and Housekeeping* had to say about venal servants, *"Boarding Out"* ratcheted the anxiety level higher still with lurid descriptions of loosened ties among kin (including husband and wife), the virtual certainty of picking up illnesses from other boarders, and an innocent child-character's slow descent into death. Ruthless in her determination to persuade ladies to manage their own homes, Hale exploited every opportunity to instill a sense of guilt; thus, in the crucial deathbed scene in *"Boarding Out,"* the "placid features" of the little corpse "plainly indicate that she has 'got home.'"[86] This kind of scene painting was so crude that it may not have been taken seriously. Be that as it may, neither it nor high prices persuaded nineteenth-century Americans to forego "boarding out."[87] Indeed, Hale herself "boarded," happily and healthily, for decades.[88]

With this information as a background, it makes sense that Emerson's letters and journals say little about transforming "Bush" into a boardinghouse; nor will it come as a surprise that this fourth and final experiment was short-lived. Fear of failure may explain the dearth of commentary. But so may dread of exposure, since Experiment #4 could have been seen as a refusal of duty on the part of both Waldo and Lidian. Less likely was anxiety that some would interpret the arrival of Mrs.

E. C. Goodwin as evidence of poverty. Yet that *was* the usual reason that nineteenth-century Americans opened up their homes to coresidents who shared expenses or paid for room and board. Hale had published a short story based on this premise in 1834, but in real life, a decade later, financial straits were the reason Calvin and Harriet Beecher Stowe shared their home. In this case, "boarding" at home was not to the wife's liking. "I wish the summer were through," she reported, "& this boarding business closed, I am heartily sick of it—It is too noisy & disquieting & harassing." Here was proof of the dictate that "in a boarding house you are thrown into all sorts of company."[89] At "Bush," the Emersons tried to control the threat of de-privatization by putting Goodwin and her children into rooms that had been once those of their cook and maid. Equally significant, there is no evidence that the Goodwin and Emerson groups dined together or reason to assume that the Emerson children were encouraged to think of the Goodwins as "family." Despite these precautions, this experiment ended when it became clear that "keeping the entries & doorsteps and parlour free from litter" burdened Lidian because Goodwin "with all her children and the boarders was very busy attending to the providing and the chambers." That seems to have been the last straw, for Waldo attempted no more "experiments." Eventually, "Bush" was served by seven nonkin employees.[90]

Thus there were four experiments, all failures, from the point of view of establishing a form of household government that was morally superior to the plantation "family." Emerson recognized the failures, for a lecture of the later 1840s admitted that tinkering would not get the job done. "I see not how serious labor, the labor of all and every day, is to be avoided," he announced, since "the reform that applies itself to the household must not be partial. It must correct the whole system of our social living. It must come with plain living and high thinking; it must break up caste, and put domestic service on another foundation."[91]

Going much further than his private dismissal of *Live and Let Live,* this critique called for repudiation of a social organizer that sentimentalists could not do without: call it caste, rank, or class, it was what made one citizen master or mistress and another man or maid. Unfortunately for his reputation as a service-labor theorist, Emerson dropped the matter there. Thoreau picked it up again when he returned to "Bush," at Lidian's invitation, while Waldo was overseas.

Thoreau's second stint of nonkin coresidence had little in common with the first since, during the later stay, he occupied the dignified and utterly male role of secretary. From this respectable position, he wrote cheekily to the master of "Bush." One letter recurred to a topic Thoreau had broached in the unhired days with regard to Emerson's son Eddy. "Mr. Thoreau," the boy supposedly asked, "will you be my father?" Bolder during his second and more elevated stay, Thoreau extended the joke. "Lidian and I make very good housekeepers," he claimed, adding that "you must come back soon, or you will be superseded."[92] Though comments of this sort could be defended as harmless joshing, their purposeful subversion of a key sentimental tactic is suggestive. That tactic was, of course, to downplay the dangers of nonkin propinquity by depicting most servant-characters as lumpen or grotesque (e.g., *Home*'s Martha and Hale's "masculine" waged housekeeper who turns out to be a crook) and pairing off the few attractive servant-characters with decent and industrious working-class mates (e.g., Lucy Lee). This expedient was devised for a readership familiar with the charge that "a very large proportion" of prostitutes "were female servants, betrayed from the ways of virtue, in the first instance, by their masters, or their master's sons, or their fellow servants of the opposite sex." Under the influence of this school, antebellum Americans were regaled—for their own good—both with stories of the traps that lay in wait for lasses who moved to the city in search of service posts *and* with abolitionist accusations that the "sixteen slave States constitute one vast brothel."[93] Thoreau's second letter did not point toward anything so dire. Yet by alluding, even in jest and indirectly, to the topic of union between a mistress and her husband's secretary, he drew attention to an anxiety that sentimental pundits had done their best to ignore, bracket, and deny.

Lidian would do something similar, interestingly enough, when Waldo was off traveling again years later. "Why don't you address a letter to your wife sometimes?" she inquired. "If you knew what a sentimental affair there has been got up between her and Mr Alcott—(or Mr Alcott and her I should say) you would write to keep good your claim; that is if you value it—."[94] More representative, though, of her evolved concept of mistress-ship is a letter written in 1848 to a man who had accused her of trying to "steal" a servant from his home. Her stiff missive with few punctuational stops informed William Whiting that

> Mary Collins was engaged to live with me whenever I should resume house-keeping and I had decided to keep house again on the strength of expecting to have her. But to oblige Mary by securing her a place, and in consideration also of Mrs Whiting's being an invalid, I gave her up. I wished Mrs W. to be sure of having her long enough to make it well worth her while to teach her the ways of the family.
>   Your daughter Jane, with her characteristic nobleness, while thanking me for resigning in your favor what I valued so much as my claim

on Mary, said "Still it may be that when you keep house, I may see your need of her to be so much the greatest, as to feel bound in conscience to give her up to you" I answered "We will see when the time comes"

I was surprised, after this, by hearing from my sister that Mrs Whiting in praising Mary added "I shall try to keep her all my life"[95]

Certain that her own need was greater and thus that the Whitings had played her false, Lidian claimed that she had done nothing but tell Collins that "if you prefer living here, engage yourself now. . . . Are you not free?" Shame on the Whitings, she concluded, to find that Collins "is not free" since "she longs to come into my family. And she dares not do it, nor even own that she does. She is a most timid spirit & is held in the bondage of fear." Nothing in sentimental advice was as openly feisty except, perhaps, Sedgwick's paean to the "republican independent dependent," another image that made the worker's volition key.

Volition was a hot topic at Brook Farm, too, especially as it informed calculations of the morality of relying on staff. "That there is a slave on my plantation or a servant in my kitchen is no evil," a Brook Farmer named George William Curtis decided in a letter of 1844, "but that the slave and servant should be unwilling to be so, that is the difficulty."[96] It could be coincidence that Curtis admired Sedgwick's didactic novellas. But it is no happenstance that he juxtaposed "free" and chattel service during the period in which Emerson was doing the same thing, for, in contrast to the Concord householder, Curtis opted for de-privatized domesticity. In chapter 3, we will see how "THE ABOLITION OF DOMESTIC SERVICE" attempted by communitarian Transcendentalists demonstrated the influence of sentimental precepts, for good and ill.[97]

3 Educated Friends, Working

The only equivalent for service, is a service in return.
—Theodore Parker, *The Dial* (1841)

Odds are, the "domestic & social experiments" probed in chapter 2 were unique. But Emerson was not the only American exercised about attendance; far from it. First and foremost, manners-mavens begged for relief. "He who shall contrive to obviate [servants'] necessity," opined *The Laws of Etiquette* (1836), "or remove their inconveniences, will render to human comfort a greater benefit than has yet been conferred by all the useful-knowledge societies of the age." Following hard on mavens' heels were proslavery polemicists who turned grousing to their advantage. "Envy of the North by the South!" one snorted in 1837. "The boot is on the other leg, perhaps."[1] Next, as if in direct response to both apologists and mavens, disciples of Charles Fourier mocked "would-be democrats" who mistakenly "accepted Domestic Service, as the ancient philosophers and modern clergymen do slavery, as an established and consequently eternal fact!" Historians of Brook Farm have overlooked this declaration, though all air opinions about the effect Fourierism had on that reform group. Neglected, along the way, is examination of Brook Farm's policies and predicaments in relation to contemporary complaints about nonkin staff—though that concern was patent, interestingly enough, to Emerson. This chapter corrects the oversight by probing attendance in the community that George Ripley envisioned as "a society of educated friends, working, thinking, and living together," yet routinely billed, then and later, as an extended family.[2]

Though it has long been recognized that Brook Farm was established to redress imbalances caused by false valuations of manual and intellectual labor, less well-examined is organizers' desire to "realize the Christian ideal of life, by making such industrial, social and educational arrangements as would . . . avert collision of caste" and thus "sanctify life more completely than is possible in the isolated household." This goal meshed neatly with the way in which Ripley described his vision of the "true church of the first-born" before stepping down from the Unitarian pulpit to cofound a Transcendentalist ministry. "It would consist," he explained, "of those who are united by no other tie than faith in divine things; by the desire to cultivate the holiest principles of our nature,—reverence, justice, and love; . . . and to connect the jarring elements of earth into materials for a pure, serene, and joyful life." Few if any memoirists of Brook Farm addressed this topic directly. Yet many left statements about one of the main ways in which jarring elements had been connected and caste-collision forestalled.[3] "[T]here were no servants—no *hired help*," one communitarian recalled decades later; instead, "all work was honorable, and . . . was done in *Groups*."[4] This assertion echoes the report that a spokesman made to a Fourierist convention in 1844. "We have an association at Brook Farm, of which I now speak from my own experience," he announced. "We have there abolished domestic servitude as one of the first considerations; it gave one of the first impulses to the movement at Brook Farm."[5]

Associationists who opposed the "odious feature of domestic servitude" as loudly as they decried slavery were bound to applaud this abolition.[6] The spokesman's point was, however, that—even before transforming their group into a Fourierist phalanstery—Brook Farmers had done more than any other reformers to realize a servant-free form of "family" life. In 1894, a male memoirist recollected what the spokesman had downplayed: "There was much hard work for the women, as it was not a well-proportioned family"; he added, though, that "poetry and enthusiasm . . . beautified the laundry and kitchen with hopes and glories."[7] Agreeing, most chroniclers praised the chivalry exhibited by Brook Farm men who helped to hang out dripping wash while vaunting the equality that the women enjoyed in matters such as voting rights. These were, indeed, innovations. More intriguing, though, to the historian of nineteenth-century U.S. labor will be what other memoirists admitted: servants *were* employed at Brook Farm, whatever boosters may have claimed. "I am almost ashamed," Amelia Russell recalled, "to own that a hired cook ruled in the kitchen when I first became a member of Brook Farm, and she continued there for five or six months afterwards. Whether the task was considered too arduous, or none felt themselves sufficiently competent to undertake it, I do not know, but I think it must have been the latter feeling, for I never knew any one shrink there from work that must be done, if she or he were able to do it." This cook left, Russell recalled, when funds grew tight, at which point a communitarian took over food preparation until the group dissolved.[8] The fact that this "noble woman" could prepare communal meals but had preferred not to is telling; so is the omission of her name. Revealing too, though in a different way, is another memoirist's certainty that "no sensible reader will expect or desire that I should give a detailed account of how many sloppy days there were . . . in the wash-room," as finances squeezed.[9] Significant finally is unwillingness, on the part of Brook Farm's female cofounder, to explain what she had hoped to accomplish in reformist domesticity.

Though most nineteenth-century sources deny Sophia Ripley a cofounder's role, chroniclers as knowledgeable as Emerson did present her in that light.[10] If more recent commentators on Brook Farm have not, then a degree of feme covert may still infect comprehension of this reform community.[11] It is understandable that Jenny Franchot, focused on Sophia's conversion to Roman Catholicism, said little about Brook Farm in *Roads to Rome: The Antebellum Protestant Encounter with Catholicism* (1994). She might have, though, insofar as repugnance to a religion that many nineteenth-century liberals despised may have shaped the community's annals—so much so, that a memoir offering information on many community members' subsequent careers, up to and including notice of the demise of a dog named Carlo, failed to mention Sophia's dedication to Catholic charities. Franchot provides strong evidence that Sophia's conversion bespeaks, among other things, resolution of a gender-inflected spiritual quest. Unanswered by *Roads to Rome*, however, is whether or how that quest informed the cofounding of Brook Farm. Helpful here is Carole Shammas's charge that attention to the erosion of men's wonted domestic authority "illuminates the preoccupations of the American leaders of the utopian communities of the 1840s . . . and their varied male constituencies."[12] I agree. Yet I think it possible to illuminate other preoccupations too, such as those of female leaders who saw opportunity in the fissures created by the erosion that Shammas charts. Leading this (tiny) cohort, I submit, was the Ripley who formulated a position diametrically opposed to the one outlined in Catharine Beecher's *Treatise on Domestic Economy* (1841). Suggestive, in this light, are references to Sophia's participation in organizational meetings for Brook Farm, decision to buy stock in the farm rather than let George handle that proprietary role alone, tireless contributions at both manual and intellectual tasks, and traumatized inability to watch fire devour the last of the money Brook Farmers had invested in their group's future. Suggestive too, particularly as regards motivation, is the letter of 1843 in which she described a Shaker woman as looking like "a saint & prophetess," two images of feminine authority not strongly tied to domesticity.[13]

Beecher was interested in feminine authority, too; indeed, her *Treatise* was intended to win recognition of mistresses' civic contribution. Waged servants' contributions were also acknowledged in the *Treatise*, especially in a defense of "free" attendants' right to demand all the market would bear. The snag is that this defense was mounted in the context of an appeal to minimize reliance on nonkin. "It is," Beecher advised, "the peculiar duty of ladies, who have wealth, to . . . make it their first aim to secure a strong and healthful constitution for their daughters, by active domestic employments. All the sweeping, dusting, care of furniture and beds, the clear starching, and the nice cooking, should be done by the daughters of a family, and not by hired servants." Passages such as these have led some to say that Beecher's advice was remarkable for "resolute unsentimentality." Yet in fact, her early publications called for affective outreach. "It is not merely by giving them comfortable rooms, and good food, and presents, and privileges," the *Treatise* opined, "that the attachment of domestics is secured; it is by the manifestation of a friendly and benevolent interest in their comfort and improvement." More crucially, no unsentimentalist of resolve would have praised *Live and Let Live* or grown as harshly *anti*sentimental as Beecher did, in time. A major difference, in fact, between Beecher's vision of homes being happier "whenever ladies manage such things, as ladies should," and the "domestic & social experiment" that Sophia Ripley co-organized at Brook Farm is that where the former assumed the need to reach across social divisions, the latter tried to create the conditions of an amity in which elements would never jar nor castes collide.[14]

Students of sentimental literature have approached the topic of outreach in diverse ways. For instance, Philip Fisher has traced a philosophical lineage, Marianne Noble worked psychoanalytically, and Richard Brodhead examined scenes of engagement with print. Yet no historian of sentimentality has looked at communitarian attempts to address the chasm between attendants and attendees, any more than students of de-privatized householding have pondered the influence of affective precepts. The annals of Brook Farm are a good place in which to probe such things, due to the heavy freight seekers of the "Newness" loaded onto the concept of friendship. The result may not have been the most spic-and-span household, since one letter from the farm deplored the shortage of tablecloths in light of a gift of molasses that children in the community were inclined to drip.[15] It was nevertheless, according to all accounts, an unusually inclusive domicile.

The kind of outreach envisioned in the early days was summarized in the letter in which George Ripley explained that Brook Farm would abjure "the services of hirelings, who are not of my order, and whom I can scarce make friends." This may sound snobbish. But George added that he planned to invite his washerwoman ("certainly not a Minerva or a Venus") to join the group. This plan met with the woman's approval because she wanted her daughters to be educated. And educated they were, at the Brook Farm school, while their mother labored at the same rate of pay allotted their instructors. Seen from this angle, the Brook Farm project developed a position set forth on the title page of *Live and Let Live*. The epigraph from William Cowper reads: "And whereas the Turkish spy says he kept no servant because he would not have an enemy in his house, *I hired mine because I would have a friend*." This idea has little in common with what daughterlike Lucy Lee experiences with motherlike and un-motherlike mistresses. Sedgwick must have liked the concept, though, since she returned to it several times. One recurrence came when *Live and Let Live* noted that Lord Chesterfield "in his last will, in making some bequests to his servants, calls them his 'unfortunate friends, his inferiors in nothing but position,'" while another came fifty pages later in a talk about the degree to which household strife "would be materially lessened if young women . . . carried into their relation to their domestics the right spirit; if they regarded them as their 'unfortunate friends,' whom it was their religious duty to instruct, to enlighten, to improve, to make better and happier." Though quotations from Cowper and Chesterfield suggest how "retro" this idea was, by 1837 nineteenth-century sentimentalists often looked to the past to promote ideas about attendance.[16] Looking instead, as conscious progressives, to the future, George and Sophia Ripley spoke of education rather than the training that Lucy Lee's good mistress provided. Education having done its work, they were certain, all might live and labor as nonjarring, because connected, elements.[17]

Fourierists also spoke of amity—"To serve and wait upon friends is a pleasure," a booster caroled—as did Beecher at times. She was, however, so uncomfortable with this term's leveling potential that a follow-up to the *Treatise*, titled *Letters to Persons Who Are Engaged in Domestic Service*, emphasized the debt servants owed those who provided them with a home. "I know many domestics," one letter states, "who have become so much attached to the family where they have long lived, that no money would tempt them to leave. They seem to feel that all that interests the family belongs to them. They share the joys, the sorrows, and the hopes of the family, and are loved and trusted by all, as kind and faithful friends, while every thing reasonable is done to make them comfortable and contented."[18] Nicole Tonkovich has tied protestations of this kind to a desire to differentiate between servants and spinster-authors that, she suggests, could have meant a lot to Beecher. Wider reading discloses, though—and not for the last time—the downside of analyzing one advisor apart from others whose work was popular at the time. In other words, while Tonkovich's argument could also be applied to Sedgwick (another unmarried woman author), it is weakened by the fact that Beecher's definition of friendship affirmed the social ranking that Caroline Gilman, a wife of many years' standing, had promoted in *Recollections of a Southern Matron*. This similarity highlights divergence among conservatives inasmuch as the South Carolina Unitarian justified rank by adducing race, while Lyman Beecher's daughter credited Providence. "[I]n whatever way it may be," her *Letters* taught, that "men gain power to rule over others, so long as they really hold this power, it is by the permission of God."[19]

This was not a position that the seekers gathering at Brook Farm were likely to approve. Nor is it clear what Beecher meant by the qualifier "really," though that term implies judgment of the righteousness of specific claims to authority that might have intrigued foes of slavery. The closest Beecher came, though, to admitting the possibility of reauthorization was when she imagined the situation "if all the domestics in this land were suddenly changed into refined, well bred, well educated persons," for should that unlikely metamorphosis occur, *Letters* admitted that "the station of a domestic would be regarded as genteel, honourable, and respectable, far more than it is now." This comment labels improbable something the Ripleys had already set out to achieve. There was truth, then, to many of the comments and claims in Beecher's *Letters*: "*Somebody* had got to do the work in the kitchen," one missive sighs.[20] The Brook Farm task was to acknowledge that truth while shunning slaves and trying to do without hirelings.

Men old enough to engage in agricultural labor found this task not only doable but, in certain cases, a matter of lasting satisfaction. Typical, then, of the happiest chronicles of Brook Farm is John S. Dwight's recollection that in the "golden years" before Fourierism, "the scholars and the cultivated would take their part also in the manual labor, working on the farm or cultivating nurseries of young trees, or they would even engage in the housework." Though that "even" suggests a degree of smugness that puts true egalitarianism in doubt, still more can be learned from tributes to George Ripley's good-fellowship that are almost arrogantly male. "We have never looked upon him," another male Brook Farmer remarked, "as a master, or an employer, but as a fellow laborer on the same terms with ourselves." Looking back on those days, Dwight concurred wholeheartedly. George's "aspiration was," he recalled, "to bring about a truer state of society, one in which human beings should stand in frank relations of true equality and fraternity, mutually helpful, respecting each other's occupation, and making one the helper of the other. The prime idea was an organization of industry in such a way that the most refined and educated should show themselves practically on a level with those whose whole education had been hard labor." This sounds like what George said he was looking for when he bade farewell to his church. "I would neither be a despot," he reported, "nor a slave, but I have lived with you as a man with men, as a friend, a brother, an equal."[21] That few of these terms could have had relevance for his wife is unlikely to have caused friction between them, considering the pains Sophia took to differentiate between her own reform interests and those of advocates for women's rights; she reported herself irked, for instance, in 1840 by the "feminists" who crowded a friend's speaking engagement "so that we who belong there could not talk."[22] The attempt to establish "friend service," the better to avert caste collision without going so far as to espouse feminism, lay at the heart of her vision of Brook Farm. Vision was impeded, however, by this cofounder's extreme personal dignity. Familiarity was encouraged to the extent that girls in the Brook Farm school addressed Sophia by her given name. Recollections of "Her Serene Highness" suggest, however, a half-hostile moniker used behind the back of an authority figure few dared tease. In striking contrast, Sophia's sister-in-law answered good-humoredly to the comic hail, "Your perpendicular majesty."[23]

I will have more to say about regal role-play at Brook Farm. First, though, it is necessary to identify two forms of gender bias in its annals. One sort made it difficult for some chroniclers to see in-house chores as labor. John Dwight's "even . . . the housework" betrays this attitude. But so does the judgment that another communitarian passed after leaving Brook Farm. "The effect of a residence at the Farm," charged George William Curtis, "was not greater willingness to serve in the kitchen, and so particularly assert that labor was divine; but discontent that there was such a place as a kitchen." This remark may support testimony that Curtis was a communitarian dilettante, since "discontent" is a strange word to apply to the existence of the main site of nourishment in most U.S. homes.[24] Dilettantism has never been attributed, though, to John Thomas Codman, another male memoirist who recalled little about the organization of the in-house chores undertaken by his sister Rebecca, among others. Memoirists' ages may be pertinent here, since several who had been boys while at the farm recall doing household tasks. No male memoirist recalled, however, being asked to tidy rooms or to "treat[] Bridget, the Irish hireling, with uniform politeness."[25]

Bias of another kind rested on expectations derived from traditional domesticity. Many chronicles of Brook Farm reveal, then, that reformist "family" life was closely monitored by onlookers and communitarians alike; only Emerson seems to have realized, however, how much pressure bore down on the shoulders of the married couple who had broken with existing norms. "At Brook-Farm," he reported in 1843, "the authority of G. & S. R. is unconsciously felt by all: and this is ground of regret to individuals, who see that this patriarchal power is thrown into the conservative scale."[26] This comment was penned when Emerson was in the midst of his own "domestic & social experiments"; experimenting too, however, was the Ripley who reported feeling disheartened by coresidents' assumption that hierarchy of some kind was natural or meet. Admitting as much to Emerson (with a degree of candor unusual in their correspondence), Sophia depicted herself as "one sitting in solitude" after "vainly looking for a man or woman where I have most hoped to find them," only to find "those who might prophesy of the next age to the present, of eternity to time, prophesying only of themselves, casting their own horoscopes, impertinently prying into their own emotions, or intoxicating themselves with the excited emotions of others; feeling the rising & falling of their own pulse, perhaps recounting its variations to the nearest friend." It was disappointing to realize that "though, faithful, like the servant, to their allotted task of the hour," most Brook Farmers "reject the human side of life, turning their back upon the world's work, even when they believe it must be done, & ennobling it not by the seer's eye & prophet's touch," but instead "casting their cares upon the merely practical men & women of society— even to the elevating of them to a height they have no title to fill[,] even that of rulers." This was not what she or George had had in mind, judging by his avowal in 1840 that the "true followers of Jesus . . . attach no importance whatever to the petty distinctions of birth, rank, wealth, and station; . . . have no struggles for preëminence" and "no desire for the chief seats in the synagogue."[27] How complicated the Ripleys' chuckles must therefore have been when they learned of a perception expressed by a child living at the farm. Seeing the boy playing, a passing adult is supposed to have asked, "Well, Tom, who is the common mother of us all?" Though the response anticipated is something like "the good Earth," the boy guilelessly responded, "Mr. Ripley."[28]

The tangle of gender expectations, domestic responsibilities, and spiritual visions outlined here shows that Sophia was looking for more at Brook Farm than a retread of the teaching career for which she had been heralded in Boston. Insufficient, too, would have been a general idea of laboring for others, since there were many ways to do so that would not have dismayed her socially prominent kin. The unspoken implication of most existing scholarship is that she acted in accord with her husband's plans, as if out of a sense of wifely resignation like that prompting some of Lidian's wry comments. Weakening the force of that assumption, though, is a pileup of testimony that Sophia was George's full partner (or even admitted superior, since a niece would recall hearing that he "seemed to look on" her "as an idol"). Central to this contention is recognition that the female cofounder of Brook Farm was not only better educated than Waldo's second wife but also childless; she was, moreover, the only Transcendental wife to publish in *The Dial*. "Let no drudgery," commanded an essay titled "Woman" that Sophia published there in 1841, "degrade her high vocation of creator of a happy home. Household order must prevail, but let her ennoble it by detecting its relation to that law which keeps the planets in their course."[29]

There is little shared ground between this advice and the *Treatise*'s claim that "whenever ladies of refinement, as a general custom, patronise domestic pursuits, then these employments will be deemed ladylike."[30] Quite to the contrary, "Woman" made a spiritual agenda patent, even as it voiced impatience with gender inequity. "[I]n the spot," this essay observed, "where man throws aside his heavy responsibilities, his couch of rest is often prepared by his faithful wife, at the sacrifice of all her quiet contemplation and leisure. She is pursued into her most retired sanctuaries by petty anxieties, haunting her loneliest hours, by temptations taking her by surprise, by cares so harassing, that the most powerful talents and the most abundant intellectual and moral resources are scarce sufficient to give her strength to ward them off." The essay was also more militant than the *Treatise* as it went on to charge that "If there is a being exposed to turmoil and indurating care, it is woman, in the retirement of her own home; and if she makes peace and warmth there, it is not by her sweet religious sensibility, her gentle benevolence, her balmy tenderness, but by a strength and energy as great and untiring as leads man to battle." Recognition of this truth mandated, Sophia concluded, education that enabled girls to "penetrate through externals to principles" the better to form their own opinions; this finding sheds light on chroniclers' observation that female education was a priority at Brook Farm. Equally important, this essay predicts some of the arguments about nonkin attendance made by later nineteenth-century "New Women" who shared Sophia's taste for using the word "sentimental" as a pejorative.[31]

Back in the 1840s, many who read "Woman" must have thought of Margaret Fuller if only because, like Sophia, she discussed women's roles without reference to child-rearing or the management of staff. Fuller and Sophia were fellow travelers, in their way. Yet, like the men with whom they debated and conferred, they marched to distinct cadences. Recognizing this, Fuller commented that though Sophia "usually goes higher and sees clearer" than George, comprehension did not always follow. "I told her the truth," Fuller reported, "that I cannot understand her mental processes." Historians of labor may be tempted to say something similar in response to the letter in which Sophia rhapsodized that the efforts of a woman named Ellen Barker, who was hired to clean up the buildings that would house the first crop of Brook Farmers, comprised "the hardest and most disagreeable work that any of them would ever have to do."[32] She was probably extrapolating, though, from what she had seen on a visit to a community called Zoar, of which she reported that "The women here are as much at leisure, so far as household affairs and tending children is concerned, as the most fashionable lady could desire." Later, when it had become exhaustingly clear that hard labor was required of all who committed to de-privatized domesticity on a straitened budget, Sophia told Emerson that he could "hardly realize, how unimportant the results of our undertaking, or any undertaking seems to me, except that of leading the noblest life."[33]

These words may have been intended as a retraction of the disappointment she had expressed a few weeks earlier in a letter to Emerson: "Clear crystal springwater is not their drink," Sophia had said then of fellow Brook Farmers, "but sweetened, diluted beverage, perhaps spiced wines." She nonetheless remained critical of fellow communitarians, for after claiming that "I do not wish or need stronger figures reposing in the shade at noon—or gazing on the setting sun"—Sophia inquired, "why do they not with clear strong vision meet his [i.e., the sun's] meridian glance & challenge him as a co-worker?" Any number of Brook Farm memoirists recalled "Her Serene Highness" living up to this call, and beyond. Most deliberate in this respect, however, is Amelia Russell's recollection of Sophia volunteering for arduous nursing chores when a student from overseas developed a dangerous and highly communicable disease. Sophia left no special record of amity with Russell, though they were close in age, worked long hours together in the farm's less-than-ergonomic laundry room, and had been acquainted before "Miss Muslin" accompanied two nieces to the farm so that they could enroll in its school. Yet because Russell's recollections are widely held to be both accurate and fair, it is important that she praised Sophia's unfailing can-do attitude. Not only does this report counter those that imply passivity on Sophia's part, but, more to the point, it implies that Russell was tired of hearing a fine person's memory dishonored by chroniclers unable to assess the courage it took for a highly intellectual woman, of distinguished if not wealthy pedigree, to agree to serve.[34]

A pithy gauge of what that decision meant appears in a letter of 1856, which announced that in "well understood common parlance," women in the still-new republic "must be regarded either as 'ladies' or as 'servants.'" By de-privatizing her own domesticity, Sophia stood out against this truism and the caste collision it justified. Knowledge of the letter she wrote to Emerson, when she was feeling discouraged and isolated, can make the blithe spirits seen in her early reports of life at Brook Farm sound naive. "More of laughing than of weeping we have had the last few weeks," she declared in the spring of 1841, "for a busy and merry household we are at Brook Farm."[35] Comments of this kind help nonetheless to measure how badly a socially conscious woman might have wanted to escape mistress-ship during the period in which Waldo felt ambivalent about mastery.

Catharine Beecher addressed reluctant mistresses in her *Treatise* but had more to say about attendance in *Letters to Persons Who Are Engaged in Domestic Service*. It seems unlikely that many communitarians would have responded positively to *Letters'* patronizing tone; offensive too, to many gathering with the Ripleys, would have been this book's promotion of the contractualist credo. Disturbing, finally, for many at Brook Farm may have been Beecher's refusal to acknowledge slavery. Taking these points in order, *Letters'* fairy-tale format was noticeably different from the tone of *Treatise*, addressed to "young ladies." Nor was there much of a relationship to real-world conditions in the setting Beecher chose to explicate the reason that some lived and labored for nonkin. There was, then, little about life and labor in the antebellum United States that matched up to her account of shipwreck survivors being granted the use of a rich palace, on two conditions: that they care for themselves and that they live without rank. "All were 'free and equal'" in the new order, *Letters* explains, and thus "equally entitled to 'life, liberty and the pursuit of happiness,' in any way each thought best for himself." Confusion results nonetheless, since "nobody wanted to cook, or wash, or sweep, or plough, or take care of horses. And yet all this work must be done, or they would be destitute of the necessaries and comforts of life. At first, the strongest tried to force the weakest to work for them, and for a while, it seemed as if the poor women and children, who had little strength to resist, would be made slaves to the strong." A pitiful scene, if one's interests lie with "women and children." Beecher's sense of who deserved pity is more clearly indicated, though, by the fact that this pathetic passage follows notice that "the servants, the soldiers and the sailors were the strongest, and so they got possession of the best of every thing." Here, servants who are not identified by gender are grouped with the brawny and masculine, as distinguished from the "poor women and children" who are terrorized by their might. The last is an intriguing turn of phrase, considering how many nineteenth-century servants were in fact poor women and children. Yet when "poor women and children" suddenly reconfigure as "children . . . and ladies," Beecher's ideal domestic order is revealed. "If your lot had been drawn," one letter explains, "by one of the girls in the parlour, she would have been in your place, and you perhaps in hers, and then you would not have thought about the matter as you do now."[36]

Though this advice was addressed to servants, it is hard to see why any cook or maid would have found it compelling. In contrast, many probably did think that the contract implied by "free" service relationships mandated compliance with employers' dictates. *Letters to Persons* promoted that perception with talk of "suitable compensation" and by defining servants as "persons who for a reward agree to perform the work of the family." Unlike *Ann Connover* (the Sunday School tract that made a similar argument in the 1830s), Beecher admitted that agreement could be murky. Regardless, though, of whether it was the attendant's "own will, or . . . the will of parents," she stressed acceptance of a contract: wage earners "put themselves freely under the direction of their employers, and agree to do their work as they wish it to be done, and they receive a reward for this service." Obviously enough, this decision subordinated servants to another's rule. Yet *Letters* advised that stations and "places" were the law of society inasmuch as "domestics in a family will often feel very much above persons who are mulattos, and refuse to eat or associate with them." The insinuation that no "free" attendant was of African descent discloses a case of tunnel vision comparable to *Letters'* heedlessness about slavery. "[J]ust imagine," one letter counsels, "the state of things in this country, if all the *homes* in the land were broken up, and all classes of persons herded together in common, like flocks of animals."[37] Since house slaves had little ability to shelter their homes from breakage—and might well *be* herded like so many farmyard beasts in cases of sale—these lines should have displeased any with a heart for attendants who were property.

As is well known, some members of Brook Farm were readers of that kind; represented, too, were anticreedalists likely to resist the idea that mistress-ship comprised a form of "home mission." Amy Kaplan has shown that Beecher's reliance on that argument established rationales, the effects of which can be traced to imperialistic domination of dark-skinned people in far-off lands. Though this valuable insight has already enhanced Beecher studies, scholars should reckon with the fact that the term "home missions" had appeared in a review of *Live and Let Live* published years before the *Treatise* appeared. Ladies "will learn," this review promised, "that there are, in the 'home missions,' where every mistress of a family is stationed, most glorious opportunities of using her faculties and talents. . . . [T]he woman who enjoys good health, and fails in her domestic duties, or who finds them a burden intolerable to her spirit, may rest assured that her mind is very shallow or her judgment and taste very, very sadly perverted."[38]

A case could be made that the Beecher family's ministerial fame gave the *Treatise* and *Letters* more proselytizing impact than anything suggested by a novelist who had left the Congregationalist fold. Operating, though, from the premise that all reading material can guide hopes and fears, I would include *Redwood, Hope Leslie, Clarence,* and *The Linwoods*—the novels in which Sedgwick had most to say about non-white servants—in the imperializing charge. Brook Farm memoirs might be drawn into this discussion, too, since a fair few were published during the first sustained period of U.S. "outreach" toward the darker-skinned populations of Cuba and the Philippines.

Returning to the 1840s, print of less global significance includes portraits of socializing attendants. A well-known example of this sort of thing was Washington Irving's "John Bull," a story that describes how tasked and heaped British masters are by residuals who cannot be sold or turned away. "Everything that lives on him seems to thrive and grow fat. His house servants," reported *The Sketch Book of Geoffrey Crayon, Gent.* (1820), "are well paid, and pampered, and have little to do." Condoling with the squire who feels "eaten up by dependants," due to the fact that "superannuated servants" take advantage of his "great disposition to protect and patronize" anyone living on his estate, Irving depicts "gouty pensioners, and retired heroes of the buttery and the larder, . . . lolling about . . . crawling about . . . dozing under the trees, or sunning themselves upon the benches at [the mansion's] doors. Every office and out-house is garrisoned by these supernumeraries and their families, for they are amazingly prolific; and when they die off, are sure to leave John a legacy of hungry mouths to be provided for."[39]

Less satiric, but more purposefully heart-wringing, was an account of lonely wage earners in New England. "I hear complaints respecting servants wherever I go," Caroline Gilman reported in *The Poetry of Travelling in the United States* (1838), "and I think it must arise from their entire separation from their friends and relatives. I have in vain looked among them to find relatives enjoying each other's leisure, and sharing each other's cares; all are strangers to each other; and in every kitchen is the isolated American girl, or stout Irish woman, or free negro."[40] Not to be outdone, advisors who espoused "free" service portrayed socializing servants, too, in *The House Servant's Directory, Home, Ann Connover,* and *Susan Pike; or, A Few Years of Domestic Service* (1839). Material of this kind is pertinent to analysis of the moment in U.S. history at which "educated friends, working," could seem like an improvement on the way in which most households were run.

A product of that moment who visited Brook Farm before it converted to Fourierism described its goals for readers of *The Dial.* "The community will have nothing done within its precincts," Elizabeth Palmer Peabody explained, "but what is done by its own members, who stand all in social equality;—that the children may not 'learn to expect one kind of service from Love and Goodwill, and another from the obligation of others to render it,'—a grievance of the common society stated, by one of the associated mothers, as destructive of the soul's simplicity." Peabody approved the program here outlined. Yet as if concerned about the ramifications of the rubric "educated friends," she warned Brook Farmers to guard against "the spirit of coterie." This caution was well considered when "fifty-four of the ninety-nine members belonged to some kinship group," with relatives of either George or Sophia outnumbering any other unit. But it made even more sense when all but twelve of the original communitarians left—taking their investments with them.[41] The number of Brook Farm residents would swell again, with the shift to Fourierism, to as high as ten dozen. Yet because few of the incomers had much money to gamble on reform, the mass departure of pre- and anti-Fourierists did less to reduce the spirit of coterie than to speed financial collapse. Nothing Peabody could have said is likely to have saved Brook Farm; several memoirists did say, however, that the community's gravest lack was a businessman at the helm. Respect kept these opinions muted until after George and Sophia Ripley had died. In contrast, criticisms of impractical leadership at a contemporary reform group were penned even before its members had convened.

Leading the critics was Abby Alcott, a chronicler of de-privatized domesticity whose reportage has stirred considerable indignation against the experiment half-baked by her husband and a friend of his from England, Charles Lane. Many of Abby's criticisms of Fruitlands are well observed. Yet fairness demands recognition that most antebellum reform communities were equally doomed from the start if they were even close to as underfinanced and thinly populated. That being said, it must be admitted that a casual attitude toward key concepts helps to explain why the Alcott-Lane group barely lasted one winter. Trouble was brewing, then, when Lane billed Fruitlands as "something really progressive, call it family or community, or what you will," insofar as this careless summation shows how little he recognized how the difference between these two terms would strike Abby.[42] She may not have cared that a major question, for people paying attention to labor snarls, was how free wage-earners could really be when forced to sell labor under conditions over which they had little control. At the heart of her trials as a wife and mother, though, was how a house could be kept sans nonkin who did not work for love alone. Brook Farm answered the first challenge by making workloads discretionary and responded to the second by committing to the principle that no member would be a household governor while another was reduced to a char. Neglecting both areas of contention, the cofounders of Fruitlands made themselves vulnerable to arraignment as, at least, poor providers: men who failed to meet obligations to kin because they turned their backs on real-world exigencies.

Things started off badly, with a misty vision: "Family is not dependent upon numbers, nor upon skill, nor riches," Fruitlands' cofounders decided, but rather upon "union in and with that spirit which alone can bless any enterprise whatever."[43] It would be rash to say that "educated friends, working," lasted longer than what this pair liked to call the "consociate family" *just* because gestures toward kinship reinforced expectations of hierarchy. Thoughts of kinship do help, however, to elucidate what went wrong for Abby, a woman sharply attuned to the distinction between a housekeeper and her "help." Not that she ever dreamed mistress-ship would preclude hard work. "Been preparing my cottage for the reception of my husband and his friends," she noted as the men planning Fruitlands wended their way back from overseas. "I would have him find his home swept and garnished. The lord of our house and life shall find that his servants and lovers have not slept or idled during his absence from the field of labour. We have toiled, and shall reap the harvest of his 'Well done, good and faithful!' This is all I could wish, all he can give, to fill me with joy and content." If Abby greeted the travelers in this mood, they must have felt bemused that less than a month later, she lost interest in housekeeping, finding her "disrelish of cooking so great that I would not consume that which cost me so much misery to prepare."[44] Noting the gap between "swept and garnished" and later "misery," Madelon Bedell has suggested that Abby felt jealous of Lane's influence over her husband and household insofar as it reduced her to the status of "general house-cleaner, dishwasher and scullery maid."[45] This suggestion is sound but heavily slanted toward Abby's preferred self-siting. "No man is great to his valet says Sterne or somebody else," she attested; "neither is he always *sublime* to his *house maid.*"[46]

This is a witty gripe. Yet wit must not be allowed to obscure recognition that Abby *liked* presenting herself as a servant to people who knew she was not. (She does so, for instance, in the "Well done, good and faithful!" entry, since this was the Bible's praise for conscientious attendance.) True, she had enjoyed little financial security since marrying a man who refused to earn. Abby seems, however, to have most resented penury when it eroded her natal rank, for that is when she was most likely to portray her position in servile terms. Significantly, this form of self-presentation predates plans for Fruitlands; thus quite early in her marriage, Abby asked her father, a prosperous farmer, for a loan. When he refused, she riposted, "Would you have me take in washing?" Sarcasm marks the social siting Abby thought her due but hints, too, at the way her assumptions contributed to consociation's fall. It may be true, then, that she had labored at Fruitlands, as she would claim, "like a galley slave."[47] Awareness of a penchant for servile troping suggests nonetheless that she was offended less by hard work than by the expectation that she attend people other than those whom she recognized as having a claim on her energies. This suggestion provides reason to return to the history of Fruitlands with new eyes. For instance, though this community famously included a female layabout, it is possible that Anna Page just refused to skivvy under Abby's managerial eye.

If that is not the way in which Page's story has been told, this is because the historical record has favored Abby's point of view ever since Bronson Alcott's journals disappeared. It may be amusing, under these circumstances, to read the chronicle that recounts that "[s]omebody once described 'Fruitlands' as a place where Mr. Alcott looked benign and talked philosophy, while Mrs. Alcott and the children did the work."[48] Yet awareness of the pro-Abby slant in the Fruitlands archives reminds us that this commentator affirmed one view, rather than the only view, of what it was that coresidents owed each other in communitarian reform. There is certainly a case to be made against exploitative use of children's labor. It would have been quite reasonable, though, to Americans raised as Bronson had been that daughters contribute to the household economy. Abby would have shared this expectation even if, in her father's home, nonkin shared the workload. More important, then, because more productive of conflict at Fruitlands, is the fact that she did not like to be managed: "I cannot gee and haw," she wrote before that household was established, "in another persons yoke."[49] These facts marshaled, it is easy to understand why Abby resisted the setup at Fruitlands: "Mrs. Alcott has no spontaneous inclination towards a larger family than her own natural one," Charles Lane reported; "of spiritual ties she knows nothing."[50] This remark does not prove that Abby tried to mistress Page. But even if she never acted that highhandedly, Lane's comment suggests that Bronson's wife expected to be in charge. Some may feel so much sympathy for the stress, fear, and resentment under which she housekept that they see no need to defend her behavior at Fruitlands. However, for any looking to justify her determination to cling to management status, a key point could be that her volition was assumed by the marriage vow.

Such assumptiveness is implied in an account of the Fruitlands community that a loving daughter published decades after consocation was abandoned as a humiliating mistake. Those familiar with "Transcendental Wild Oats" will remember the drubbing Louisa May Alcott gave the only female Fruitlander who was not her kin. "Sleep, food, and poetic musings were the desires of her life," she recalled, "and she shirked all duties as clogs upon her spirit's wings. Any thought of lending a hand with the domestic drudgery never occurred to her." More culpable though, in this rendering, are Bronson and Lane, both of whom come in for criticism when their unfounded optimism swamps Abby's common sense. Louisa's difficult relationship with her father had much to do with his rejection of the usual paternal roles; thus, on being asked her definition of a philosopher, she is said to have shot back, "A man up in a balloon with his family at the strings tugging to pull him down."[51] This anecdote casts doubt on the impartiality of her representation of Fruitlands, as do, of course, the affection and pity she felt for Abby. It is clearer now, in sum, than it would have been from a daughter's vantage that Anna Page had her own story to tell. History does not tell us why she chose to consociate and what kind of information she had been given about the group before she moved in; helpful, too, would be information as to what Abby thought of Page's reasoning, since she had followed rather than joined after her husband and his new best friend ignored signs that all was not well. When Bronson and Lane did notice Abby's unhappiness—at last—they decided "they have been wrong in . . . lauding the Maternal instinct, & the Family, &c. These," Emerson gibed, "they now think are the very mischief."[52] Though this comment was made tongue-in-cheek, it shows that two male cofounders came to see what turmoil de-privatization could bring to a wife and mother with children to raise.

Abby learned things too as, in the wake of Fruitlands, she tried her hand at running an employment agency for servants. Though Bronson thought the for-profit endeavor a terrific joke, his guffaws provide one of the clearest gauges of his own ignorance about service labor, household management, and "family" life.[53] Abby herself did not initially grasp the nature of the "intelligence offices" that brought together homemakers in need of attendants and persons seeking service posts.[54] Indeed, by running such an office, she may be said to have retraced Thoreau's footsteps; she came to see, as he had, the importance of paying wages to those who served outside their own kinship groups. Yet Abby's office soon closed its doors. She may have felt the sting of critics: "Those offices," one source griped, "which profess to recommend good domestics, are '*bosh*,—nothing.'" But she was definitely bothered by the idea that, as a South Carolina writer claimed, a Northern intelligence office was "more like a slave market at the South than any thing else I can compare it with," for she admitted as much when she refused to be "even remotely associated to the false relations of mistress and maid" on similar grounds: "The whole system of Servitude in New England is almost as false as slavery in the South," Abby would avow.[55] This remark shows the influence of concern about "wage slavery." Yet deeper convictions are probably articulated in the way Mrs. Bronson Alcott justified her return to private life. "It is more respectable," she decided, "to be in my family—than a Servant of the Public in any capacity—and to be used by it [i.e., the public] is ignoble."[56] This was a safe position to uphold at midcentury. By choosing, though, to work "in my family" rather than at gainful employment, Abby affirmed values that Fruitlands had been intended to discredit. Affirmed, too, was the split between "lady" and "servant" that Sophia Ripley was trying to transcend.

No memoir of Brook Farm put her project in those terms. It is highly doubtful, though, that many coresidents knew or cared what

The Intelligence Office (1849), by William Henry Burr, promotes the "wages slavery" line that aspects of waged attendance compare to the treatment given servants who are property. No. 1959.46. Collection of the New-York Historical Society.

motivated Sophia. All memoirists paid respect to her, with most focusing on her character and pedagogical gifts. Of more interest, though, to most memoirists—understandably enough—were their own remarkable experiences: "There it was," beamed a former student in the Brook Farm school, "that I first learned to iron towels." Stressing the family-like manner in which communitarians labored, Arthur Sumner added that "there was the kindest feeling of brotherhood among the members," so that "it did not need that a man should be a scholar or a gentleman to be received and absorbed." A female communitarian agreed but challenged the masculinist emphasis: "with us," recalled Rebecca Codman Butterfield, "it was brother and sister working together at labors which were all equally honorable."[57]

These fond glances back toward vanished youth may not look like refutations. Yet they rebutted an earlier memoirist's claim that Brook Farmers had sometimes taken "friend service" to a fool's extreme. In one of these episodes, Georgianna Bruce Kirby recalled, "the desire of each to wait on every other had resulted in some confusion" since "it seemed so selfish to eat, while others as hungry stood to serve." In the end, she said, the community was obliged "to call a meeting to settle the question of griddle-cakes or no griddle-cakes, since those eating their breakfasts declared that they could not enjoy the hot cakes while oppressed by the thought of two or three friends leaning over the stove cooking them."[58]

The whiff of ridicule notwithstanding, this anecdote honored a domestic regime unlike that in which Kirby had been raised: born in England and brought to the United States as a children's nurse, she tried to show that amity through education was no dream. There is no way to be sure, now, why she spoke of friendship where other memoirists remembered siblinglike ties. While it is probably pertinent then that, for example, Rebecca Codman had lived and labored alongside her brother John, historians must also bear in mind the impact of natal rank. Noteworthy in this respect is unwillingness on the part of two Celtic women to dine with communitarians characterized (by one of Sophia's adoring female students) as "of good New England blood" but also refusal by a one-time valet, named John Cheever, to become a stock-holding member of Brook Farm.[59] Scholars who ignore these reluctances may accept Kirby's account of the disruption occasioned by the shift to Fourierism: "there could be no congeniality," she sighed, "between the newcomers and those who had been so united under the first dispensation."[60] Knowing, though, that the unity of Brook Farm had already been fractured by holdouts such as Cheever and the Celts, others will wonder whether protestation comprised a form of posturing. It would not necessarily follow that amity through education was a chimera. Rather, it would hint that Brook Farm memoirs reflect social prejudices complicated, perhaps, by defenses of chroniclers' current status and fame.

Having nothing to defend once Brook Farm closed its doors forever in 1847, Sophia left no clear record of her aims, accomplishments, or defeats. Her best biographer, a descendant named Henrietta Dana Raymond, reconstructed a sense of her efforts to live as a socially conscious intellectual who made stringent demands on herself while sharing lavishly of her time and energy. The woman depicted in *Sophia Willard Dana Ripley: Co-Founder of Brook Farm* (1994) is admirable in many ways. Viewed, however, alongside what we have seen of Emerson, Thoreau, and Bronson Alcott, she comes across as yet another Transcendentalist trying to rethink service in ways reflective yet subversive of sentimental postulates. I have already mentioned how Sophia's situation differed from Lidian Emerson's; even more edifying, though, is the contrast between her goals and Abby's, since the letter that rejected the role of "ruler" says that Sophia did not yearn to mistress. This finding is relevant to the fact that she never disparaged her spouse or complained of laboring like a "galley-slave." Yet it is just as pertinent to memoirists' recollection of a call that female Brook Farmers paid, in the early days, to area wives, since these visits imply a degree of proselytizing fervor that Abby did not share. Resemblances between calls of this kind and the intrusive "home visit" are not incidental. More suggestive, though, for students of the literature of nineteenth-century U.S. service is recognition that visits to wives who lived near Brook Farm recall the gender consciousness of "Woman." Abby agreed with Anna Page that their sex was oppressed: both knew, then, that "a woman may live a whole life of sacrifice, and at her death meekly says, 'I die a woman,'" while "A man passes a few years in experiments in self-denial and simple life, and he says 'Behold a God.'"[61] However, neither Fruitlander seems to have dreamed of rising above that disparity, much less of blurring mistress-ship with servitude.

A more organized, but less gender-alert, way to engage in outreach was offered by Fourierists who queried the benefits of conceptualizing of service in terms of kin-likeness. "[I]t does not become those," preached an Associationist newspaper published at Brook Farm, "who daily live by civilized slavery, who have it in their kitchens, their workshops, and their manufactories, to use loud words of denunciation against those who live by barbarous slavery, which is only the elder sister of the same monstrous family." As this was the official Fourierist line, historians of service will note particularly its image of a freakish clan. Associationists did trope familially at times; society being "but one family," one explained, "all men are brothers."[62] More than most contemporaries, though, they challenged received truths about what *Letters to Persons* called "that most important institution of God, *the family state.*" This aspect of the French scheme repelled Emerson. "In reference to the Fourier formula," he told his journal, "one should remind the projectors that people cannot live together in any but necessary ways."[63] This is a strange observation insofar as Emerson could have said the same thing about his own coresidence with Thoreau. More attuned, then, than Emerson to the oddity of defending structures that might betoken norms as opposed to need, Brook Farmers brought the era of "educated friends, working," to a close by voting to turn their group into a phalanstery.

Various explanations have been adduced for the shift to Fourierism. Yet when the focus is Sophia's project at Brook Farm, it may have been of paramount importance that Associationists had much to say about communitarian homemaking. "There will be no more servants," promised *A Popular View of the Doctrines of Charles Fourier* (1844), "yet everybody will be served with the utmost zeal, intelligence, and promptitude." That this was an outreach program is clear from comparison with another Associationist text. "Those whose minds are cultivated and manners polished, cannot really associate with . . . servants," taught *The Phalanstery* (1841), as such people are "generally corrupted by the conditions of their servitude."[64] Yet Fourierist outreach was not the same as that attempted at Brook Farm in the early years since—as Carl J. Guarneri has explained—the Associationist goal was "harmony between classes rather than the removal of all inequalities of wealth and power. Fearing that 'communism' would stifle freedom," he adds, followers of Charles Fourier "made allowances for gradation in members' investment and accommodations" in reform communities. Allowances having been made, reformers imagined, phalansteries would become households in which "those who serve are ready and willing friends, who are themselves served on other occasions with equal zeal and skill."[65] This was "friend service" as imagined by Associationists; it pleased some. What it was not was a program of amity through education, much less the "true church" of the Ripleys. I do not know how Sophia viewed the Associationist promise, "domesticity is but an exchange of services."[66] It is nevertheless clear that the contractual nature of this axiom was a far cry from her wish to see Brook Farmers strengthening gifts as seers and prophets. Missing from Fourierism, then, for a seeker such as Sophia was attention not to service but to the "selfism" that prevented Brook Farmers from transforming labor for others into a stepping stone to glory.

Information unearthed by Henrietta Raymond about Sophia's upbringing and young adulthood supports this contention by revealing that she felt grateful and respectful affection for two gently bred aunts who had dedicated themselves to kin service on her behalf. The fact that many of those memories would have concerned laundry room chores such as ironing may help to explain why Sophia scoffed at the idea that reformist homemaking was an act "requiring high, heroic valour," since "it has never seemed to George & myself anything but the simplest, most every-day affair possible." Strengthening this perception, Raymond has pointed out, could have been the scriptural directive quoted in one of Sophia's *Dial* essays: "let him that is greatest among you be as a servant." Almost certainly, this verse motivated many Brook Farmers' willingness to labor sweatily at unaccustomed chores. The goal of serviceability may, however, have had special significance to a visionary who, after having been raised in an atmosphere of loving kin service and marrying an idealistic minister, quite possibly out-stripped him in her commitment to a radical revisioning of "the family work." I emphasize this point because Sophia's report, after leaving Brook Farm, that she found it "inexpressibly sweet" to do the Catholic clergy's bidding as if "I were a servant or a little child" could sound like the whimper of a crushed spirit. Contradicting that interpretation, though, is her tireless lobbying to establish an order of nuns and provide a refuge for "fallen" women. Neither a power monger, then, nor a "very troubled person" drained by adversity, Sophia was a selfless reformer impelled by dreams of feminine transcendence.[67]

An intriguing sidelight on this argument is notice of that faction, among nineteenth-century advisors, who passed on the image of "home missions" because they preferred to speak of "home-queens."[68] I have found no evidence of Sophia using that term. Memoirists did recall, however, that she had appeared at Brook Farm masquerades in costumes that bespoke female power. The most reliable account of this sort has her playing the part of a gypsy fortune-teller, a role quite in keeping with her expression of interest in seers and prophets. Pertinent too, though probably erroneous, is the memory that she dressed as England's Elizabeth I at another community fete. I consider this memory less trustworthy, not only because some say that the Brook Farmer who arrayed herself as Good Queen Bess was Sophia's sister-in-law; even more salient, the monarch who ordered the execution of Mary Stuart would have been a strange choice for a person attracted to Catholicism. If, as seems likely, memories grew blurred over time, it is nonetheless fascinating that Sophia was remembered as having emulated the Virgin Queen since on the one hand Georgianna Kirby sniped that the appeal of "Papistry" lay in its worship of a woman who had conceived immaculately, while on the other, Sophia made no bones about admiring the Shakers, a celibate religious group founded by a seeress.[69] If this sidelight returns us to the question of what could have led a woman noted for her elegance and reserve to blue other people's linen, the answer must, I think, be a form of the idealism that led a prosperous householder to unhire a college graduate and a young bachelor to ponder serviceability before going to live alone by a pond. There was, unfortunately, a huge drawback to the way in which Sophia put her ideals to the test: this was the tendency for life in a small community to decrease her chances of coming into contact with others as elevated as she. Recognizing this, she complained of a meeting at which Brook Farmers proved to be callously judgmental of "natures, particularly reserved & delicate ones"—so much so, she told Margaret Fuller, that "much that you would esteem a necessary & pleasing manifestation of a superior nature, is set down to the account of faults."[70] Since this letter bears no date, it cannot tell us if Sophia's nature was less appreciated in 1843 than in 1842 or 1845. She seems, however, to have been significantly less important to young female chroniclers after the shift to Fourierism.

One such chronicler, the "sweet Lizzie Curson" who deplored stained tablecloths, does not seem to have interacted with Sophia at all; this is an interesting finding since, after marrying another Brook Farmer, she went to live and labor in a Fourierist phalanx.[71] A friend of Lizzie's named Marianne Dwight saw more of Sophia, perhaps through the influence of Marianne's brother John. Yet relations between Sophia and the chronicler called the "Pollyanna" of Brook Farm were never warm, though the latter had also been a teacher and was no intellectual slouch. Nor was she a reluctant laborer, for her letters are one of our best accounts of the rigors of de-privatized domesticity. "[M]y business is as follows," Dwight noted in 1844. "I wait on the breakfast table (1/2 hour), help . . . clear away breakfast things, etc. (1 1/2 hours), go into the dormitory group till eleven o'clock,—dress for dinner then over to the Eyrie and sew till dinner time,—half past twelve. Then from half past one or two o'clock until 1/2 past five, I teach drawing in Pilgrim Hall and sew in the Eyrie. At 1/2 past five go down to the Hive, to help set the tea table, and afterwards I wash tea cups, etc., till about 1/2 past seven." This statement has Dwight working harder, if only because of responsibility to more coresidents, than most women of her age, education, and social background. She knew it, too, for this letter goes on to say that "We need more leisure, or rather, we should like it. There are so many, and so few women to do the work, that we have to be nearly all the time about it." Dwight probably found pleasure in compiling a longish labor litany. There was pleasure too, however, for this particular Brook Farmer, in working with and for others according to Fourierist precepts. "For myself," she declared in 1845, "I would not exchange this life for any I have ever led. I could not feel contented again with the life of isolated houses, and the conventions of civilization." Dwight's contentment highlights the misery recorded by a "free" servant who wrote a longing letter home in 1848. "[Y]ou cannot tell how I want to see you & the rest of the family," this young worker mourned. "I cannot bear to think about them[,] I want to see them so much . . . time looks long but it will soon slip away."[72]

Caroline Gilman might have nodded with an "I told you so" air at this corroboration of her concern about lonely Northern servants. If, however, such nodding did occur, Dwight could have prized it as unsolicited testimony to the merits of communitarian domesticity—and been rebuked for her radicalism by writers such as George Fitzhugh and Sarah Hale. The latter was a proslavery polemicist so bombastical that one commentator has accused him of indulging in a "sheer love of the perverse." There is considerable truth to this charge, as even passing acquaintance with Fitzhugh's prose goes to show. "A Southern farm," he opined in 1854, "is a sort of joint stock concern, or social phalastery, in which the master furnishes the capital and skill, and the slaves the labor."[73] If, as seems likely, many intended readers dismissed this nonsense, it was harder to ignore ladylike ridicule, from the esteemed editor of *Godey's*, of Fourierist redefinitions of home and "family" life. Much can be learned about antebellum attitudes toward colonization from Hale's *Liberia; or, Mr. Peyton's Experiments* (1854). More germane, though, to those who would know how Association looked to its antebellum critics is Hale's decision to have a fatherlike slaveholder try to help freedpersons achieve self-reliance by establishing them in a phalanstery. By having Mr. Peyton's group fail because former property keep running to him for guidance, Hale predicted Fitzhugh's claim that "Fourierite Phalansteries" along with "Mormon and Oneida villages" can "succeed so long as . . . despotism lasts," because "when the association loses the character intended by its founders, and acquires a despotic head like other family associations, it works well, because it works naturally." Fitzhugh rode this hobbyhorse for years. "The Family is threatened," he ululated in 1857, "and all men North or South who love and revere it, should be up and a-doing."[74]

Throughout all this fuss, the acclaimed badness of U.S. servants was presented as a looming threat to domestic bliss. "Not a day passes over our heads," *Godey's* claimed in 1844, "that we are not thrown into hot water about something or other, with our abominable servants." With complaints of this sort on the rise, it is not surprising that, two years later, Hale's periodical approved the report that some privileged New Englanders were homemaking without "help." *Godey's* did not attribute this shift to the servant-averse program of Beecher's *Treatise*; instead, it credited a desire to housekeep with "true republican simplicity." Demurring a few years later, a Swedish traveler explained the phenomenon by referencing "the difficulty there is in getting good servants" in the North and gesturing toward "economic causes" she did not elucidate.[75] Fredrika Bremer was silent as to whether the households in question sent out laundry, employed seamstresses, or hired staff seasonally. Nor did she seem to realize that the majority of U.S. households had always managed without attendants. What she implied, instead, was dissatisfaction with "free" service so intense that some chose to ultraprivatize—and thus, in our terms, de-sentimentalize—their homes. This trend was forecast by a criticism that the *Knickerbocker Magazine* brought against Sedgwick's "well-meaning little domestic stories" in 1842. Signed by "A Sufferer" who found servant management trying, this essay found an episode from *Live and Let Live* "quite *outré*, even for fiction": this vignette has a kind mistress sending a costly laxative to a cook who acts irritably because she is ill. Away with the coddling of attendants, "A Sufferer" scorned; better to have homemakers do their own chores. "God be praised," s/he trumpeted, "we live in a land where men must learn to be their own servants, since every man can and will be his own master."[76]

The idea that U.S. servants had extraordinary opportunities to rise socially irritated some Americans very much; citing de Tocqueville in 1872, an essay in *The Galaxy* charged that "the transition state in which the servants of a republic live" is "one very unfavorable to the peace and order of a household." At the same time, "the liberty and equality idea" inspired some; it is safe to assume, for instance, that the ironies embedded in "A Sufferer"'s conclusion were patent to a fan of *The Linwoods* named William Wells Brown.[77] Irony may have been at work even earlier, though, in the vision of servant-free households advanced at the end of *Recollections of a Housekeeper*, if Gilman meant to twit Clarissa by having her dream of "grand cooking-establishments . . . scourers . . . window-cleaners, &c." as a corrective to "the mortification and embarrassment of our present system"; the jape would be, of course, that the wage payer was looking for ways to wriggle out of responsibilities.[78] Whatever Gilman intended, this dream had long-lived appeal since Melusina Fay Peirce vaunted it after the Civil War, as did, decades later, Charlotte Perkins Stetson, the Beecher great-niece who promoted "kitchenless houses." Caroline Gilman links these reformers inasmuch as Peirce was her great-niece and Stetson became a Gilman when she married for the second time.

These advisorial genealogies have their interest (and not only in relation to de-privatized domesticity). Yet when the topic is communitarian reform in the 1840s, the more central finding is that Marianne Dwight was as contented in the Brook Farm Association as Abby was miserable at Fruitlands. If Dwight did not perceive herself as losing status, that is probably because, as an as-yet-to-be-married woman, she could not feel the diminution of mistress-ship not yet enjoyed. Equally edifying is recognition that when Brook Farm's prospects looked rocky, she took the initiative of devising a business plan. "I must interest you," Dwight announced in 1844,

"And so, Jane, this is Missis Jones's new Bonnet! Cost only ten Dollars! I'd be ashamed to be seen with such a thing on!"

"If there ain't Missis Jones, with that Bonnet on! Don't let's see her, Jane!"

"I tell you, I won't have any body pokin' about *my* kitchen. You or I has got to keep out!"

"Yes, Ma'am, I'm goin'. I won't poke myself up in the country. Folks as I lives with allus goes to Newport in September."

More humor from Harper's New Monthly Magazine *(1856), a "family" publication heavily reliant on middle-class readers. Special Collections, University of Virginia Library.*

in our fancy group, for which and from which I hope great things,—
nothing less than the elevation of woman to independence, and an
acknowledged equality with man. Many thoughts on this subject have
been struggling in my mind ever since I came to Brook Farm, and now,
I think I see how it will all be accomplished. Women must become pro-
ducers of marketable articles; women must make money and earn their
support independently of man. So we, with a little borrowed capital
(say twenty-five or thirty dollars; by we, I mean a large part of the
women here), have purchased materials, and made up in one week
about forty-five dollars worth of elegant and tasteful caps, capes, col-
lars, undersleeves, etc., etc.,—which we sent in to Hutchinson and
Holmes, who have agreed to take all we can make. If they find a ready
sale, we shall be greatly encouraged,—and be able to go on extending
our business, as far as our time and numbers will allow.[79]

"By and by," this plan continues, "when funds accumulate (!) we may
start other branches of business, so that all our proceeds must be applied
to the elevation of woman forever. Take a spiritual view of the matter,"
Dwight concluded. "Raise woman to be the equal of man, and what
intellectual developments may we not expect?"[80] Gestures toward spir-
ituality notwithstanding, nothing about this position suggests adherence to the ideals advanced in "Woman." Perhaps Sophia had already
trained herself to sit contentedly in solitude, uncaring that—following
Brook Farm's formal pledge of allegiance to Fourierism—many parents
removed their teenaged daughters from her tutelage. She has to have
noticed, though, that she thereby lost the company of several female
students who remembered feeling "worshipping infatuation" for her; of
the courtly male coresident who is said to have regarded her as his
"mother-confessor"; and of almost every individual who had joined the
Ripleys hoping to establish the "true church."[81] Last but not least, she
lost the occasional visit from Margaret Fuller, a real friend as opposed to
the sort developed through fostered amity.

Marianne Dwight could never have seemed a fit substitute for
that daring mind. Yet she devoted herself to the kind of reform she
understood and admired. "The great doctrines of Association fire my
soul every day more and more," Dwight attested in 1845. "I am awed
at the vastness of the schemes it unfolds, I am filled with wonder
and ecstasy."[82] Amelia Russell was less rapturous about the French
program. Yet she and Marianne enjoyed each other's company despite
significant disparity of age. Their friendship would have made it
more glaring that Sophia's relationship with the best-educated young
women at Brook Farm was more courteous than relaxed—a sad come-
down from her vision of an ennobling, and specifically feminine, form
of servitude.

And what of other Brook Farmers, male and female, once the "true church" gave way to the schematics of a phalanx? For Amelia Russell, that shift was best understood in literary terms: as the "new Fourierite system began to be organized," she remembered, "the poetry of our lives vanished." This rendering of the situation affirms Georgianna Kirby's memories as well as those of Arthur Sumner, for the towel-ironer grew to be a man who still seemed angry that "some very unpleasant people" had abruptly "appeared on the scene." These were the sort, he recalled, who chose to "collect together in the great barn, and grumble; when the others passed through, the malcontents eyed them with suspicion, and muttered, 'Aristocrats!' all because they knew themselves to be less cultivated and well-bred." How unfriendly, his tone implies. Comparable, though less mewling, is Russell's allegation that existing friendships caused ructions that impeded the spread of amity. "The moment," she asserted, "that the idea of an aristocratic clique entered into the mind of any one, that moment the harmony of Brook Farm was at an end; the break was bridged over, but the spirit that made us one was gone." From there on in, she added, "[i]nstead of the voluntary labor we had before enjoyed, there was now a compulsory feeling which gave you a sensation of not belonging to yourself."[83] House slaves could have had something to say to that sensation; so, perhaps, would "bound" workers. By the time Russell's recollections were published in 1878, both forms of attendance were obsolete. Yet because their disappearances did not bring an end to tension with servants, analysts would do well to realize that "Home Life of the Brook Farm Association" did not appear in print until pundits had begun to teach: "Too much sentiment is wasted on the modern servant." Russell's memoirs lent support to this position when published in *The Atlantic Monthly* and again when reprinted in book form twenty years after her death. Since the only reasonable inference to the later publication is that someone thought *Home Life of the Brook Farm Association* (1900) would have current interest, reprinting may imply support for the anti-sentimental gospel that rationalization was the only way to ease the "painful servant problem" still rankling throughout U.S. homes.[84] If so, the thrust of Russell's memoirs, but also Sumner's and Kirby's, was that Brook Farm had foundered on a version of that social ill.

Though Fourierism lived on (with help from a few ex-Brook Farmers) for a while longer, it was clear to most observers by the later 1840s that the communitarian ideal thrived best in fiction. "Ah," breathes a man of the future, "you did not begin to live in your benighted nineteenth century! Just think of the absurdity of one hundred housekeepers, every Saturday morning, striving to enlighten one hundred girls in the process of making pies for one hundred little ovens!" To today's eyes, this story predicts Edward Bellamy's surprise best-seller, *Looking Backward: 2000–1887* (1888). But when first published in 1848, it must have sounded like a defense of Association. "What fatigue! What vexation!" the man of the future gloats, for in the attendant-free future he reveals, kin dine together in a great hall, served by a huge kitchen and a corps of cooks. This is the truer domesticity, he contends, because it is more protective of kin. "The family and the home are indeed sacred," the visitor from the nineteenth century is told, "and the bond broken only in death." Two decades later, another fictionalized treatment of communitarian domesticity culminated in the advent of Miss Moonshine. This "Transcendentalist-lady" dislikes the term "servant," though nonkin attendance is the job for which she has come to interview; her preference is for the more elevated "daughter of labor." When asked what she expects of the position, the idealist replies: "A moderate stipend, a seat at your fireside, a place in your hearts (*sighs*), an opportunity to devour the works of the masters . . . to mingle in sweet commune with congenial souls (*sighs*)."[85] If this conflation of sentimentality and Transcendentalism amused Waldo Emerson, it probably made others—including, perhaps, Russell, Sumner, and Kirby—wince.

Far more grating for any who recognized mounting unhappiness with nonkin attendants was how little communitarian experiments had done to ease domestic tension on either side of the Mason-Dixon Line. Not that critics of de-privatized homemaking had done any better. "[W]e love our slaves, and we are ready to defend, assist and protect them," Fitzhugh asserted, while the Northerners he pretended to address "hate and fear your white servants, and never fail, as a moral duty, to screw down their wages to the lowest, and to starve their families, if possible, as evidence of your thrift, economy and management." It would be rash to say this allegation lacked support. Yet when the issue is the development of service-labor theory, affective amplification of such intensity suggests stagnation of thought. A second-generation Transcendentalist confirmed the persistence of old imagery in 1864. "Not long ago," Moncure Conway reported, "in conversation with a strong defender of Negro Slavery, I found that the corner-stone of his theory was an impression that there was in the homestead of the South a simplicity, a patriarchal relationship between the servants and superiors, which contrasted favourably with the corresponding conditions in other communities, where, he maintained, the relation between servant and master being purely and at each moment mercenary, the ties must be galling to both parties."[86] Though Conway did not say as much, the fact that communitarians had railed against "free" service yet failed to provide a viable alternative to it could have strengthened this impression.

Nonsense, insisted sentimentalists; all that was needed was more love. As thoroughly stagnant, then, as anything in Fitzhugh's shrill output is "Lydia's Wages" (1854), a story in which a white native-born servant becomes so family-like that her employer is as embarrassed to pay her as she is to accept her due. "It cost Mr. Purdy more thought than anything which had happened for a long time," this sketch recounted, "when he offered her the first instalment of her wages"; then, though "[i]t didn't 'pear right to him, no how," he leaves the money "in hard dollars" on a kitchen cupboard while she is elsewhere. "Lydia blushed when she discovered it was for her, though she was all alone," since "'[i]t 'peared' to her very much in the same light as it did to Mr. Purdy." More innovative was a tale that made fun of an Irish cook who plots to extort a pay raise and relished her eventual discomfiture. "I'll work for ye, misthress, dear; I'll be yer bound slave and niver mintion the pay," the miscreant promises upon realizing what she stands to lose. "I'll serve ye on me knees, an' ye'll take me in again. Och! woe for me! the big fool I've been!" The exact amount of her recompense, this servant-character has realized, is less important than the immeasurable boon of a good mistress: "Niver spake," she begs, at last, "o' the wages, plaze."[87] This depiction of attendance is not free of disdain. Yet "Labor; or, Striking for Higher Wages" (1859)—as its title emphasizes—drew attention to the fact that servants are employees. Noteworthy from this vantage is the mistress-character's reliance on a servant with the Anglo American name of "Jenny," since her loyal assistance is utterly family-like. Edifying in this respect is the Irish cook's failure to mention increased devotion; rather, she speaks of more profound abjection in a heavy, "comic" brogue.

No doubt, the image of a deeper genuflection pleased some middle-class readers. Yet there was more to the "servant problem" at midcentury than struggles over social status, since affect remained one of the chief criteria by which attendants were judged. Catharine Sedgwick tried to extend the life span of this criterion with a short story that emphasized Celtic servants' warmheartedness. "I buy Margaret's services," the grateful mistress-character in "The Irish Girl" (1844) reports, "and she throws in her love." For readers who remembered the perjurious Conolly in *Clarence,* this was not a completely new move. Yet inasmuch as it *was* a departure from paeans to native-born "help" such as *Redwood*'s Deb and *Home*'s Martha, it is pertinent that Sedgwick would soon confess in a private letter to preferring an Irish immigrant: "I would not exchange her," she reported, "for all the service I could distill in Yankeedom."[88] We can only speculate what might have happened if Sedgwick had written a didactic novella to this effect rather than a brief tale in which the servant-heroine dies tragically. That, however, would have been a brave gesture considering the many and varied charges brought against Irish immigrants once they started to dominate the U.S. service-labor pool. As seen in "Labor; or, Striking for Higher Wages," greed was one such charge. "You are right," a Midwestern homemaker told a grown daughter, with specific reference to Celtic attendants. "I believe with you, that nothing will bind them but Dollars and cents." Incompetence was another favored accusation, and brutishness a third; thus, in 1851 the same mistress congratulated the same correspondent on finding "a *woman* rather than a headlong, Irish, heedless animal." Sarah Hale tried to rebut these criticisms by having *The Ladies' New Book of Cookery* (1852) teach that Irish women "are neither stupid nor ungrateful." On the contrary, she judged, "if they are taught in the right manner, they prove very capable, and are most faithful and affectionate domestics."[89] Criticisms stayed current nonetheless for another generation, since 1875 found a respected author of children's books classifying Irish servants as "that inefficient, untrustworthy, unstable horde who come fresh from their training in peat-bog and meadow, to cook our dinners, take care of our china dishes, and adjust to the nice little internal arrangements of our dwellings." How Sophia Ripley would have blanched to see such ugly words appear as the doctrine of the woman who had run the Brook Farm nursery school.[90]

Though insults of this kind are usually taken as reflective of the fact that Celtic peasants were immigrating in unprecedented numbers, another variable to keep in mind is the sort of print for which antebellum editors would pay. Ever alert to this aspect of the world of letters, James Fenimore Cooper in a novel of 1846 had a character mourn "the domestic slave, who identified himself with the interests, and most of all the *credit* of those he served, and who always played the part of an humble privy counselor, and sometimes that of a prime minister." In 1859, an advocate of renewing the African slave trade concurred. "I love the simple and unadulterated slave," Edward A. Pollard sighed; "I love to look upon his countenance, shining with content and grease." No such love could be felt, he shuddered, about "the 'genteel' slave" who, because "inoculated with white notions, affects superiority, and exchanges his simple and humble ignorance for insolent airs"; this sort Pollard classified as his "especial abomination."[91] Whatever social historians may say about whether servants really had grown more difficult at this time, students of the literature of U.S. service will see that one effect of the convergence of complaints such as these would have been to encourage yearnings for native-born attendants at precisely the point in U.S. history when native-born whites were turning their backs on service work.

Just as the escape-route of mills, factories, and so on began to be available, Beecher's *Treatise* taught homemakers to see management responsibilities as God's holy plan: if mistresses had trouble with cooks and maids, she instructed, that was because Christians were sent trials to fortify their souls. After midcentury, though—and with scattered jabs at communitarian reform—she advised differently in essays that harangued against "coarse and vulgar servants, who live in the cellar and sleep in the garret." This position may sound like the old exasperation with "the ungracious, capricious, sluggish, disrespectful, and, at the very best, ill qualified nature of American attendance" that had been standard since the early national period, and to some extent it was. Complaints signified in a new way, however, once "friend service" was no more. "It annoys me," a Philadelphia man reported in 1850, "to feel how entirely one's comfort depends on servants."[92] Some pundits counseled resignation. "As we can not dispense with her strong arms," one of the nineteenth-century's few male advisors opined in 1864, with specific reference to Irish servants, "we have to endure her ignorance, her uncouth manners, her varying caprices, and her rude tongue." No such thing, retorted Beecher in essays that would be republished in *The American Woman's Home* (1869); the solution was the *"close packing of conveniences"* capable of decreasing reliance on household employees by as much as 75 percent.[93] Germane to this retort were her interest in genteel country "cottages" that provided no living space for staff and *Godey's* admiration for a Southern farm house in which "servants' apartments and kitchen offices are so disposed that, while connected to render them easy of access, they are sufficiently remote to shut off the familiarity of association which would render them obnoxious to the most fastidious." Praise of this sort recalls a complaint voiced in 1828. "One thing that assists," a visitor then reported, "in depriving their parties in the South of any appearance of style is the nasty, black creatures whom they have for servants. . . . You can't imagine how disagreeable it is to have so many of those creatures going about. They are so stupid and so indolent, always in the way when not wanted."[94] Oversupply was not the usual gripe in the "free" states. Taken together, though, complaints about waged and chattel servants shed new light on the gnarled emotions that might have accompanied images of "a house divided" after the midcentury.

U.S. architects in the mid-1800s acceded to the taste for division by building back stairways for nonkin coresidents and installing speaking tubes and dumbwaiters that distanced servitors from "family" life. Objection was made to these innovations in liberal venues. "What genteel Christian family would buy a house," carped the *Massachusetts Quarterly Review* in 1848, "which had not a separate back-entrance, and a back staircase for the servants?" Sarcasm was no answer, though, to the anger expressed in a household ledger of 1845 that describes one servant as "Industrious, but obstinate, Self-willed & meddles with things in which she has no right." Worse yet, this worker was "Famous for going about the house at night with a lamp for want of employment and conciets that she Knows more of the arrangements of the family concerns than her employers."[95] Family-like trust and warmth may have prevented such things from occurring in certain homes. Yet the tenets of sentimental outreach also strengthened the moral imperative of heeding reports from servants who had witnessed immoral acts. Privatizers' best recourse under these circumstances was a powerful expedient: legal restriction on servants' speech. Restrictive laws directed at servants were on the books, North and South. Yet after lawyers began to challenge the rules of exclusion in the 1830s, abolitionists picked up on the idea that there were cases in which it was right and proper to flout the rules of evidence in the name of a higher good. By the mid-1840s, venues as diverse as lecture tours, newspaper columns, books, and U.S. courtrooms were open to nonkin staff.

Many of the accounts that emanated in these settings included familial passages such as the one from *Linda; or, Incidents in the Life of a Slave Girl* (1861) in which a former house slave recalls her first mistress as "almost like a mother" to young female property. Elizabeth Fox-Genovese has claimed that ex-slave narrators deployed language of this sort to "hold . . . white folks accountable to their professed ideals." This is careful wording, but it is misleading since whites expressed disparate ideals and thus disparate significations for gestures toward familiality. Then, too, even if strategic concerns put phrases such as "almost like a mother" into antislavery print, the collaborative provenance of sponsored witnessing makes it hard to be certain who was deploying what— or whom. Chapter 4 explores "testimony . . . from the kitchen" to gauge the extent to which ex-slaves' narratives challenged sentimental conceptualizations of servitude.[96]

4 Kitchen Testimony
and Servants' Tales

A talkative servant is never considered a desirable inmate in any family.

—*Plain Talk and Friendly Advice to Domestics* (1855)

The man quoted at the end of chapter 3 objecting to "testimony . . . from the kitchen" knew that his own name would come up in the divorce suit that thrust servant-witnesses into print in 1850 and 1851. Recognizing in a later situation that his interests had been protected, he reacted differently, calling his daughter's former nursemaid "as much one of my family as I am" although she had published an account of her experiences in service that disclosed information about his own home.[1] Perhaps N. P. Willis was grateful that Harriet Jacobs used pseudonyms in *Linda; or, Incidents in the Life of a Slave Girl* and said nothing about what she had seen and heard when she was his coresidential employee; perhaps, too, he was gratified that she represented his first and second wives (i.e., her two mistresses in the North) as caring and kind. If, however, such things motivated Willis to award Jacobs the supreme sentimental accolade, he must have deemed the chapters in *Linda* that touched on his own life congruent with the rule he set forth during the aforementioned divorce suit. This was a rule advanced in many nineteenth-century servants' manuals. "If, by chance, you have witnessed family scenes of an unpleasant nature," taught the book quoted in this chapter's epigraph, "as a member of the family, honor should forever seal your lips."[2]

   Willis's tribute to Jacobs may seem predictable in light of the energy that sentimental advisors had put into promoting the standard of family-likeness. Yet when pondered alongside his alarm about kitchen testimony, "as much one of my family as I am" measures the success with which *Linda* negotiated several tricky traverses. These traverses ranged from homemakers' hopes concerning nonkin coresidents who served to antebellum attendants' increasing access to print, and from a growing appetite for inside information about the home lives of the rich and famous to the emergence of respectable sponsors. The passage of ex-slaves' narratives through these straits merits praise. At the same time, their intervention in the fight against slavery had a less positive aspect insofar as, structured by forces over which former and fugitive slaves had no control, many narratives affirmed family-likeness as the criterion to apply to nonkin servitude. This tactical "give a little" is highlighted by Willis's expression of confidence in Jacobs, a method of articulation that echoes her own claim that a former mistress had acted "almost like a mother" when she was young.

   These findings contextualize Jacobs's worry, while she worked on the manuscript of what would become a powerful report of near-obsessive harassment, that her employer would disapprove of her reportage. If Willis knew what she was doing, she fretted, he "would tell me that . . . he was sorry for me to undertake" the role of kitchen witness "while I was in his family."[3] Jacobs may not have known that the last person to "go public" with news of Willis's "private" life had been a fair-weather friend.[4] But if—like many another servant in human history—she kept a watchful eye on her master's prospects, she would have known how heavily Willis's wealth and fame rested on willingness to market scenes of his own domesticity. The best probe of his "sentimental commerce" with adoring readers is found in Thomas N. Baker's *Sentiment and Celebrity: Nathaniel Parker Willis and the Trials of Literary Fame* (1999), the study that also provides the most complete account of the Forrest trial that got some so exercised about the wisdom of letting "free" servants testify in court. Baker's research (which was invaluable to my own investigation) will be examined presently. The point to make here is that when Jacobs worried about Willis's objections to her life-writing, she knew that his "sorry" could mean summary dismissal. Viewed from this perspective, her decision to write in secret, late at night, shows how little room she saw in midcentury visions of good and faithful service for laborers' speech, even as it reveals determination to oppose unjust silencing. Her editor was determined too, for Lydia Maria Child, a radical abolitionist of many years' standing, wanted the world to know how it felt to live as a slave. Several scholars have pondered these women's collaboration.[5] Yet none asked whether Child's determination to win a hearing for experiential testimony about bondage could have led her to drown out Jacobs's opinion of sentimental precepts concerning "free" attendance. Nor have any wondered about the pressure that reports such as *Linda* could have brought to bear on received notions of servants' rights. Yet indeed, no contribution to the literature of U.S. service has been as disruptive.

Concern about tale-bearing servants did not start with the Forrest trial, for, looking only at antebellum fiction, the topic had been broached in *Clarence* and *Live and Let Live* and negotiated, between the two, in a bogus ex-slave's narrative titled *The Slave; or, Memoirs of Archy Moore* (1835). In 1837, Catharine Beecher joined the discussion. "A nursery maid may see," she explained, "that a father misgoverns his children and ill-treats his wife. But her station makes it inexpedient for her to turn reprover. It is a case where reproof would do no good, but only evil." Since this argument appeared in a text that tried to dissuade ladies from supporting abolition, it was not long before an antislavery activist made a counterclaim. "I cannot agree with thee in the sentiment, that the station of a nursery maid makes it inexpedient for her to turn reprover of the master who employs her," Angelina Grimké told Beecher in 1838. "This is the doctrine of *modern aristocracy,* not of primitive christianity," she explained, because "so far from her station forbidding all interference to modify the character and conduct of her employer," that "station peculiarly qualifies her for the difficult and delicate task, because nursery maids often know secrets of oppression, which no other persons are fully acquainted with." As this was the abolitionist justification for sponsoring ex-slaves' narratives, Grimké made sure to clarify that she included chattel attendants in this claim. "I have myself," she attested, "been reproved by a *slave,* and I thanked her, and still thank her for it." Karen Sánchez-Eppler is right to point out that of Grimké's expression thanks to an unnamed slave reinforced the rule that privileged people were the proper permitters of underlings' speech.[6] To the extent, however, that questions about permission arose in households attended by the waged and bound, Grimké's control of a conversation with a servant would have sounded good to homemakers in the North.

Students of the ex-slave narrative have not approached this body of reportage as "testimony . . . from the kitchen" for several reasons. First and foremost, ex-slave narrators did not focus salaciously on masters' and mistresses' affairs, as the servants called as witnesses in the Forrest trial did perforce; equally significant, witnesses such as Robert Garvin,

John Kent, and Anna Flowers were not asked to expound on the morality of their servitude. Most important, none of the New York servants were presented as members of an oppressed group. These points of divergence are not trivial. Yet when the object of scrutiny is the literature of U.S. service during the period in which "free" labor was still new, it is most crucial that ex-slaves' narratives were part of the world in which Americans pondered objections to lawyers' use of servant-witnesses and, in the face of such protests, chose whether or not to read transcripts of the Forrest trial. Noteworthy in this respect is the pride a North Carolina newspaper expressed in a form of editorial censorship. "We are pleased to notice," preened the Wilmington *Daily Journal,* "that no Southern paper short of New Orleans has republished the disgusting evidence in this most disgusting case."[7] Even more illuminating, though, of antebellum readers' perception that ex-slaves' narratives comprised a form of kitchen testimony is a midcentury craze for speeches by attendant-characters who shared opinions about their working lives. One of the few book-length examples of the minigenre I call "servants' tales" is actually a hybrid, Harriet E. Wilson's fictionalized autobiography, *Our Nig; or, Sketches from the Life of a Free Black, in a Two-Story White House, North* (1859). There are, however, passages in several midcentury books and stories, including *Walden* (1854), that play with the contours of a form of storytelling which suggests that some saw ex-slaves' narratives as a subset of "backstairs gossip" justified by appeals to a higher morality.

I will discuss examples of kitchen testimony and its ventriloquistic double in due time. However, two clarifications are necessary first, one having to do with the modifier "nonkin" in relation to service and the other having to do with my decision to distinguish between ex-slaves' narra*tives* and ex-slave narra*tors.* Regarding the first point, there is no doubt that some house slaves were the sons, daughters, and siblings of those they attended. At the same time many weren't, and of the ex-slave narrators who were related to their masters and mistresses (e.g., Frederick Douglass), few probed that fact while writing under the auspices of never-enslaved sponsors. Taking the touchiness of this topic as reason to distinguish between the opinion of an ex-slave narra*tor* and the arguments advanced in the narra*tive* that bore his or her name, I credit authors where I am certain and otherwise attribute agency to texts. It is no minor emendation to say "Jacobs intended" but "*Linda* argues." On the contrary, this approach acknowledges that when waged, "bound," or chattel servants tried to tell what they knew, in the middle of the nineteenth century, few gained untrammeled access to print.

Thus, it is well to be wary of attributing thoughts (or silences) to Jacobs that may reflect Child's views.

The ramifications of this position will become clear later in this chapter when I discuss specific examples of kitchen testimony and servants' tales. Yet my focus on literature is not intended to bracket the many nonprint variables that changed, and were seen as changing, in the 1850s. Among the most salient of these were increasingly visible class stratification, especially in larger cities; more elaborate housekeeping and thus, in wealthier homes, larger nonkin staffs; and a shift from "help" (a form of labor that smacked of the village and farm) to more genteel "domestics." Germane to all these changes was the anxiety that accompanied privileged Americans' perception that foreign-born servants outnumbered native-born attendants and uncertainty as to whether Americans of African descent were to be regarded as fellow citizens. All of these sources of confusion should be borne in mind when thinking through midcentury complaints about Irish "Biddies." They have relevance too, however, for those who would unearth a sense of the variety of ways in which Northerners responded to the Fugitive Slave Law of 1850 and the literature inspired by this politically polarizing statute.

Amidst shift and uncertainty, the eruption of kitchen testimony was emblematic, not least because to many U.S. homemakers it would have seemed like an abrupt change. It was only a few years, after all, since Anna Cora Mowatt in her play *Fashion* (1845) had made a joke of the information servants accrued by coresidence. "I'se refuse to gib ebidence," a footman named Zeke announces in that hit farce, "dat's de device ob de skilfullest counsels ob de day! Can't answer, Boss—neber git a word out ob dis child—Yah! Yah!" A decade earlier, William Gilmore Simms had had even more fun in *Guy Rivers* (1834) with a lawyer so addled as to try to use his chattel manservant as an alibi. "Hob—Hob—Hob—I say—where the devil are you?" the foolish advocate shouts.

> "Hob—say, you rascal, was I within five miles of the Catcheta pass to-day?"
> "No, mosser."
> "Was I yesterday?"
> The negro put his finger to his forehead. . . .
> "Speak, you rascal, speak out; you know well enough, without reflecting." The slave cautiously responded—
> "If mosser want to be dere, mosser dere—no 'casion for ax Hob."
> "You black rascal, you know well enough I was not there—that I was not within five miles of the spot, either to-day, yesterday, or for ten days back!"

"Berry true, mosser—if you no dere, you no dere. Hob nebber say one ting when mosser say 'noder."

The unfortunate counsellor, desperate with the deference of his body servant, now absolutely perspired with rage.[8]

These passages may not raise laughs today. Yet they imply how controlled servants' speech had felt while sentimental advice was in the ascendant and how unsettling kitchen testimony could seem to privileged homemakers when this form of reportage was new. More evidence of the shift appears in a *Harper's* cartoon of 1857 in which a kitchen witness is given a hearing in a court of law. When the judge credits the woman's lying tale, her employer is left looking not fatherlike but instead like a silly weakling who can only scuttle home, tail between his legs.

Another way to measure the depth of the dis-ease caused by kitchen witnesses is to notice how small a role race- or ethnicity-based imputations played in denunciations of this form of chronicling. Prevalent, then, in household manuals are condemnations of talkative servants who could be of any skin color or ethnicity. "Incredible mischief to the peace and reputation of excellent families has been done," taught *Plain Talk and Friendly Advice to Domestics* (1855), "by the indiscretion of servants; who, for the poor pleasure of appearing to know all the affairs of the family, have undertaken to give a full version, supplying all blanks with a ready invention, when they were wholly ignorant of all the attending circumstances, and reasons for matters which to them were mysterious and unaccountable."[9]

N. P. Willis put the matter more forcibly during the Forrest trial. "[T]here is not a . . . gentleman's house, waited on by servants," he avowed, "where the hospitality may not be sworn to as debauchery."[10] Though Willis was (rightly) worried about his own reputation, someone else saw things the same way. "There is neither safety nor peace to expect in society hereafter," railed "An American," again in the *Herald*, "if the low-bred, morbid and indecent thoughts and inferences of servants . . . are to be applied to the actions of those whom they serve, and their most innocent acts distorted into crimes, and published to the world." The generality of these accusations contrasts with the novel of 1860, which found "it . . . truly wonderful that civilized, educated, Abolitionists, could be so daft as to believe the monstronsities fulminated by lying runaway negroes, against their masters." Yet even *The Black Gauntlet* downplayed the Africanist slant when it grouped the testimony of "running back negroes" with reports by "Irish and Dutch servants," as if to show that rank rather than bloodlines was the real issue.[11]

Mr. Simpkins's Experiment in Housekeeping.

Mr. Simpkins applies at an Intelligence Office for a sober, tidy, respectable servant.

The Keeper sends him one, with first-rate recommendations from her last place.

Mrs. Simpkins wonders why Bridget will always draw corks with her teeth.

The cork-drawing mystery is solved—not to Mrs. Simpkins's satisfaction.

Mr. Simpkins insists that Bridget shall leave the house at once.

Attempting to carry his order into execution, a slight misunderstanding ensues.

Harper's New Monthly Magazine *returned to a favorite theme in October 1857, though here the jab is directed at a householder rather than a mistress unable to control her staff. Courtesy, American Antiquarian Society.*

Dis-ease about coresidential nonkin was nothing new in the 1850s. "Servants should be trusted to a certain extent," *A Manual of Politeness* had warned in 1837, "but not too far." Nor was the specter of speaking servants, since English-language literature had long relied on servant-heroes such as Tom Jones, servant-narrators such as Nelly Dean, and servant-interlocutors such as any number of characters in

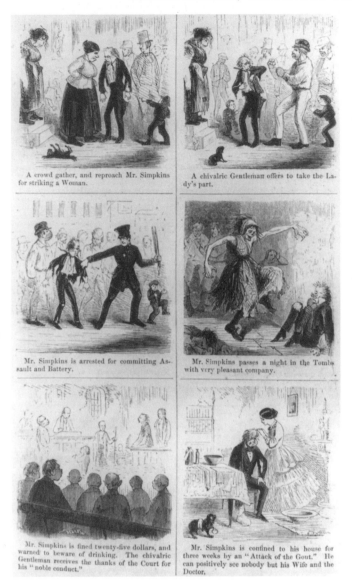

A crowd gather, and reproach Mr. Simpkins for striking a Woman.

A chivalric Gentleman offers to take the Lady's part.

Mr. Simpkins is arrested for committing Assault and Battery.

Mr. Simpkins passes a night in the Tombs with very pleasant company.

Mr. Simpkins is fined twenty-five dollars, and warned to beware of drinking. The chivalric Gentleman receives the thanks of the Court for his "noble conduct."

Mr. Simpkins is confined to his house for three weeks by an "Attack of the Gout." He can positively see nobody but his Wife and the Doctor.

Dickens's large and cherished output. Closer to home, *Live and Let Live* had exploited appetites for the sorts of scurrilous stories to which servants were made privy, so much so that, I suggest, this didactic novella deserves to be seen as a factor in the development of ex-slaves' narratives *and* the midcentury flurry of "servants' tales" that responded to them. Leaving that conjecture aside, though, to focus on the sorts of influences that authors of servants' tales are likely to have admitted to, the simultaneity of the Forrest trial and *Uncle Tom's Cabin* (1852) is a topic never probed. It repays scrutiny, however, because while Harriet Beecher Stowe's best-seller includes several worker-narrated discussions of piety, submission, and the desire for freedom, it does not give house slaves such as Eliza, Dinah, and Adolph a chance to say what they think of their workloads, self-images as attendants, or good and bad mastery. Servants' tales responded to this gap, with most contributions emanating from proslavery writers eager to expose Stowe's blind spot. "'Free! I wonder what they call free?'" asked a white wage earner in Caroline Lee Hentz's *The Planter's Northern Bride* (1854), "feeling of the knots and callouses of her toil-worn hands. 'I know I ain't free, or I wouldn't work, like a pack-horse, from one year's eend to another. I'm obliged to work to live, and to make others live, and God knows I'm willing; but . . . Albert says the niggers sing and dance as much as they please, when their work is done up. I wonder how I would look singing and dancing!'" Use of the Yankee-ism "eend" recalls the story of Lucilla, the white wage earner pitied near the end of *Recollections of a Southern Matron*. Echoing Gilman, Hentz insisted on the contrastive tactic that Stowe had abjured. "I'm ten times more of a slave, this minute," a waged servant-character in *The Planter's Northern Bride* tells a contented chattel valet, "than you are, and have been all my life."[12]

Like the sentimental advice surveyed in previous chapters, servants' tales reproached homemakers who failed to embrace nonkin menials familially. "Oh, dear, dear! Wonder if my mistress knows I'm made of flesh and blood?" Fanny Fern had a waged attendant ask in "Soliloquy of a Housemaid" (1852). "I've been up stairs five times, in fifteen minutes, to hand her things about four feet from her rocking-chair!" N. P. Willis's estranged sister may have noticed a dearth of servant-characters and just explored it with a professional writer's eye for something fresh; alternately, here as elsewhere, she may have chosen to express sympathy for working Americans who were poor. There is reason to wonder, though, since Fern was not always so positive about servitors and because the "Soliloquy" was published soon after a maid and two footmen had embarrassed brother "Nat" on the witness stand.[13] Another point of interest about the "Soliloquy" is its use of standard English, since proslavery servants' tales heaped up dialect. Waged attendance "diddent suit my turn of mind," one anti-*Tom*'s fictive Jonathan recalled, "any how you could fix. They axed me tew dew ever so many nasty things, which turned my free-born stomach. I went to service; so I thought I would tucker it eout. But I coulddent dew it. . . .

The hull thing went right straight agin my notions of equal rights and no monopoly. The hull consarn was a monopoly from A to izzard. The best things went up stairs, and skersely the least mossel came down except the bones. They done nothing, and we did everything, from rocking the cradle to blacking boots." This peroration concludes with a defiant Yankee twang: "*Master* indeed! *Servant*, indeed! I jist walked off, and I've never bin in sarvice since." Though an antebellum reader did not have to be strongly proslavery to find this kind of thing amusing, the effect of this passage can only have been calculated in relation to characters shown to be devotedly family-like. "Wa' you lib, Cato want to lib," a chattel character claimed in a novel of 1853, "an' wa' you dead, Cato want to dead."[14]

Protestations of this kind were designed to rebut the desire for freedom voiced by several enslaved characters in *Uncle Tom's Cabin* but expressed even earlier by ex-slave narrators who challenged the notion that slavery was in any sense family-like. Some ex-slave narrators exposed the sadism wreaked upon the defenseless, while others suggested an emotional crippling that made a mockery of affective claims. Representing the first faction is a scene of abuse found in the *Narrative of the Sufferings of Lewis Clarke* (1845). As Marion Wilson Starling has noted, the depiction of Clarke's mistress, "the incomparable shrew, Mrs. Banton, is the high point" of this account "from a literary standpoint." This is true. Yet Mrs. Banton's excesses must have been at least as intriguing to those who wondered if slaveholders really did commit themselves to family-like care of human property. Not in the Banton household, Clarke reported, for there

> A very trivial offense was sufficient to call forth a great burst of indignation from this woman of ungoverned passions. In my simplicity I put my lips to the same vessel, and drank out of it, from which her children were accustomed to drink. She expressed her utter abhorrence of such an act by throwing my head violently back, and dashing into my face two dippers of water. The shower of water was followed by a heavier shower of kicks; but the words, bitter and cutting, that followed, were like a storm of hail upon my young heart: "She would teach me better manners than that; she would let me know I was to be brought up to her hand; she would have *one* slave that knew his place; if I wanted water, go to the spring, and not drink there in the house." This was new times for me; for some days I was completely benumbed with sorrow.[15]

Adding to Clarke's trials was the fact that he was allowed to see his mother, who lived thirty miles away, just three times in ten years. None can say whether the impossibility of confiding in her was harder to bear than the kinlessness recalled in *Narrative of the Life of Frederick Douglass, an American Slave* (1845). "The ties that ordinarily bind children to their homes," this testimony reported of the Maryland estate on which "Fred" spent most of his childhood, "were all suspended in my case. I found no severe trial in my departure" though he left siblings and a pleasant-enough mistress behind. "My home was charmless," this passage concludes, "it was not home to me; on parting from it, I could not feel that I was leaving any thing which I could have enjoyed by staying." Four years later, William Wells Brown depicted the situation more wryly. "Do you not call me a good master?" he recalled one of his owners inquiring, to which the forthright slave replied. "If you were you would not sell me."[16]

No one knows how many antebellum Americans investigated ex-slaves' reportage in books or lectures. Well attested, however, is widespread knowledge that former and fugitive bondspeople were testifying to terrible suffering caused by owners' callousness and greed. Antislavery activists were committed to this effort. Yet few if any had reason to want to break down traditional strictures on nonchattel servants' revelatory words. Certainly Grimké spoke of servants in the abstract when responding to Beecher. Yet if Eric Gardner is right about the way in which abolitionists reacted to *Our Nig*, then members of this group strove to limit the parameters of kitchen testimony so that the focus would be on chattel attendants rather than on those who were "bound" or "free."[17]

They had their work cut out, even a full decade after the scandalous Forrest trial. In *Sentiment and Celebrity*, Thomas Baker provides an excellent account of the ruckus that grabbed headlines when Edwin Forrest, America's leading Shakespearean actor, tried to divorce his British wife, Catherine, and she countersued. As might be expected under these circumstances, there was widespread interest in the testimony offered by a servant-witness who suggested that relations between Mrs. Forrest and N. P. Willis were adulterous. Trying to untangle fact from reportage, Baker emphasizes the multiple interpretations that could be put on a manservant's testimony that he saw Willis, in dishabille, bid "goodnight dear" to Forrest when she was an overnight guest.[18] More significant, though, to Harriet Jacobs—a worker employed in a position much closer than John Kent's to the Willises' "private" life—must have been how affronted Willis felt by testimony that, if legally inconclusive, was quite embarrassing. She probably did not know that he liked a bit of doggerel that blasted servants' venal ways.

> Born in the garret, in the kitchen bred,
> Promoted thence to deck her mistress' head;
> Next—for some gracious service unexprest,
> And from its wages only to be guess'd—
> Raised from the toilet to the table, where
> Her wondering betters wait behind her chair:
> With eye unmoved, and forehead unabash'd,
> She dines from off the plate she lately washed.[19]

Regardless, however, of whether Jacobs had heard of this versifying, she would have known without needing to be told that few if any servants of African descent achieved such "promotion" due to race-based restrictions about who dined where in genteel U.S. homes. Realizing the same thing, Willis is unlikely to have worried about Jacobs imitating the servant in the poem. More positively, the fact that he classified her as a member of his family *after* she had published a book-length narrative bespeaks appreciation heightened by awareness of the information she could have shared—and chose not to.

One of the servant-witnesses who testified during the Forrest divorce trial, the Scottish housekeeper Christiana Underwood, tried to be as circumspect. It was much more fun for trial watchers, though, that an Irish immigrant named Robert Garvin did his best to foster prurient suspicions (possibly having been paid to do precisely that). A one-time Forrest employee who does not seem to have worried about future employment while he got laughs in the witness-box, Garvin interspersed comic ripostes with scandalous reports of having seen Catherine Forrest and Willis "laying on each other" while he washed windows on the piazza.[20] Though Garvin testified that his mistress told him to go away and clean the windows later, he added that he entered the room after the couple had departed and "noticed some hairpins and an elastic garter in the room; they were not there when I dusted up the drawing room in the morning." Trial watchers knew that servants were supposed to peer into corners and pick up items that had gone astray.[21] Yet the garrulous Garvin admitted that he had tried to peep on another occasion and had given up because he could not see into the drawing room. He was luckier, he said, another afternoon when he entered a room in order to light the gas and found his mistress on a Captain Calcraft's knee, "with one arm leaning on his shoulder, and the other across his breast rather."[22] Such stories required deliberation. Were they true? Did they reveal malice? Had Garvin hoped to catch his mistress in flagrante delicto? But they were so obviously juicy that Catherine

Forrest's lawyer tried to put the lid on tattle in his opening address. "You are not here for the purpose," he told jurors, "of circulating family secrets and family discords." Very noble—yet all knew that one-time coresidents in the Forrest and Willis homes were going to do exactly that, with journalists poised to peddle their kitchen testimony to all who cared to buy.[23] Thoughtful observers recognized, too, that servants risked more than others who revealed aspects of the Forrests' "private" life. Thus, when Dr. John Rich defended his late-night visits to Catherine Forrest's bedroom, his words were not categorized as "dentist's testimony," much less defamed and opposed. The specific hurdle for servant-witnesses was that information they imparted was open to the charge of breaching domestic sanctities.

This hurdle loomed high for Anna Flowers, a witness who embodied the few servant-related fears that Garvin's testimony missed. A former chambermaid in the Forrest home, Flowers claimed to have information that only an extortionist could profit by. As Flowers told it, she and her mistress got along agreeably until Mrs. Forrest asked the teenager to share her bed when a male guest spent the night, only to leave Flowers behind to join Captain Howard in another room. Flowers's relationship with her mistress did not suffer from this experience, she said, though things changed when the philandering wife left New York, Howard showed up at the door and demanded entrance, and then raped the chambermaid. This story is coherent, since rape could deter a person with information suited to blackmail. What is more, Howard admitted that he had had intercourse with the Forrests' maid. There is no evidence, however, apart from Flowers's testimony, that the intercourse was forced.[24]

Whatever happened between Flowers and Howard was seamy. Yet the only reason this encounter, or Garvin's discoveries, gained wide attention is that a celebrity couple went to court for reasons of their own. This aspect of the case makes it possible that hunger to be heard, rather than venal greed, explains Flowers's decision to come all the way from Louisiana to testify. Unfortunately for her, the trip was injudicious if she had hoped to serve nonkin again, since damaging testimony gave Catherine Forrest's lawyers no option but character assassination. The assault proved easy to mount. First dredging up a former employer (who reviled Flowers), counsel then examined an ex-colleague with whom she was said to have had sexual relations (he appeared in court filthy, ragged, and probably drunk) and made sure jurors heard about her stint in a home for juvenile delinquents. This attack strategy says a great deal about nineteenth-century fears of live-in workers but shows, as well, that Beecher was right: it often *was* inexpedient for servants to speak out, even in a good cause. The most widely approved reason to do so was a moral obligation that few middle-class trial watchers were likely to attribute to a servant hired from a New York House of Refuge; more probable, many would have concluded, would have been hope of gain from Edwin Forrest or his legal team. Perhaps money did change hands, since Flowers's fare from Louisiana would have been costly. Yet for whatever reason she agreed to testify and however she may have been recompensed, no faction shielded her from ferocious efforts to discredit her report.

The testimony of early ex-slave narrators had been attacked, too. Yet once abolitionists learned to choose witnesses wisely and stand behind their selections, a clash between moral obligation and the dictates of privatized domesticity became inevitable. Which side to take, in this conflict, was a real conundrum for people accustomed to the idea that coresidence abrogated servants' right to speak of what they saw in nonkin homes, but also for any who considered "family" life the bastion of religious, ethical, and civic training. In this respect, kitchen testimony posed a huge challenge to sentimental visions of nonkin attendance, not least because the things that servants saw and heard could be highly marketable. It was not charity, then, but a profit motive that most likely impelled Eliza M. Potter to publish a servant's-eye view of fashionable affairs.

Though neglected by literary and cultural historians, *A Hairdresser's Experience in High Life* (1859) won a large local audience with an exposé-style report of disreputable carryings-on among the elite. With no personal axe to grind, Potter testified more like Robert Garvin than John Kent; however, she does not appear to have been sponsored to speak. Good evidence that self-initiated reportage left her feeling vulnerable is found in the defenses she offers of her decision to testify. The first was affirmations that her trade is special. "[N]owhere," *A Hairdresser*'s introduction states, "do hearts betray themselves more unguardedly than in the private boudoir, where the hairdresser's mission makes her a daily attendant. Why, then, should not the hair-dresser write, as well as the physician and clergyman?" The second was a disclaimer. "I hope," Potter prays, that "the few incidents mentioned by me in these pages will *injure no one*. I merely write them out for the amusement of those who may wish to indulge themselves in a little gossip which has no evil intention in the world." The upshot of both remarks is presentation of this servant-writer as a moral activist, a placement borne out by stories that present her foiling assignations, upbraiding philanders and reproving matrons who long to pass on the latest "dirt." When, for example, a client asks Potter if she can keep a secret, the hairdresser allows herself a little sarcasm at the lady's expense. "I told her most assuredly that I could," she testifies, "but I could keep it better if it was not told me." This was a recurring refrain, for Potter insisted that the type of work she did put her in a position that was none of her asking. "I have often wished," she sighs at one point, that "I could absent myself from conversations that I knew ought to be confidential, and that I had no business to hear; but I could not tell ladies to shut their mouths." Indeed, she adds, on deciding "to settle down and be quiet—to see and not to see, to hear and not to hear"—she found "it was impossible to do this and continue my occupation as a hair-dresser." In line with this posture, Potter's use of what one commentator called "a code of genteel disclosure" (in which discreet dashes occluded the identities of rouged ladies and genteel thieves) suggests desire to avoid the epithet "tale-bearer."[25]

Avoidance of this charge was a difficult proposition for a writer situated like Potter since she attended nonkin in the manner of a lady's maid, sometimes worked as a maid and governess, and intermittently coresided with employers. Equally germane for antebellum readers, she pictured herself as of mixed-race descent. Not that readers are likely to have cared about racial issues while Potter's news was fresh; on the contrary, her self-published book sold like hotcakes for a while. Soon, though, Potter disappears from the historical record. She may have died. But it is just as likely that she learned, as Anna Flowers had before her, that talkative servants had better have somewhere to go when they stepped down from the witness stand.

Safer by far was composition of a "free" servant's tale such as *The Greatest Blessing in Life* (1850) or a chattel servant's tale such as *Autobiography of a Female Slave* (1857); riskier but more interesting were anomalous works of kitchen testimony such as *Walden* and *Our Nig*. If this list did nothing else, it would imply that trouble with attendants spurred literary innovation at midcentury. This is a significant finding insofar as creative forms of storytelling, which focused attention on servant-authorship and included eccentric forays into life-writing, preceded and may have shaped the collaborative composition of *Linda* and, later, the disastrous reception of *Behind the Scenes; or, Thirty Years a Slave, and Four Years in the White House* (1868).

One of the sprightlier responses to ex-slaves' narratives was that found in the novel *The Greatest Blessing in Life*. The title of this fictive servant's tale was confrontational since it mounted a challenge to those keening that nonkin attendants comprised "the greatest plague in life."

Yet its moral was the familiar claim that faithful servants conferred a blessing on the homes in which they labored; pacifying too, to many readers, would have been *The Greatest Blessing*'s nonchalance about "wage slavery." Both findings should be drawn into rumination about why whoever wrote this novel signed him/herself a "Servant of Servants." Perhaps, though, a desire for anonymity reflects calculation of the shock value to the proposition that a white and native-born waged housemaid could find common cause with slaves.

By way of overview, since this novel is not well known, *The Greatest Blessing* recounts the adventures of a "free" white Northern servitor. Willing and able to attend efficiently, Catherine earns her wages in every post. Yet as a grown woman who is not working to support dependent kin, Catherine is an independent laborer who feels compassion toward servants who are enslaved. Taking and making opportunities to speak out against slavery, teach chattel to read, and assist the efforts of the Underground Railroad, Catherine somehow finds the time to locate and serve a good mistress who is pleasant and considerate (though sisterly rather than motherlike). After all this, her energy undiminished, Catherine leaves nonkin service to marry an antislavery activist. As this plot summary shows, *The Greatest Blessing* was audacious—perhaps too much so, since it does not seem to have attracted much attention. Thus, this novel's interest for the historian lies less in its cultural impact than in the challenges it mounted toward received notions of servants' "place" in nonkin homes. Most intriguing, in light of the growing popularity of ex-slaves' narratives, is the scene in which Catherine overhears a wage-paying mistress bewailing the disappearance of old-fashioned disciplinary methods. "[H]ow I wish," this woman sighs, "the whipping post could be revived in New England, and I had power to bring my servants up to it."[26] Scenes of servants eavesdropping were not new; here, though, since the sigher is aware of Catherine's proximity, *The Greatest Blessing* suggests the arrogance of expecting servants to pretend not to hear words uttered in their presence. Simultaneously, this scene forces *The Greatest Blessing*'s heroine to decide whether to speak her mind, and speak she does, only to be angrily scolded for doing so. With angry female scolding being a strong indicator in nineteenth-century U.S. fiction that the scolder is out of line, the clear implication is rebuke of wage payers who long for harsher methods of servant control.

No student of the literature of U.S. service should overlook *The Greatest Blessing in Life*. Yet its offbeat contributions have been drowned out by the massive popularity of *Uncle Tom's Cabin* and scholarship that analyzes Stowe's novel within a narrow framework. Starting with the popularity, it is possible that this international best-seller pleased as many as it did because it offered a range of service-labor theories familiar from earlier works. Thus, where Tom's steadfast faith recalled *The African Servant* and Phillis in *Trial and Self-Discipline*, river-crossing Eliza shares much characterological ground with Rosa in *The Linwoods*. In addition, though one could compare the Harris family's departure for Liberia to Magawisca's decision to live out her life with the Pequots, no servant-character in *Uncle Tom's Cabin* is given the training so central to Lucy Lee's experience as a maid. Equally significant, a few servant-characters in *Uncle Tom's Cabin* (most raucously Sam and Andy) are treated with the patronizing superiority seen in the *Recollections of a Southern Matron*, while another, the foppish Adolph, recalls the parasites that Washington Irving pictured in "John Bull." My argument is not that Stowe lacked originality, since the Christlike death of Tom was unprecedented in the literature of U.S. service. It is, instead, that literary historians who fail to reckon with lineages and analogues are unlikely to notice the limits she imposed on her depictions of attendants. These limits can be defended: slavery was a heinous wrong. Yet from the vantage of the early 1850s, *Uncle Tom's Cabin* was vastly partisan insofar as it had much to say about family-like slavery but nothing concerning attendance that is "free."

Groundbreaking scholarship on this sentimental blockbuster has contrasted the "heart-services" of the Quaker kitchen to the horrors of bondage. Thus, in *Sensational Designs: The Cultural Work of American Fiction, 1790–1860* (1985), Jane Tompkins argued that "by resting her case, absolutely, on the saving power of Christian love and on the sanctity of motherhood and the family, Stowe relocates the center of power in American life, placing it not in the government, nor in the courts of law, nor in the factories, nor in the marketplace, but in the kitchen." Though Lora Romero critiqued this approach on the grounds that it relies on a simplistic opposition between power and resistance, she shared Tompkins's willingness to let Stowe bracket all the kitchens in which kin service was supplemented or supplanted by the labor of wage earners. The same blind spot characterizes Gillian Brown's analysis of the Quaker household. "Good motherhood," Brown asserted in *Domestic Individualism: Imagining Self in Nineteenth-Century America* (1990), "manifest[s] the proper relation between caretakers and their charges, whether households, children, or slaves."[27] This statement of the case is correct but slanted, since nonslave attendants were also important to Stowe's intended audience. Indeed, insofar as the immobilization of chattel staff was a leading reason employers found "free" service annoying, studies of *Uncle Tom's Cabin* remain incomplete until they grapple with the extent to which Stowe's first novel distracts attention from the downside of waged attendance. Equally important, studies of this novel will be of little use to historians of U.S. labor until it is recognized that Stowe tried to pluck the mote out of her neighbor's eye while ignoring the beam in her own.

Alert to such mote-plucking, detractors pounced. "I have never seen half the happiness North," the novel *Antifanaticism* (1853) had a traveler avow, "among the servants, that I saw South." As this was hardly a new claim, one could expect Stowe to have erected some defense against it. The fact that she didn't suggests an inability that opponents harped on mercilessly. "I tell you now," a white Northern servant-character decided in a short story of 1858 that took her to a slaveholding state, "I had rather be a slave here myself, and know when I get old I shall be taken care of, than to go back to the North, work as long as any one will employ me, and when I am too old to work either starve in some miserable cellar or garret, or else end my days in the poor house."[28] Much later, Stowe acknowledged the comparability of "free" and chattel attendance. "The condition of domestic service," she told readers of *The Atlantic Monthly* in 1864, "still retains about it something of the influences from feudal times, and from the near presence of slavery in neighboring States," so much so that, she added, that "the essential *animus* of the slave system still exists, and pervades the community, North as well as South," with "a latent spirit of something like contempt" for live-in staff.[29] This statement of the case was alert. But it came years too late to forestall the perception that *Uncle Tom's Cabin* had implied that only chattel service was open to critique.

A more bizarre contribution to the literature of nineteenth-century U.S. service did something similar while promoting the sort of misogyny in which the "servant problem" fell beneath the notice of male householders. *Walden* was and is anomalous as an advice guide inasmuch as its brand of domesticity was unlike that proposed by any other nineteenth-century manual. Yet it was at least as peculiar as kitchen testimony insofar as Thoreau revealed nothing about nonkin lives. The most significant aspect of this idiosyncratic composition, for our purposes, was Thoreau's self-siting: "Having been my own butcher and scullion and cook," he jokes at one point, "as well as the gentleman for whom the dishes were served up, I can speak from an unusually complete experience." Raillery of this sort let Thoreau insist on his own privileged status despite a low income, in the manner of Abby Alcott posturing as a servant to those who knew she was not; erudite allusions did much the same. At the same time, raillery on this topic brought *Walden* into conflict with those certain that service labor could and ought to be family-like. Today, scholars know that pondside solitude was eased by weekly visits home to enjoy Mom's cooking and superior laundry facilities. Yet as long as Thoreau withheld that information, most readers would have pondered *Walden*'s quips and claims, knowing its author as a protégé of the writer famed for advocating self-reliance. Thoreau encouraged this framing with passages that name the woodland breeze a "priceless domestic" that reliably "swept the floor and dusted the furniture and kept the things in order" and that find "Fire" a "cheerful housekeeper" for a cabin home. The result may have been a style of homemaking suited to supporting the argument that most men lived lives of quiet desperation. But it was no answer to the troubles with attendants that homemakers found so deeply vexing (even if Thoreau's description of a household modeled on a medieval Great Hall had some one-time Brook Farmers sighing for what had been). Putting the matter in its starkest terms, nothing about *Walden* rebuts the Philadelphia homemaker who thought waged servants' mobility annoying enough to justify the frustrated claim that "Slavery is not without its merits."[30]

Quite different was Mattie Griffith's *Autobiography of a Female Slave*, a book-length servant's tale that delighted radical abolitionist Lydia Maria Child. A fascinating but still neglected text, *Autobiography* measures the perceived importance of sentimental precepts by confronting them head-on. Central to this confrontational stance is denunciation of Christian ministers who judge human bondage "just, right, and almost available unto salvation. I cannot think," Griffith's chattel heroine asserts, that people of this opinion understand slavery "in all its direful wrongs. They look upon the institution, doubtless, as one of domestic servitude, where a strong attachment exists between the slave and his owner; but, alas! all that is generally fabulous, worse than fictitious. I can fearlessly assert that I never knew a single case, where this sort of feeling was cherished." If asked why slaves seemed happy, Griffith had an answer. "As I was passing through the room," the heroine of *Autobiography* recalls, "I could catch fragments of conversation anything but pleasing to the ear of a slave; but I had to listen in meekness, letting not even a working muscle betray my dissent." Later, when asked her opinion of an antislavery speech, Ann understands the wisdom of staying mute. "Too well I knew my position to make an answer; so there I stood, silent and submissive." These passages throw light on Griffith's use of scenes of eavesdropping (one of which introduces her heroine to the admirable qualities of Frederick Douglass). Ultimately, though, the most important result of eavesdropping is that it enables Ann's mistress to learn of her servant's fidelity.[31] This reversal—a mistress eavesdropping on a servant—put a spoke in the wheel of etiquette experts who labeled servants "domestic spies, who continually embarrass the intercourse of the members of a family, or possess themselves of private information that renders their presence hateful, and their absence dangerous."[32] So did the scene in *Linda* in which a jealous mistress tries to trick a sleepy slave girl into confessing a wrong.

Some may think that the episodes mentioned in earlier chapters, in which novelists portray servants conversing, constitute examples of mistresses eavesdropping on employees. Comparison reveals a far more surveillance-minded attitude, however, in the advice guide of 1855 that depicts attendants advising each other how to gain pay raises and sneak food out of an employer's pantry. Quite obviously, the brief dialogues in *Plain Talk and Friendly Advice to Domestics* were not written to edify workers; instead, they were directed toward the "American Housekeepers, whose trials and difficulties have enlisted the author's sympathy." It was mistresses, then, rather than cooks and maids who were expected to get something out of skits such as "The Difference between Mary and Jane" and "Elizabeth Lawney's Club—Her Evil Counsels." The former is a chat between servant girls, the handier of whom was "bound out" as a young girl to "as good a mistress as ever lived. She was as kind to me," the grateful servant-character reports, "as any mother to her child, but very strict." The latter skit is spicier because it describes how one bad Irish servant may corrupt a roomful. All ends well, however, since evil counsels are foiled by a good servant whom the would-be corrupter mocks as a "half-breed Irish girl." Dilution of the blood is no trivial matter in this instance, because Sarah defends fidelity to employers who show kinlike affect. "Isn't my mistress kind and good as a mother to me?" she inquires, with a slight but noticeable brogue. "You must love your mistress—oblige her," she continues, "for that you like to see her happy, and a smile on her winsome face, and her bright eyes thanking ye all the time. Live with her till she feels and you feel that you belong to her," this sermonette concludes. Though this counsel sounds like parts of Beecher's *Letters to Persons*, *Plain Talk* insisted with *Live and Let Live* that privileged women have duties to live-in staff. "As mistress," this guide teaches, "you stand in stead of parent to them, and are responsible for their good conduct, and the correction of their faults, to the extent that your rightful authority over them, as members of your family, entitles you to act." This precept still had adherents. But its charm had begun to fade. "It's all very well," a *Godey's* story shrugged in 1857, "that we are to turn parish school-teachers to every ignorant, awkward soul we stumble over at the intelligence office—but who believes it?"[33]

Though, as noted, many factors spurred skepticism about sentimental tenets, resistance to kitchen testimony makes it crucial to gauge the impact of abolitionist publications that made it plain that professions of family-likeness could rob workers of much that made life dear. Lydia Maria Child mounted this charge in *The Patriarchal Institution, As Described by Members of Its Own Family* (1860) by juxtaposing comments such as a passage from the *Charleston Courier* that asserted, "Slavery is with us a parental relation," so superior to waged relations that the "tender care and protection of the master elicit an affectionate attachment from the slave, which will be looked for in vain from the hired servant of a more Northern clime," to the testimony of whites who held other views. One of her sources was a South Carolina native who recalled the heartbreak of a childhood in which the slaveholder's "wife and . . . daughter sometimes find their homes a scene of the most mortifying, heart-rending preference of the degraded domestic. . . . Let these few hints suffice to give you some idea of what is daily passing behind that curtain, which has been so carefully drawn before the scenes of domestic life in slaveholding America."[34] Again, charges of this kind needed to be brought, since it was past time for slavery to be brought to an end. There was deliberate restriction, nonetheless, to the fight against slavery that made it difficult to address the problems posed by nonchattel forms of labor. A former "bound" girl named Harriet Wilson addressed this snarl in 1859.

Barbara A. White has explained Wilson's circumstances in ways that illuminate her decision to blend kitchen testimony with the "servant's tale." More recently, though, discussion has moved to the labor theory advanced in *Our Nig*, with Thomas B. Lovell saying that this book (along with *Linda*) calls for more familial relations within "free" labor and Gretchen Short replying that Wilson more broadly charged that "domesticity in the North needs to be reconceived as well, to account for the possibility of remunerative, recognized domestic labor."[35] I appreciate this discussion yet am disturbed by the ease with which both scholars bypass the chance to consider *Our Nig*'s arguments in terms of the history and literature of U.S. service. It is right, then, to think of Wilson as a labor theorist. Yet much energy will be misspent, I believe, if it is not recognized from the outset that her frame of reference was less domesticity in general or even indentured labor than, specifically, "bound" servitude. Insisting, under these circumstances, on *Our Nig*'s delineation of a vision of service relationships within the context of ideas advanced by earlier writers, I find Wilson's ideal as affective as Catharine Sedgwick's yet as unflinching as Maria W. Stewart's reminder of the fatuity of hoping that faithful attendance would pave the way to a brighter future for Americans of African descent.

Stewart's cautionary note is illuminating in the context of a book that, according to Robert Reid-Pharr, charged that "sentimentalism and interracialism are antithetical."[36] This is a valid assessment of the way in which the Bellmonts treat their "bound girl." I wonder, though, whether it accurately reflects Wilson's views, or those of her servant-heroine Frado, since novelist *and* character advocate affective relationships between the serving and the served. Indeed, Wilson affirms much of the advice found in *Home* and *Live and Let Live* when she finds Frado's employers failing to provide a family-like work environment, to offer family-like nurture and affective sustenance to a live-in servant, and, worst of all, to extend family-like concern to the "bound" girl who becomes ill through overwork. Wilson does show that several of the Bellmonts were harsh even toward kin. That, however, does not persuade her to abandon the sentimental standard, probably because she had nothing to put in its place. Almost certainly, the trauma of having been abandoned by her own mother had an impact here.[37] At the same time, the difficulties that a mixed-race heritage presented for a young, poor, female resident of a smallish New England town could have left Wilson with gnawing hunger for a place in which she felt she belonged. Too, there is every possibility that she knew, or had had occasion to hear about, "bound" children who were treated humanely by the nonkin with whom they coresided.[38] If so, then Wilson had little reason to contest affective precepts about "good" mistress-ship and "good" service except—and this is a huge "except"—that they could not be enforced. This, of course, had been Stewart's position in the lecture of 1832 that begged black parents to keep their children out of service work.

Enforcement is a topic of particular significance because, as *Our Nig* shows, servants may be brutally silenced, even from weeping; screamed at or threatened with grievous bodily harm if they dare to complain of ill-usage; and, most pertinently, heeded or not when they do speak out according to the tenderheartedness of those who listen. It is not that all served Americans are callous; after one ugly scene, one of the kinder Bellmonts "came to hear the kitchen version of the affair." Rather, Wilson demonstrates, it is that anything a service worker chooses to say about coresidential nonkin may be construed as speaking out of turn. Under these circumstances, it is no accident that *Our Nig* reveals Frado's feelings about her lot in a scene of overhearing by a member of the served family. "In the summer I was walking near the barn," the eavesdropper recalls, "and as I stood I heard sobs. 'Oh! oh!,' I heard, 'why was I made? why can't I die? Oh, what have I to live for? No one cares for me only to get my work. And I feel sick; who cares for that? Work as long as I can stand, and then fall down and lay there till I can get up. No mother, father, brother or sister to care for me, and then it is, You lazy nigger, lazy nigger—all because I am black! Oh, if I could die!'"[39] It can be no accident that the *Autobiography of a Female Slave*—a servant's tale that pretends to be kitchen testimony—has a served American overhear chattel to protect a ladylike slave from the imputation of fawning, while *Our Nig*—a work of kitchen testimony that adopts many of the characteristics of a servant's tale—uses this device to protect Frado from the charge of trying to elicit pity.

Some time ago, Elizabeth Breau made the provocative suggestion that *Our Nig* had much to say about gags and silencings because Wilson intended her novel as a harsh satire on "the white-abolitionist-assisted liberation of black speech." This charge gives students of the literature of U.S. service reason to ponder the degree of narrative autonomy that ex-slave narrators managed to preserve when forced to submit to editorial supervision. That question is of wide and enduring interest. Yet it has particular importance in the case of *Linda* because Child is known to have deleted material from Jacobs's manuscript. The story that remains relates a tale of resistance to ceaseless harassment that includes an illicit liaison; a long period of living in hiding, which put loved ones at risk; and more dangers after the imperiled "slave girl" escapes to the North. Each of these trials (and more) confirms Child's argument in *The Patriarchal Institution* that the notion of a "plantation family" was a pernicious myth. Standing up against that image, though, is the line in *Linda* that comes near the conclusion that Child had asked Jacobs to amend. It is impossible to be sure, now, how sincere was the tribute to "free" service that must have pleased many wage payers. "Love, duty, gratitude . . . bind me to her side," this paean asserts of the second Mrs. Willis. "It is a privilege to serve her." I am less sure than P. Gabrielle Foreman that this line expresses Jacobs's "barely checked anger." More certain, though, is adherence here to the sentimental posture that writers such as Sedgwick had marked out years before.[40] Child denied making substantive corrections to Jacobs's text. Yet the vital importance of the claim that ex-slaves' narratives were written by people who had been property casts doubt on never-enslaved abolitionists'

Alfred Jacob Miller's The Marchioness from Dickens *(ca. 1860) put a well-known fictional character, and one of served Americans' more pressing anxieties, on display in oil. Walters Art Gallery, Baltimore.*

denials of having altered their sources' reports in any way. Equally germane, Child may not have felt obliged to acknowledge changes she thought minor, judging by the thought or ink required.

Relevant to this line of inquiry is consideration of information that *Linda* did and did not reveal. There was ample justification, then, for disregarding sentimental strictures on servants' speech when a master or mistress used near-psychotic strategies to maintain the upper hand. There would have been justification too, for at least some onlookers, for exposing the cruel pressure driving Jacobs's decision to take a lover. Permissions of these kinds are important; highlighted by them, though, is how little sanction there was to name people who had done a kitchen witness no wrong. This point should be borne in mind when pondering Child's decision to mask the identities of those Jacobs served in the North. The reason offered for this intervention—"delicacy to Mrs. Willis"—has been attributed to the "easy expendability of black identities."[41] This suggestion is alert to real-world exigencies. Yet it ignores other factors that could have guided Child's reasoning, such as the fact that N. P. Willis had "walked out" with her years before, when Miss Lydia Francis was a rising literary star; that he was a power in the world of East Coast publishing, with a stable of reviewers in his pocket; and that he was widely known as a womanizer (a reputation that could have blunted the force of *Linda's* indictment of *enslaved* women's sexual vulnerability). Perhaps Child knew, too, when she counseled self-censorship how brief a success *A Hairdresser's Experience in High Life* had enjoyed or how badly Anna Flowers had been treated on the witness stand. Yet, of course, she need not have heard of either to have understood the role of kitchen witness for any who needed to earn a living after disclosing information about nonkin to whom they were thought to owe family-like willingness to keep mum.

It may seem as though I want to give Child authority over Jacobs's life-writing. Yet my argument calls for a tweak rather than wholesale revision. The reason the tweak would be significant, if it did occur, is that it made *Linda* find "free" service more affective than chattel attendance. This argument could have been of great use to the antislavery cause. Yet it may reflect ambivalence in Child's mind about a group whose stupidity she mocked in a joke she shared in 1838. "Where do you live now, Nancy?" this jape has a former mistress inquire of a former employee. "Please, ma'am, I dont live anywhere now," the girl says, "I'm married." Noteworthy, too, is a vision Child shared in 1874 of Heaven as a place without "house-rent, servants, &c." These passing comments need not indicate a settled dislike of "free" servitors. Child's sense of humor does need to be mentioned, though, as evidence of ideas that were in the air when she set to work on Jacobs's manuscript. However, nothing indicates that she would have agreed with a comment Stowe had a hero make in her second novel, *Dred: A Tale of the Great Dismal Swamp* (1856). "I see no reason why the relation of master and servants may not be continued through our states," he announces, "and the servants yet be free men."[42] On the contrary, there are marked differences between the conclusion of *Linda* and the episode in *Dred* that finds an enslaved character refusing to be freed since he can think of no happier fate than to go on serving beloved white charges.

Returning to Jacobs, a kitchen witness who had been both a chattel servant and a wage-earning attendant, it was probably she (rather than Child) who mounted *Linda's* understated plea for a rethinking of service that would allow domestic laborers to commute to work. I say "understated" and "plea" because the wistful reference to a home for "Linda" and her children is voiced from her employers' attic. However, there is nothing shy about *Linda's* revelation that a faithful residual may grieve over the constraints placed upon her by a live-in job. The reason I attribute this comment to Jacobs is that she had more reason than Child to be keeping up with the emergence of a form of labor that allowed some domestic workers—especially black women—to earn an income without having to forego privacy or personal time, social activities, and homemaking.[43] The impact of the rise of "day service" on U.S. domesticity was gradual but vast, since it reordered expectations of women's and domestic labor; raised the possibility of dual incomes in poorer families, with all that increased income could entail; altered the responsibilities given children whose mothers labored in other people's homes; helped break down the idea that service workers belonged under household control; and reduced the porosity of the antebellum concept of "family." Equally important, the shift to "day service" widened the distinctions between service in middle-class homes and the residences of the rich while heightening nostalgia for "good old days" in which attendants were denied the right to leave a post at will. The closing lines of *Linda* do not foresee all of these eventualities. They nevertheless go significantly further than anything in domestic advice literature written before the slaves were freed.

To conclude this examination of *Linda*'s "Love, duty, gratitude" claim, I must add that professions of affection for nonkin in works of kitchen testimony must sometimes have been statements of fact. "Who says I'se free?" a freedwoman interviewed after the Civil War demanded. "I warn't neber no slabe. I libed wid qual'ty an' was one ob de fambly. Take dis bandanna off? No, 'deedy! dats the las' semblance I'se got ob de good ole times." Farther North, an immigrant from Parish Kilusty, near Tipperary, told employers that the temporary post she took (to be near her dying father) was a stopgap. "I like it very well," Margaret Maher reported. "But it is not my home[;] my home is with you."[44] These protestations may be construed as flattery. Yet nothing proves they are anything other than reliable statements of certain workers' sense of belonging. The variables that would have affected that sense include such things as age, race, religious training, natal provenance, and location of or affection for kin. All of these things, and more, shape the affect claimed in three book-length works by servant-authors: *A Lifetime with Mark Twain: The Memories of Katy Leary, for Thirty Years His Faithful and Devoted Servant* (1925); Alice Childress's *Like One of the Family: Conversations from a Domestic's Life* (1956); and *Idella, Marjorie Rawlings' "Perfect Maid"* (1992). By exploring the love, duty, and gratitude attested to in these texts (two of which were edited, one of which was not), we can erect a background against which to probe the most outrageous work of kitchen testimony produced in the nineteenth century, the "Literary Thunderbolt!" known as *Behind the Scenes.*

Appearing first in this cohort of three, *A Lifetime with Mark Twain* makes the most sentimental claims. "I'm not living among strangers," Kate Leary testified after coresiding with the Clemenses for decades. "They're my family." The book that reports this assertion does not seem to have been written at the initiative of the Clemenses' long-term housekeeper; instead, it appears to have been solicited by a friend of Twain's daughter Clara when the humorist had been dead for fifteen years. The friend, an actress named Mary Lawton, shared a witticism that some servant-readers might not have found amusing: "Why Katy," Mark Twain is supposed to have said, "she's like the wallpaper; she's always there." Though this was a comic restatement of the sentimental goal, *A Lifetime* reveals that Leary was dispensable when her employers went broke. *A Lifetime* recalls the period of unemployment, when Leary was forced to live with her own kin, as dull and lonely; all is brighter when the Clemenses return, wealthy once more. Obviously enough, memoirs of the rich and famous are usually slanted in this way. Some kind of editorial agenda must nonetheless be reckoned with, if only because *A Lifetime* has the U.S.-born Leary speak with a brogue that her surviving relatives do not recall. Motivation for this kind of "enhancement" probably rested on the expectation that early twentieth-century Americans would be charmed by the memories of a family-like Celt. Charming, too, to this audience would have been the idea that a servant's life stopped when death breaks up the employer's household. "Nothing matters any more, now that the family is gone," *A Lifetime* has Leary sigh at its close, "and it comes back every day—the wonderful life I had with them. It's always in my thoughts them years we had together, way back in the beginning, stretching up to now. It seems like a long, long road to me, but all of it was happiness, and when I shut my eyes, or even when they're open, I can see them all around me again. . . . And although it's terrible lonely when I get to thinking about the past, I have the comfort of having them with me in my thoughts, anyway. And sometimes it almost seems as if they was right here in the room. . . . [J]ust as they used to be, and I can go on serving them to the end."[45] Leary's surviving relatives do not remember their great-aunt as having been miserably lonely when her services were no longer required by the Clemenses. But the cited protestation was not made up out of whole cloth, either, since kin do recall her pride and happiness at having shared her life with the family of Mark Twain.[46]

Thirty years after *A Lifetime* was published, Alice Childress admitted the possibility of unabashed warm feelings for an employer in a sketch collected in *Like One of the Family*. First-person monologues by a straight-talking "day worker," Childress's work is intentionally brash. "I am *not* just like one of the family at all!" Mildred tells an employer who has foolishly made this claim. "You think it is a compliment when you say, 'We don't think of her as a servant. . . .' but after I have worked myself into a sweat cleaning the bathroom and the kitchen . . . making the beds . . . cooking the lunch . . . washing the dishes and ironing Carol's pinafores . . . I do not feel like no weekend house guest. I feel like a servant, and in the face of that I have been meaning to ask you for a slight raise which will make me feel much better toward everyone here." Refutations this direct make it all the more telling that Mildred remembers another employer fondly. "It didn't happen all of a sudden," she recalls, "but one day it suddenly came to me that I thought a awful lot of Mrs. L . . . and that if she ever came to my door I'd be glad to invite her in without feelin' a strain." When Mrs. L. moves to California, Mildred acknowledges the loss. "Yes," she concludes, "I'm sorry she moved because I really liked workin' at that place." This story affirms deferential etiquette since Mrs. L. addresses Mildred by her given name and the day worker does not follow suit. It shows too, though, that Childress (who knew "day's work" firsthand) wanted to stress that affect begins with respect on the part of mistress *and* maid.[47] Good results extend in both directions, Mildred concludes. "I found myself doin' little extras now and then and when she had a party or somethin' like that I really put myself out to make it a nice affair because I was interested," she recalls. Indeed, "by and large I believe I did more work for that woman than for anybody that I've ever worked for."[48] Sentimentalists were to notice, we may assume, that this worker evaluates service relations not on the basis of family-likeness but on their tendency to augment her pleasure in a job and on an employer's satisfaction with her own parties.

Third and last in this clutch of servant-writers, Idella Parker shared memories of working for a white Floridian known best for a novel, *The Yearling* (1937), and an autobiography, *Cross Creek* (1942). The impulse to life-write seems to have been Parker's, however much prompting she received from Marjorie Rawlings's friends or fans. Yet because Parker worked with an editor, it is not clear who decided to use a line from *Cross Creek* in the title of these memoirs and again in the book's opening line. "Marjorie Kinnan Rawlings called me 'the perfect maid'," *Idella* recalls. But, "Let me say right off that I am not perfect, and neither was Mrs. Rawlings, and this book will make that clear to anyone who reads it." This work of kitchen testimony is particularly rich because it relates a historicized understanding of the person Parker had been in the years when she cooked and cleaned for a difficult mistress. "I enjoy telling" about the past, *Idella*'s preface explains, "because the youngsters in particular are always so amazed to hear how things were between the races back then. It may seem like ancient history to you of this generation, but it is true. These were the days of the Depression, when most black people were afraid of whites. I was one of those that feared. I think fear caused us to be obedient and do as we were told." Several stories in *Idella* clarify what kept Parker quiet while she was young. "I didn't answer," she recalls of one blowup, "for let's not forget that this was years before civil rights, and I was a long way from home. Humble and quiet was my way of life."[49] Hinted, too, is that the basis of Parker's dozen-plus years with Rawlings was that this job let her live near kin to whom she could go for companionship or relief when her employer drank to excess. "I was sorry for Mrs. Rawlings, and my love for her grew because it seemed she had only me and her dogs to depend on," *Idella* recalls. "This is maybe one of the reasons I kept leaving and coming back, for she did depend on me." That "maybe" is important, but so is the fact that Parker—who claimed kinship with Nat Turner—pitied her employer. "The person she hurt most was herself," *Idella* explains. "So our relationship was a close one, but it was one that often felt burdensome to me. Still, I did my best to protect her and help her as much as I could. I loved her then, and I love her still. What else could I do?"[50]

Analysis that reduces these words to an expression of false consciousness is impoverished. More perceptive is recognition that while *A Lifetime* uses familial language to describe a relationship forged in the later nineteenth century, Childress mocks this way of conceptualizing nonkin service and *Idella* eschews it altogether. Equally noteworthy, *A Lifetime* has nothing to say about pity or respect; emphasized instead are kindness and the excitement of living in the household of a famous man. Editorial agendas must have shaped some of these decisions. But biographical variables should be adduced, too, since Leary never married or had children while Childress and Parker both chose that route, and this consideration could have influenced how each felt about family-likeness to employers. Highlighting this point is the fact that no claim of family-likeness is voiced in *Behind the Scenes*, though Elizabeth Keckley was alone in the world.

An onlooker so well informed as to recognize that the memoirist named was not the Abraham Lincolns' servant might reasonably inquire why such a claim should be expected. The answer lies less in the pages of *Behind the Scenes* than in responses to the book that shriek dismay about Keckley reporting what she had observed of the Lincolns' family life. Some shriekers acknowledged racial hierarchies, while others didn't. Common to all, though, was denunciation of a freedwoman, turned fashionable modiste, who dared to reveal what she knew about a former First Lady's demanding nature and lack of control. There is nonetheless more to the outrage effected by *Behind the Scenes* than its showing—nothing new, after all, by 1868—that nonkin members of a household who can hear may witness in print. In *Disarming the Nation: Women's Writing and the American Civil War* (1999), Elizabeth Young agreed with James Olney that the outrage was narratological, a product of generic indeterminacy. Yet in *Race, Work, and Desire in American Literature, 1860–1930* (2003), Michele Birnbaum credited Keckley with irruption on a grander scale, claiming that "what she breached is not literary form but the shape of social reality."[51] This phrasing is dynamic. But the claim is questionable in more than one way, not least for its failure to grapple with Frances Smith Foster's evidence of encroachment on Keckley's work by a never-enslaved editor and profit-hungry publisher.[52] Unfortunately, Birnbaum is not the only scholar to scant the complexities of book production, though they may help to explain why a book that recalls testimony such as Robert Garvin's when it presents Mary Lincoln as a "peculiarly constituted woman" who indulged in "little jealous freaks" that pained her war-weary spouse rather contradictorily takes a lofty tone in a story about Keckley shielding the Lincolns' privacy from an adventuress who asked for help securing a chambermaid's post in the White House so that she could "learn its secrets, and then publish a scandal to the world." As it happens, this anecdote recalls one that Catharine Sedgwick had told about Elizabeth Freeman, in an essay quoted in chapter 2, and a very comparable one that Caroline Gilman had related at the start of *Recollections of a Southern Matron*. But when the topic is not white authors' portraits but African American self-representation (with or without aid), it is more important that *Behind the Scenes* depicts Keckley in a range of roles: as a harried slave then self-possessed free worker, independent businesswoman, and trusted factotum who eventually rises, according to Elizabeth Young, to the status of shadow president.[53]

Why, then, characterize these memoirs as an example of kitchen testimony? One reason is provided by word choices in the text: "To defend myself," an early passage avows, "I must defend the lady that I have served."[54] Another is found in the decision to share memories of the president's preference that "Madam Elizabeth" brush his hair, his wife's insistence that "Lizabeth" arrange her gowns, and the watching that "Yib" volunteered to do at Willie Lincoln's sickbed. In these recollections of personal attendance, a successful tradeswoman favored by an elite clientele traverses social ranks in ways that could raise doubts as to whether these memories were shared because she was proud to be of service to the Great Emancipator or because they showed how easy her affections were to exploit. There is, Keckley scholars know, more to *Behind the Scenes* than the episodes noted. The (self?)-sittings mentioned were, however, more than enough—when recounted amidst midcentury notions of black women's capabilities and social roles—to let detractors portray a prominent and sought-after dressmaker as a member of the Lincolns' staff.[55]

Calculations of both capabilities and roles can only be hampered by the *post*sentimentality of much that has been written in response to *Behind the Scenes.* I will have more to say about postsentimentality in chapter 5, since this halfhearted revamping reached its fullest expression in the 1870s. To demonstrate, however, that postsentimentality should not be dismissed as the silly vaporings of a distant era takes little more than notice of the twentieth-century writers who vilified Keckley for perpetrating "an appalling breach of friendship and good taste."[56] Defying this faction, Jennifer Fleischner strove for evenhandedness in *Mrs. Lincoln and Mrs. Keckly: The Remarkable Story of the Friendship between a First Lady and a Former Slave* (2003). Yet precisely because, like most biographies that probe developmentally, this study personalizes strongly, it lends firm support to those who applaud Keckley's act of "revenge" and Mary Lincoln's consequent "unmasking."[57] Determinative here is neither sentiment nor sentimentality but instead postsentimental eagerness to laud service relationships that are family-like by heaping abuse on those that are not. A stylistic, rather than a theoretical, innovation, postsentimentality foments the development of warring camps and, in the process, blinkers scrutiny of affect that strains against preconceptions and norms. In the case of *Behind the Scenes,* moreover, postsentimental commentary tends to imply (purposefully or not) that Keckley was justified in putting in print her own life and times not by admirable accomplishments or a unique vantage on national trauma but by nothing more glorious than Mary Lincoln's overheavy leaning on the familial creed. Putting this thought differently, my position is that whatever one thinks of the service-labor theory promoted by Sedgwick, Gilman, and others, cheers for *Behind the Scenes*'s shocking revelations can be understood as implying that Keckley's life-writing was justified not by life itself but by a famous client's errancy. Contesting this position is Lori Merish's attempt to draw attention away from imputations of gossip to focus on the production and use of highly desirable clothes. The unsentimentality of *Sentimental Materialism: Gender, Commodity Culture, and Nineteenth-Century American Literature* (2000) is welcome not because nonkin affect has no claims or because sentimental service-labor theory is the worst imaginable but because dispassion brings to light the many reasons that Keckley had to record her life in print, among them achievements that had little to do with clients, good or bad.[58]

As we will see when exploring the work of postsentimentalists in the 1870s, sentimentality can be hard to shake even by reformers who recognize its shortfall. Here, though, to close out a chapter that finds conservative values enmeshed in outrageous print, I want to respond to Carolyn Sorisio's charge that *Behind the Scenes* "splinters the fragile veneer of middle-class culture" by suggesting that little was endangered by a book available to few since it was severely suppressed. Where danger did lie was in commentary provoked by *Behind the Scenes*, some of which Sorisio has unearthed from the archives. I appreciate the long hours in libraries that have turned up commentary such as the Massachusetts *National Intelligencer*'s sigh for a world in which "Bridget and Dinah take[] to writing books . . . and select for themes the conversations and events that occur in the privacy of the family circle."[59] My appreciation rests, however, not on unneeded confirmation that served Americans disliked talkative attendants but on the large audiences reached by self-pitying avowals that service relationships were in flux. In this respect, reactions to *Behind the Scenes*—rather than the book itself—offer a gauge by which to judge the merits of the reforms discussed in chapters 1, 2, and 3. This gauge is an evaluation of each scheme's tendency to admit or deny servants' right to recount their own lives. This perspective acknowledges how unwilling advisors such as Beecher were to grant full civic standing to servants but suggests, as well, that sentimentalists were moving in the wrong direction insofar as their hope of absorbing servitors into nonkin households tended to increase the valorization of privileged privacy. That direction was fine with Waldo Emerson. But it was contradicted by Brook Farm memoirs that eschew the "code of genteel disclosure" except insofar as certain episodes and opinions were ignored. The main drawback to "educated friends, working," for a homemaker in need of assistance was that friends could not be compelled to stay at their posts. This was, after all, why Abby threw in the towel at Fruitlands: she was worn out by a domesticity predicated on the labor of "family" members who were free to go and had no incentive to remain.

Freedom to leave was, of course, the reason sentimental advisors had set to work back in the 1820s. Reason mushroomed, though, for many white Southerners as soon as the slaves were freed. Thus, a Tennessean was sorrowful but resentful, too, at the realization that a freedman called Tom "is the first to leave me & had thought would have been the last one to go."[60] So dramatic a break with prewar practice gave rise to emotions that ranged, on homemakers' part, from virulent to bleak. "The houses, indeed, are still there, little changed," a Virginia essayist observed, though "the light, the life, the charm are gone for ever. 'The soul is fled.'" Impatient with looks to the past, by 1884 another man rasped that appeals to affect had had their day. "The sentimentalists advise to minister much to the comfort and enjoyments of maid-servants," he remarked, "but everybody knows that such a course would be madness" due to the fact that "slavery is a condition and the only condition which secures absolute permanence of good service."[61] Leading this thrust was journalism that instructed homemakers to repudiate "the sickly sentimentality which tries to squeeze a tear over the fate of a stout, able-bodied young woman who has three hearty meals a day, a comfortable home to live in, every thing provided for her, good wages, and no more work to do than, if taken continuously, could be got through in five or six hours."[62] This startlingly scornful opinion bespeaks the mood of a new era characterized by loss for some, gain for others, and change for all.

5 Stupid Sentimentality

> No axioms or theories of the past have any present
> application.
> —Helen Campbell, *Prisoners of Poverty* (1887)

The source of this chapter's slate-wiping epigraph was a some-time novelist who left belles lettres to train, teach, and publish as a home economist. She retained her flair for powerful phrasing, though, to such an extent that she would go on to promote "day service" by labeling coresidential arrangements an "open contradiction to that privacy on which rests the essential thought of home."[1] These facts merit scrutiny because, in certain ways, Helen Campbell was the Sedgwick of her generation although she used excerpts from interviews with former maids to expose how unlikely served and serving Americans were to achieve a family-like relationship. Campbell may not have been responsible for the fact that the book that disseminated this argument was titled affectively. But as she is presumably the person who decided which of her interviewees' observations to share in *Prisoners of Poverty: Women Wage-Workers, Their Trades and Their Lives* (1887), students of the literature of nineteenth-century U.S. service will notice this book's concern that the attempt to find out how it felt to attend nonkin would be dismissed as "stupid sentimentality." This phrase jumps off the page because, while seeming to find affective appeals inane, it leaves open the possibility that sentiment might edify if linked to waged attendance in some nonstupid way.

Failure to discern ambivalence of this kind has thrown analysis of nineteenth-century advice literature out of true. Yet so has scholarship that brackets *Prisoners of Poverty* from the counsel to which it responded.[2] Bracketing is understandable since *Prisoners* contributed to discussions of the "labor question" more explicitly than did work such as Marion Harland's *Common Sense in the Household* (1871). Yet once nonkin service is admitted to be labor, bracketing grows hard to defend. To resituate Campbell's thoughts on nonkin attendance within the context of advice published after the slaves were freed, this chapter ponders *Prisoners* alongside a question Harland posed. "Do we understand, ourselves," she asked, "what is the proper place of a hired 'help' in our families?" Claiming that she did understand, an advisor named Harriet Prescott Spofford commended "those families who," though fair and kind, "do not quite make their servant a part of themselves."[3] Such delicacy was anathema to Melusina Fay Peirce's uncompromising advocacy of an "entire reorganization of the domestic interior" designed to "almost entirely blot out from our domestic life the servant element!" Campbell's counsel was almost as blunt, though she started from the other end. "[T]o learn the struggle and sorrow of the workers is the first step," *Prisoners* punned, "toward any genuine help."[4]

Work such as Campbell's was overdue when it appeared in 1887. "How came it to pass," *Godey's* had asked back in 1855, "that the cordial bond of affection which at one time existed between the master and the servant is being gradually weakened, and estrangement and feelings akin to hostility taking its place?"[5] But *Prisoners* was not up to its declared task, in large part because Campbell failed to realize her slate-wiping claims. To gauge the confused state of advice literature written after the slaves were freed, this chapter explores Gilded Age counsel to reveal debts to the past such as are suggested by the facts that:

* "Zina" Peirce defended the servant-expulsive idea of "cooperative housekeeping" by making glowing reference to the "kind solicitude, life-long help and trust, and feeling of mutual interest which subsisted between mistress and servant under the old slave system, and veiled many of its deformities";
* in response to which Harland paid tribute to *Live and Let Live* in a cookbook/guide that sold extraordinarily well;
* after which Spofford sniped about "pseudo-philanthropists who are on the look-out for a grievance" while insisting that "a member of your family, as the servant is," deserved a pleasant, airy bedroom as well as "wages, a home, consideration, and kindness";
* in the wake of which half-old/half-new counsel, Campbell had *Prisoners* advance a vision of nonkin service in which rejection of sentiment was to foster "a far closer tie" between the serving and the served.[6]

Regional allegiances may seem like a good way to organize these didacts. Yet that system breaks down quickly, since if Spofford and Campbell were rock-ribbed New Englanders, Peirce was a New Englander with kin living in the South, and Harland (whose real name was Mary Virginia Terhune) moved to the North after having been raised in the Old Dominion by Yankees. Publication histories are as confused, since while Spofford and Harland had enjoyed prominence as romancers, Campbell had tried her hand at novels and children's stories, and Peirce was no litterateur. Most clarifying, then, is realization that where Peirce promoted her radical visions with near-frenzied "hype," Harland asked mistresses to bear and forbear with nonkin staff, and that while Spofford bewailed the unlikelihood of locating family-like attendants, Campbell tried to quash self-pity by drawing up rules of conduct that have the flavor of a contract. Attention to this variable illuminates authorial decisions such as Harland's use of a brisk yet prosaic advisorial persona, especially as that "voice" selection contrasts with Peirce's attempt to foment a sense of crisis. Peirce's approach won an audience over a considerable span of time. Yet no writer discussed in this chapter—and few discussed in any other—topped Harland in book sales. Her success exposes some of the inner workings of worry about the charge of "stupid sentimentality."

Scholarship on nineteenth-century U.S. service has not probed this topic. Instead, it has situated the frustrations of served and serving Americans within social structures such as the shift from "help" to "domestics" and the midcentury influx of Irish immigrants who made no secret of their desire to locate high-paying posts. Research of this kind is valuable. Yet when brought into conversation with studies of the impact that antislavery agitation had on attitudes toward all forms of labor, it does much to suggest that the latter stages of the "household civil war" Carole Shammas has explored were most strongly shaped by the movement to end slavery. Amy Dru Stanley's assertion that "through their attack on slavery," abolitionists "transformed the cultural meaning of wage labor, dissociating it from domestic dependency" and thus "removing the free labor contract from the household's shadow," is highly pertinent to the postemancipation finding that what the *Century Magazine* called "one of the most puzzling practical problems of the day" was not a man's affair.[7] "If there is any subject which belongs exclusively to the domain of women," another "family" magazine opined, "it is the perilous one of domestic service."[8] Slurs on "stupid sentimentality" affirm this position by blaming women (or womanish attitudes) for failing to resolve in-house ills. What they occlude is the huge role men played in creating the conditions in which the ills arose, developed, and spread.

Further complicating the "servant problem" after the midcentury was loud rejection of "moral suasion" claims. In *Women and the Work of Benevolence: Morality, Politics and Class in the Nineteenth-Century United States* (1990), Lori D. Ginzberg showed how decisively Gilded Age intellectuals lobbied against individualized charitable activities. Accenting the positive, Gregory Eiselein has portrayed the 1860s as a period of particularly rich opportunity. "Multiple contending possibilities opened up in humanitarianism," he has affirmed, "making the historical moment rich with diverse, inventive, and unconventional conceptions of benevolence." This statement of the case is not wrong but may be misleading, since Eiselein downplayed the bewilderment fomented by contending possibilities. Recognizing the possibility of confusion, in the 1830s Catharine Sedgwick had warned against conflating schools of advice that shared little except being guided by affect; to make this point, she had one character in *Home* describe another as "not in the least sentimental" and then refine the message: though "[n]ot foolishly sentimental," the woman in question is praised for her "strong feelings."[9] This degree of precision concerning the term "sentimental" is absent from writings by "new humanitarians," so much so that one of the few structuring elements in that body of print is unquestioning use of that modifier as a pejorative. Unanimity on this point had impact. It might have done more for workers, though, if "new humanitarians" had distinguished between sentimental advisors whose work varied widely and between that group and the *post*sentimentalists who made family-like service seem a precious rarity.

Leading the postsentimental charge was Harriet Beecher Stowe, in a series of *Atlantic Monthly* columns short on advice but long on expressions of ire and spite. Cause for such things will seem obvious enough to any who have flipped through the cartoon pages of "family" magazines. Recognizing, though, that print was never so simple a thing as reflective of real-world conditions, students of the literature of nineteenth-century U.S. service will want to consider the fact that the 1860s found Stowe living in an elaborate and expensive house, struggling to understand that fame might not be accompanied by wealth—after decades in which mistresses had watched servants gain leverage and felt their own dominance decline. A sense of decline had impelled antebellum writers such as Cooper, Gilman, and Sedgwick. It grew exponentially, however, once the demise of the plantation household made every U.S. servant "free." This is a crucial finding, because if Mary Louise Kete is right to say that the "fundamental subjects of sentiment" are "homes and families under the condition of loss," then the historical record should show that affective advice gained its second wind as reports proliferated that freedpersons "are very troublesome servants to keep."[10] I contend that energy did burgeon forth in the 1860s and 1870s, guided by *post*sentimental plaints about the near impossibility of achieving a family-like state of servitude.

To make this point, the "House and Home Papers" (1864–65) and "The Chimney-Corner" (1866) lavished abuse on cloddish "Paddies" and contempt on "half-and-half" attendants who expected to be treated as social equals even as they accepted wages for doing the lowest chores. Nonkin service was not the only topic Stowe addressed in these columns. But it was one of her main concerns, as month after month she attacked the attendant who "expects, of course, the very highest wages" though "her object is to do just as little as possible, to hurry through her performances, put on her fine clothes and go a-gadding." Even more disturbing, Stowe's mistress-character reports, "She is on free and easy terms with all the men she meets, and ready at jests and repartee, sometimes far from seemly. Her time of service in any one place lasts indifferently from a fortnight to two or three months," leaving destruction in its wake. "[T]he very spirit of wastefulness is in her; she cracks the china, dents the silver, stops the water-pipes with rubbish; and after she is gone, there is generally a sum of half her wages to be expended in repairing the effects of her carelessness." This destructive force owed

HIBERNIAN MAIDEN. "I'm afther lookin' for a place, Mum, where there is an ould couple wid Property, bud widout Childer, who would Look upon me as a Daughter."

In 1874, Harper's Bazar *ridiculed Irish servants in a way that poured at least as much mockery on sentimental bromides. Courtesy of Special Collections, University of Virginia Library*

much, Stowe added, to native-born white women's refusal to serve in nonkin homes. "I would almost go down on my knees to a really well-educated, good, American woman who would come into our family," she had a male character confess, "but I know it's perfectly vain and useless to expect it."[11] As concise a statement of postsentimental discontent as ever was committed to print, this statement ties a nativist fantasy to a grumble in disguise.

Stowe's complaints do not guide overtly. Yet they may have encouraged homemakers to consider a scheme that sister Catharine had been promoting for some time: a shift to "daughter service" that was deeply antisentimental in intent. This program did not make much headway while affective ideals comprised the measure of a good mistress. "I wonder," a piece in *Godey's* submitted in 1864, "that women who seem to be good, affectionate wives, and tender mothers, can speak so unkindly of those who eat of their bread, and drink of their cup, and dwell beneath their roof." Yet Beecher had begun pushing an antisentimental line back in the 1840s, and she moved more boldly once her "True Remedy for the Wrongs of Woman" (1851) described a "perfected state of society" as one in which there "will be no resource . . . but the daughters in each family."[12] Stowe did not say "yea" or "nay" to this vision in her *Atlantic* columns. Instead, as if certain that nonkin attendance would continue to be a fact of life, she alternated broadside attacks on cooks and maids with expressions of scorn for young wives too enervated to manage their own homes. This charge must have been approved, since it made money in columns and when reprinted in book form. Yet it was resented, too, since it drew a "cease and desist" in 1871. "I know all about our noble grandmothers," groaned satirist Gail Hamilton as if begging relief from a nag.[13]

Hamilton would have had even more to say if she had been privy to a letter Stowe wrote to her unmarried twin daughters in 1863. Deciding that Hattie and Eliza were old enough, at twenty-seven, to be put to daughter service, Stowe recounted her domestic burden and explained the imprudence of hiring a housekeeper to take it on. She then asked the twins to "resolve for *this year* that you will make the care of the family as much of an object as I do," an exercise she presented as "*your* interest more than mine." The single best-known proponent of affect-based outreach and women's "innate" moral sway, Stowe had tried this argument before and encountered resistance, for her letter acknowledged "the energy with which you often say that you detest housekeeping—that you hate accounts & *cant* keep them[,] that you dont like to write letters and cant write them—that you hate sewing—that you *cant* take care of sick people. . . . [A]ll these," she explained, "leave a load upon me which

if you were differently inclined you might take off." Then, as if despair-
ing of this duty-oriented approach, she added an emotive threat, advising
the twins to take up the household chores "or else—*another mother
may come in.*" This passage can be linked to the fact that Roxana
Beecher had died while Harriet was still young. But it also provides context for expressions of frustration with gadabout domestics and fatigued
younger mistresses since, Stowe advised, both augured ill for "family"
life. Meanwhile, the ever-present potential for affective appeals to turn
coercive was realized when she asked her twins to submit to kin service
on the grounds that "while you have your mother you have it in your
hands to keep her by taking from her the burdens which draw her life
away." If emotional blackmail sheds light on Stowe's advice columns, it
also illuminates Beecher's insistence that the best homes were attendant-free because "when there are servants enough to do the work, the
daughters of a family can not be made to take their places."[14]

Read in the context of a culture that had begun the long process of
creating "more work for Mother," knowledge of Stowe's and Beecher's
Gilded Age advice reminds us that advisors born in the 1830s (and thus,
to the eyes of Stowe and Beecher, approximating the age of daughters)
had reason to think carefully about denouncing the idea that service should be family-like. If, that is, the alternative was that daughters
would cook and clean, then women in the age group of Spofford, Harland,
Peirce, and Campbell could be in trouble, especially if they did not marry
(or, like Campbell and Peirce, ended childless marriages in divorce). As
the degree of danger would necessarily decrease with advancing age, it
may be relevant that the married-but-childless Spofford would publish a
tribute to daughter service in 1891.[15] However, the creation of anxiety
about one's individual fate was not the only way in which Beecher and
Stowe put pressure on younger writers, for it could have been even more
important that both depicted "family" life as a hotbed of strife. Marion
Harland rejected such emotionalism and won a huge following. "I am
inclined to believe," *Common Sense in the Household* smiled, that "if
one-half I hear of other housewives' trials be true, that I have been highly
favored among American women."[16] This comforting note made Harland wealthy and famous. There was courage to her stand, nonetheless,
since the sentimental standard had been under attack for some time
when she chose to advise in terms of a sense available to all.

Attacks on sentimental service-labor theory may have started with
pundits certain that all societies included some version of a "mudsill
class." But they were signally advanced, by liberals impatient with the
hierarchy that sentimentalists confirmed. "Our domestics are not

members of our families," readers of the *Massachusetts Quarterly Review* learned in 1848; "they are among us, but not of us; they know this, and we know it; and families and societies are all ajar in this respect."[17] Prominent "new humanitarians" picked up this line of argument in the 1860s and 1870s to clamor that "privileged" domesticity was a battlefield. Domestic service entailed "a relation which almost necessarily forbids all sentiment," the *Nation* announced in 1865; "there can be no patriarchal character to it, and seldom even common personal attachment." Fear-mongering about health was drawn into this debate—"Some of the best houses in New York have been suddenly peopled with vermin in variety," a one-time antislavery activist shrilled, "by the coming of a new housemaid with her carpetbag" from an urban tenement—and certain groups were deemed specially intrusive. "How can I let them come in," a *Scribner's* essay of 1871 had a mistress-character cry, "and spoil everything, and know that I am all the time living in an atmosphere of dirt and disorder? . . . How *can* I endure to put a dirty Irish girl, with perhaps a host of attendant vermin lurking in her bags and bundles, into a nice room like this?"[18] Whatever comments like this did to readers' impressions of Celtic staff, students of the literature of service will see how neatly images of threatening "foreign" bodies mapped onto social upheaval in the South. "We have had a constant ebb and flow of servants," a South Carolina woman noted in 1865, "some staying only a few days, others a few hours, some thoroughly incompetent, others though satisfactory to us preferring plantation life." Soon afterward, an "Old Virginia Gentleman" made freedpersons' restless mobility the topic of a short story. "We-ell," he ruminated, "if ever I put faith in a nigger gal again, you may shoot me."[19]

So sounded the voices of the aggrieved middle class. Complementing them, though, was "testimony . . . from the kitchen" that emanated from Northern *and* Southern homes. Much of this testimony was nonverbal; one can only imagine, then, what it was like to share one's home with a wage earner as sorrowful as Elizabeth Wilson represented herself in the pages of her diary in 1865. "[M]ine is a hard & lonely life," she wrote; "day after day comes & brings it's work. [I]t seems that my life is made up of nothing but long long days for nothing but work work and dig for others."[20] Farther South, repudiation of homemakers' expectations was visible even before peace was declared—"Answering bells is played out," a still-enslaved woman avowed—and grew bolder after emancipation. "You betta do it yourself," a former bondswoman is supposed to have retorted when scolded for cleaning a pot improperly. "Ain't you smarter an me? You think you is—Wy you no scour fo youself."[21] Fury is understandable from a population that quickly measured the limits to the freedom granted Americans who were black and poor. But there was a safer response that made quondam slaveholders wax at least as wrathful: the exchange of what one Southerner called "a veneering of fidelity" in return for cold, hard cash.[22]

Having watched people they had known from childhood leave with joy, stay in the neighborhood and refuse to serve, or agree to serve on a "live out" basis that allowed workers a measure of control over their working lives, Southern whites had much to say about freed attendance.[23] "I am not fit to manage negroes now, at least hired servants," an Alabama woman despaired. "They, nor I either, are prepared for the changes in our situation." A mistress in Texas agreed: "To be without them is a misery," she decided, "& to have them is just as bad."[24] But so did an Atlanta journalist. "The common experience of all is that the servants of the 'African-persuasion' can't be retained," that city's *Daily Intelligencer* reported in 1865. "They are fond of change and since it is their privilege to come and go at pleasure, they make full use of the large liberty they enjoy."[25] Some homemakers enthused about the delights of being relieved from "the plague, vexation & expense of so many idle, worthless & ungrateful house servants," while others tried to hire white servants "at all hazards, at any price."[26] Yet problems arose here too. "Many families here entirely discarded the blacks & get industrious Irish women," a South Carolinian woman noted, only to find that they "too often prove to be Drunkards &c &c." Perhaps, then, the answer was not immigrants but the local poor? Remarking on this expedient, the *Charleston Courier* reported that some ex-slaveholders were learning to "adopt into their families some young white persons of humble circumstances as a 'help,' and this arrangement succeeds well and saves them from many annoyances which the other class of servants under present teachings are so apt to occasion." This sounded good but was not the solution to all household ills. "I tried to hire some white women to live with & assist my family with their work," another South Carolinian reported. He found, to his dismay, that poor whites could be even less happy about the new dispensation than were former masters, since "They do not like the idea of becoming 'Help.'"[27] Others were less temperate in their comments about waged attendance. "What a gratification it must be to the North," one complained, "to see us fumbling and *internally* whispering *cuss talk* over our disorganized and patience trying system of 'help.'" Perhaps some Northerners felt gratified, in fact. It must have been upsetting, all the same, to any who relied on nonkin staff, to realize that U.S. servants were gaining power. In response, a Southern homemaker called for affect-free management: "All feeling must be discarded," he avowed.[28] Surely many more agreed, without committing their views to print.

As sure that warm feelings for nonkin staff were obsolete, Melusina Peirce published a series of articles about "cooperative housekeeping" that mounted allegations to the effect that servants constituted "outrageous little kingdoms of insubordination, ignorance, lying, waste, sloth, carelessness, and dirt" that mistresses must "subdue afresh every day, and every day more unsuccessfully."[29] A highly educated woman who had grown up "shabby genteel," Peirce married a brilliant man so improvident that she was compelled to take all meals with her parents-in-laws for the first eight years of her married life.[30] If that experience chafed, it also motivated her to work out a form of income-producing labor suitable for women such as herself. What Peirce came up with was a collective program capable of freeing the bright and talented from in-house responsibilities so that they could pursue further education, retail trades, and careers in medicine and the arts. This plan had ties to the vision of service industries that Peirce's great-aunt Gilman had proposed at the end of *Recollections of a Housekeeper*. But it had more recently been mooted in *The Atlantic Monthly*: "the solution of the American problem of domestic life," Stowe taught in 1866, "is a wise use of the principle of association."[31] The difference between Peirce and Stowe is not only that the younger advisor worked out what the elder had only pointed to; more significantly, Peirce spurred doubt about even minimal reliance on servitors. Not that she ever spoke of substituting daughters for employees; instead, she proposed that women who enjoyed housekeeping act as managers for communal laundries, kitchens, and dining halls. Plans of this sort could have recalled Brook Farm as much as they built on appreciation of the management responsibilities for which many middle-class women had volunteered during the Civil War. However, in Peirce's postbellum program, women's managerial labor would be waged.

Interest in cooperative housekeeping must have owed much to realization that this plan would give middle-class women the opportunity to pursue more elevated or income-producing activities. Yet the student of advice literature will focus on the gusto with which Peirce denounced "the inefficiency, insubordination, and fickleness of our servants."[32] These charges were not new. But in 1868 and 1869 they were pushed with no apologies about privileged women's ability to govern. Rather than gesturing, then, toward innate maternal qualities that made management of nonkin staff "natural" in a way unthreatening to male authority, Peirce defended "cooperative housekeeping" by sketching a history of service that zooms from slavery and serfdom to Elizabeth I, pauses at Cromwell, and goes on to decry "the disorganization begun by emancipation" that "has culminated in our American chaos, where from its very foundation the domestic temple sways and fluctuates uneasily on its ever-changing basis of ill-trained and unprincipled service, creating an antagonistic feeling which renders the relation of mistress and servant but a cold-blooded bargain, formed in suspicion and dissolved with pleasure on the slightest provocation." The solution, Peirce concluded, was to banish servants. "With the exit of the servant element from our families," she promised, "would come a great calm and freedom of spirit. The house would be, as it were, empty, swept, and garnished, and ready for all pleasant spirits to enter in and dwell there." This echo of Matthew 12:44—the story in which Jesus talks about how to keep cast-out devils out—bespeaks knowledge of Scripture but, more crucially, willingness to turn the Bible against the view of master-servant relationships used by sentimentalists. We know that some of that school defended slavery while others promoted waged attendance. Writing, though, soon after all U.S. slaves had been freed, Peirce spoke of "emancipation" (to talk about what would more accurately have been identified as the demise of feudalism) in terms of the profound "disorganization" it entailed. This questionable linking could explain why she deemed the South the best place to initiate the new domesticity: "surely, if there is a corner of the globe to which co-operation at this time seems especially appropriate, it is there." It is not clear whether Peirce knew that aspects of her program accorded with the sorts of things that some ex-slaveholders were telling their diaries. "I am perfectly independent of having Negroes about me," a rice planter rejoiced in 1868. This achievement pleased him because his feeling was that "if I cannot have them as they used to be, I have no desire to see them except in the field."[33] Concurring, though, with this man's desire to distance repugnant servitors, Peirce envisioned a future in which women such as herself would not have to get their own hands dirty or feel their tempers fray.

Responses to cooperative housekeeping ranged from attempts to implement Peirce's vision to extractions from it that look, today, like calls for service industries. "May the day hasten," *Putnam's Magazine* cried in 1870, "when housekeepers, young and old, will be convinced that we are hampering and wasting our domestic peace by persisting in labors which do not belong to the home, but should be outside callings exclusively."[34] What Peirce did *not* inspire was the outrage visited on Fourierists before the Civil War; mocked, instead, were sentimentalists who failed to register the realities of nonkin servitude. To be sure, the piece titled "Wanted: A Domestic" is a spoof. Its message was serious, nonetheless, since this story recounts the experiences of a minister-character so naive as to insist on affect from his wage-earning cook and maid. "I don't want anybody in the house," this foolish man twitters, "that don't belong to me." This comment could have looked innocent at first. Yet the joke lurking in the dual meaning of "belong" became patent when the conclusion of the sketch exposed the minister's hopes as fatuous.[35] Perhaps it is coincidence that just two years later, Louisa May Alcott published a reminiscence of having worked for a minister who promised—quite unreliably—that the person who agreed to serve in his home "will be one of the family, in all respects."[36] There was nonetheless definite skepticism about the "home missions" line by this time, as even Stowe admitted. "The mistresses of American families," she taught in 1864, "whether they like it or not, have the duties of missionaries imposed upon them by that class from which our supply of domestic servants is drawn." A writer named Kate Gannett Wells offered a sunnier view when she revived this line two decades later: "servants are our children," she sentimentalized in 1885; "home is a missionary field." Soon, though, she was promoting a harder-nosed stance: "our homes are never theirs," she told readers of *The North American Review* in 1893, "'de facto or de jure.'"[37]

Reasons to sing a new song in the 1890s include Wells's "New Woman" concern about the exploitation of domestic workers. Pertinent too, though, to her shift from sentimental to legal turns of phrase is a Gilded Age innovation; by 1871, the old emotive phrase "the family work" had given way to a de-affective substitute: "housework." The fact that this neologism arose during the period in which homemakers were taught (by Catharine Beecher, among others) to fear sicknesses that went by the moniker "house diseases" has been tied to new ideas in medicine. Looking ahead, though, it is at least as intriguing that by the time Wells abandoned sentimentality, wealthier Americans had started calling their nonkin attendants "house girls" and "house boys." In the era of Reconstruction, and writing in the leading weekly for middle-class women, Harriet Spofford gave that initiative a boost when she envisioned a good servant as one who coresides as "an intelligent and capable friend of the house."[38]

Pertinent to this lexical shift was insistence on servants' ineradicable foreignness. Natal provenance was one aspect of that xenophobic tag. "You will have to take a Paddy," one character tells another in the great midcentury romance *The Morgesons* (1862); "the old housekeeping race is going." Yet birthplace was not the only criterion for writers who shrieked about the burden on homemakers "forced suddenly to receive into their houses a great body of aliens." On the contrary, "new humanitarians" were happy to extend this argument to people of certain ethnicities who had been born in the United States. "These Irish and German girls, as we are accustomed to call them," an essayist pondered, "who are in our families as second girls, as nurses, and even as general servants, what proportion of them ever saw Ireland or Germany? They are, in fact, of the second generation. They are one remove from foreigners. Yet, though born among us, our general instinctive feeling testifies that they are not wholly of us." By showing that foreignness could lie more in the eye of the beholder than in an objective criterion such as place of birth, this remark affirms Amy Kaplan's charge that "foreign" is a concept meaning little more than "not domestic" and thus inappropriately associated with "family" life.[39]

Once the truth of Kaplan's charge is acknowledged, Gilded Age interest in "Chinese John" looms large although few Chinese men worked as household staff outside California during the 1860s and 1870s. Yet that very fact reveals the oddity of articles such as "China in Our Kitchens" being published in *The Atlantic Monthly* in 1869. The best explanation for this essay, at this time and in this venue, was desire to rebut Peirce's vituperations by exoticizing faithful service in much the same way early twentieth-century painters would juxtapose beautiful, demure servant girls to articles of homely household use. Oil paintings such as Gari Melchers's *The China Closet* (1904–5) and William McGregor Paxton's *The Kitchen Maid* (1907) were the work of a period later than that in which "China in Our Kitchens" appeared. The path toward such *post*sentimental renderings was nevertheless paved by articles that glowingly described the service of "pig-tailed John."

To gauge the postsentimental program of "China in Our Kitchens," it is helpful to recognize that this anonymous look to the past starts by invoking Old New England as a rich source of country girls eager to serve in Boston. This was a happy era, the essay avows, "those good old times when there was respect between employer and employed, and when respect and confidence often ripened into friendship and affection." This tribute toward a vanished past acts as a foil for the postsentimental finding that "the times are not as they were, neither are the servants. The farmers' daughters have disappeared; we ne'er shall look upon their like again. The new servants have come; we never looked upon their like before." The result is enmity: "a tale of antagonisms rather than of good-will, and there is very little sympathy or esteem between employer and employed." This sounds awful, and was intended to, the better to highlight the proposition that even if most Gilded Age servants were ineligible for family-like trust and care, a few rare specimens did serve affectionately. In "China in Our Kitchens," rarity is highlighted by the fact that the servants commended have names such as Hop Kee and Woo Choo. "During our residence of ten years in China," recalls the American who employed this pair, "we hardly ever had occasion to dismiss a servant; in nearly every case a strong attachment sprang up between them and us; and in more instances than one, I have felt personally grateful for services and attentions which I could not reasonably have required, and which were all the more gratifying because rendered spontaneously and heartily." The postsentimentality of this claim lies in the fact that its missionary-author finds faithful attendance as strange as opium pipes or crushed and swaddled "lily feet." Therein, a "new humanitarian" would reply, lay the inutility of yearning for an influx of Chinese servitors. "[A]las!" one sighed, "how fleeting were the delusive joys of Chang-Wang, son of the Sun."[40]

Published concurrently with such things was a less positive take on Chinese service: doubt as to whether the "heathen Chinee"—always figured as a man—belonged within God-fearing U.S. homes. John Kuo Wei Tchen has found a play of 1873 treating this issue as farce. But the service of Chinese men was no laughing matter in middle-class "family" magazines that put moral issues first. "Sagacious and expert as my automatic cook proved to be," a writer reported, "I was forced to believe that most of his virtues were the result of fear. I never knew him to become attached to or interested in any person or thing for love's sake."[41] Affirming this summation, a California homemaker added a few caveats. The Chinese manservant, she wrote, "has his good points to be sure," but "John, after all, is not a saint, and to change from Irish to Chinese is *not* to pass from purgatory to paradise." That was partly, she taught, because "John" was just as likely to grow difficult and greedy as any other servant and partly because there were doubts about the wisdom of letting him gain proximity to white girls. The Chinese manservant was, this housekeeper warned, "an unknown quantity" whom no middle-class mother "thinks of trusting . . . as we trust our own, or the negro race." The racial typing here is as fascinating as it is crucial, since it informs the gender typing that sometimes made "John" feminine and sometimes a heterosexual threat. The larger topic addressed is nonetheless how trust stacks up against efficiency. "No matter how kind you may have been, no matter what obligations they may be under," the California

housekeeper concluded, "they seem to lack the moral sense which rec-
ognizes ingratitude."[42] Intended readers did not need telling that a central sentimental tenet was the idea that because every human is born
loving righteousness, sentiments had only to be awakened to become
powerful determinants of behavior. For homemakers guided by this
view, the claim that members of a given group were devoid of morals
meant nothing more or less than that members of this group were inhu-
man, to a greater or lesser degree. The fact that the California housekeeper wrote as if she allowed servants with this lack into her home
marks her as a *post*sentimentalist who released herself from the obligation to "mother" attendants who were essentially immune to affect.
Postsentimental too, though in a different way, was the piece in the
Ladies' Repository that depicted "John," in 1870, as "a good automaton
which, wound up, would go silently and surely through the week."[43]
These claims were postsentimental, as opposed to antisentimental, insofar as they left open the inference that privileged U.S. women stood
ready and willing to mistress in a motherlike fashion if servants responsive to that kind of relationship could be found.

As a counter to antisentimental advice, postsentimentality had its
merits: most obviously, it left open the possibility of warm relationships
between the serving and the served. This was no minor point during an
era of uncertainty about what it meant for laborers portrayed as ineradi-
cably foreign to coreside at the heart of home. Nevertheless, postsentimentality could never assuage homemakers' frets and woes. Certainly
it weakened the force of the dictate that mistresses should extend
embracing outreach. Yet its greatest creative energies were expended on
finding ever-more forceful ways in which to describe bad servants'
annoying ways and good servants' rarity. Rebuking those who engaged in
this expenditure of time, thought, and talent, the *Nation* found "something childish in continually wailing" about bad servants in 1874. What
this writer failed to note is that Marion Harland had already addressed
the advisorial gap by instructing mistresses that "Bridget, Chloe, or
Gretchen . . . may have her own sensations, and draw her own inferences—*being human like yourself.*"[44]

Though born and raised in the South, Harland left before the fall of
Richmond and learned to manage "free" servants in Massachusetts,
New Jersey, and New York. In the process, she reversed Caroline Howard
Gilman's transition from North to South to become the later nineteenth-century's staunchest advocate of the sentimental creed. The wife
of a Presbyterian minister as well as a tireless self-promoter who made
much of her own happy marriage and motherhood, Harland counseled

THE TABLES TURNED.
How our Streets will look next Summer as the result of the Chinese invasion.

Which would be more intrusive, Frank Leslie's Illustrated Magazine *wondered in 1880, those brutish serving-women who dress more elaborately than their mistresses or the Chinese manservants who uphold ancient traditions of deference? Special Collections, University of Virginia Library.*

kindness toward nonkin staff. "Be kind, pleasant, always reasonable and attentive" to servants, she advised, "willing to hearken to and meet any lawful request" a cook or maid might make. At the same time, she did not paint mistress-ship as an idyll, for *Common Sense in the Household* added that servitors who are likely to be "ignorant and illogical" will generally be impelled by self-interest rather than a desire to earn employers' love and trust. Shirley Abbott has said that Harland offered readers the solace of a "fireside chat," and that may be true.[45] Where solace lay, though, was precisely in her dismissal of post- *and* antisentimental postures in a new narrative format. Contemporaries who misunderstood this innovation mocked Harland for crafting a "composite, not to say hybrid, order" of literature structured according to the plan of "a chapter of novel alternating with a chapter of receipts." Yet fans cherished this form of address. "I like her off-hand, familiar, friendly fashion of talking straight to the young and perplexed," an admirer confided.[46] Certainty that the "familiar talks" scattered throughout *Common Sense* were both "namby-pamby and incoherent" was dismissive of fans' appreciation for the "little interpolated essays" in which Harland provided "insight into the motives and governing principles of human nature as exhibited in the household."[47] Dismissal provides, nonetheless, good evidence of the disjuncture mentioned earlier between those who mocked the efficacy of individualized benevolence and those who saw no better way to cope with a form of labor that was confined to unusually small and scattered "shops." Attention to this aspect of the "servant problem" explains why—despite open ridicule in certain venues—U.S. homemakers flocked to Harland's guides.

A precocious talent, Harland's first national publication, at the age of sixteen, was in *Godey's Lady's Book*. Then, while still a teenager, she wrote an extremely popular sentimental romance, *Alone* (1854). More novels followed apace, her eighth appearing before the Civil War came to an end. Harland did not lose her touch when the slaves were freed, for she charmed again with a sequel to *Alone* titled *Sunnybank* (1866). A brief delineation of the visions of mistress-ship and servitude proffered in these two romances sets the scene for Harland's success as an advice writer to homemakers confronting the fact that the "plantation family" was no more.

Alone is the story of Ida Ross, a Southern white girl who finds friends, love, and evangelical conviction of a personal relationship with Jesus Christ. The proselytizing component of Harland's novel is central to *Alone*'s account of a Christmas morning on which Ida's chattel attendant surprises her with a gift. Rachel's love for her mistress is the more touching in that the belle's wealthy but cold-hearted guardian gives her nothing by which to commemorate the day of Jesus's birth. Equally pertinent, the enslaved attendant spends "coppers" given her by a thoughtful mistress (for what we are not told). This story illuminates Ida's management strategies when she decides to give up comfort and a loving social circle to return to the plantation that had been her childhood home. The imperative that drives her—duty—is not put in terms of a motherlike relationship to servitors, nor are Ida's bondsmen and -women said or shown to be childlike. In contrast, she is warned to think long and hard about the white lady who will teach at the school for poor whites that she plans to start, since this employee "is to be a member of your family."[48] *Alone* shows, predictably enough, that Ida's human property love, esteem, and thank her. Harland adds, however, that all decent characters in the novel cherish Ida just as much, once she devotes herself to doing right. Ida continues to be adored by right-minded characters when she returns in *Sunnybank*, a novel that begins just before the Civil War and ends with the conflict resolved. The timing of this conclusion freed Harland from having to describe the effects of emancipation. As if aware, however, of interest in this topic, her story of life on the home front makes passing reference to a few chattel who run away and expounds at length about Ida's entire confidence in the attendants who remain.

Obviously enough, this account of two incident-filled novels is gapped. Yet it is sufficient to suggest what readers would expect to find in domestic advice from Harland. *Common Sense in the Household* taught that because mistresses govern from duty, affect may or may not be their reward; that because servants are needed labor, they require assured management from those who are their social superiors; and that servile assertion cannot disturb the mistress who is wise. "[D]ear sister," readers were told, "do not add to the real miseries of life by regarding the annoyance of a careless, slothful, or impertinent domestic as a real trouble. Class it with petty vexations which are yet curable as well as endurable, and live above it—a noble, beneficent existence in the love of your fellow-creatures and the fear of God." This calm and calming counsel was worlds away from Peirce's maledictions of "these creatures who come to us we know not whence, and flit away we know not where." At the same time, it was almost equivalently removed from *Bessy Conway, The Irish Girl* (1861), a revamping of *Live and Let Live* spiced with a dash of *The Greatest Blessing in Life*. *Common Sense in the Household* shows traces of Sedgwickian thinking, too. Yet it focused attention on mistresses, advising them to keep a level head. "Your servants will remain with you longer," this guide concluded, "and be better-tempered while they stay, if you show that you appreciate the fact of a common humanity; that you owe them duties you are resolved to fulfil during their sojourn under your roof, however mercenary may be their performance of those devolving upon them."[49] The jab at "mercenary" servants was nothing new. What *was* innovative was Harland's gift for displacing sentimental tenets in such a way that the family-like relationship fostered was that between her and her grateful fans.

Crucial to this displacement was an authorial strategy all her own. "When she proposed a 'Cookery Book' to Mr. Carleton, who had long been her lucky publisher, he laughed outright," one of Harland's admirers recalled.

> He was poisoned by the popular prejudice, you see, and he suffered for it, for, not caring to be ridiculed when she proposed to give to American housewives her precious, oft-tried store of receipts, she went quietly to Scribner and offered the volume. Mr. Scribner was a semi-invalid at the time, and lying on the lounge in his private office; he heard from a partner her proposition. It struck him also as a little comical, a little hopeless and unfeasible, but he knew the lady's reputation and power. So he

said, "Tell her we shall be glad to publish it," but added: "It will probably be a loss, but in that case we may get her next novel!"[50]

Comparable incomprehension of the market for advice literature is seen in the fact that *Harper's* republished *Live and Let Live* in 1876. One can only wonder what Peirce thought of the new edition and of Harland's leaping sales as attempts to establish "cooperative housekeeping" foundered, one after another. More disturbing, though, to any who cared about service workers would have been postsentimentalists' proliferation of inflated images of good and bad attendance.

"No well-ordered house has noisy servants," a guide of 1875 fantasized. "The housekeeping in every department should move like perfect, well-oiled machinery, with invisible wheels." Though Harland taught her readers to reject such guff, Harriet Spofford dotted columns of the leading U.S. weekly for middle-class women with equally exaggerated paeans. A gifted romancer in her youth, Spofford turned advisor when lush interior dramas such as "The Amber Gods" (1863) fell out of critical favor.[51] She nonetheless retained a flair for rich descriptive passages and a taste for characters who embodied moral absolutes. "You may think," one of her columns advised,

> that nothing could be worse than your Irish girl, till you get an African one; the Swede who takes the latter's place is only good while she is fresh—she needs to be in the country but six months before she knows all the "tricks and manners;" the sprightliness of the French maid is as aggravating in its own way, and the stolidity of the German makes you long for the blarneying tongue of Bridget once again. It is true that Bridget's masses upset the whole household arrangements, but so do Dinah's praise-meetings, for the matter of that; and you feel that it would be better for you and Fifine together if her masses did too; while if, in disgust with the whole sisterhood of them, you at last secure an American, her familiarity makes you wish you could do the work yourself.[52]

More humorous than the work of Peirce or Harland, though unabashedly barbed, advice from Spofford's pen sniped in one passage to make tributes in another more glowing. Thus, in an upbeat mood, she paid tribute to the Celt who labored not as "a servant merely" but rather as

> a friend, a great-hearted, warm-hearted friend; one who feels your interests as her own; whose industry is faithfulness, whose faithfulness is devotion, whose sympathetic soul and sweet, blarneying tongue are like sunbeams through the house; in the light of whose superiority differences of religion and nationality seem but contemptible trifles; to whom the children run; to whom you turn yourself; whom you counsel with rather than command; whose clean and wholesome ways are ways

of pleasantness, while if all her paths are not paths of peace, she clears off after a flare-up so brightly that reconciliation is a pleasure; and whom if, when her days of usefulness are over, you forget, then should God forget you![53]

The *Catholic World* appreciated this passage when reviewing the book in which Spofford collected her *Bazar* essays but found her "remarks . . . not always consistent."[54] That was because had the reviewer but realized it, Spofford was not at all sure what she wanted to say about affect between employers and employees. She claimed to be tough-minded. "That kindly souled old Greek, Plutarch," Spofford announced, has "declared his conviction that there was once a golden age in whose era there was neither master nor slave. If he really believed it, he had a far more favorable opinion of the original grace of human nature than we ourselves are able to nourish." This was outspoken rejection of the sentimental premise that because all humans come equipped with a moral barometer, appeals to affect would win through. Having made this point, though, Spofford turned it into reason to heap *post*sentimental laurels on the servant who wins her employers' regard: "The good and faithful American servant is always a part of the family," she opined, to such an extent that "the family that knows her, that has once enjoyed her, would not feel itself really a family without her."[55]

Here is the snag: advisors such as Spofford had nothing to say on the vital question about how a homemaker might locate "a different class of persons from those that, ignorant and unused to our comforts and refinements, seek us from foreign shores . . . [;] who, if not enjoying our luxuries, at least appreciate their purposes and comprehend the need of our refinements; who sympathize with us religiously and as a people; who have many of the same motives and notions and wants as ourselves; [and] who could be infinitely more agreeable members of our families than those now in place there." This passage is illuminating because it shows how little Spofford's preferences had to do with natal provenance (since gestures toward religious sympathy exclude U.S.-born Catholics) or indeed any defined set of qualities or attributes (since "appreciation" and "same notions" could be turned against any employee on a given day). Rudderless leadership could not counter the work of antisentimentalists. Yet one must ask whether it had been intended to since, all things considered, postsentimental advisors were the most wishful of didacts. In the 1890s, *Good Housekeeping* noted this Achilles' heel. "The question," it pointed out, "is not what kind of servants do we prefer, but how can we get the best service out of the kind of servants that offer themselves to us."[56] The fact that Sedgwick, Gilman, and others had written reams to help mistresses realize that goal affirms the importance of recounting who said what and when in advice literature directed at the heart.

Admittedly, the distinction between sentimental and postsentimental advice could be tenuous; it is not immediately apparent, for instance, how to classify the "wish list" published in the *Christian Union* in the early 1870s. "Not one in a hundred—and that we fear is a high proportion," Eunice B. Beecher there avowed,

> of all the Irish that come to our country can, by any amount of care, patience, or indefatigable teaching, be transformed into a neat, energetic, faithful, truth-telling servant; and as for gratitude . . . for the most part all this vanishes like morning dew, at the first chance for easier work or higher wages.
>
> The English and the Scotch, as far as our observation goes, are more inclined to make their employers' interest their own. . . . The Swiss and Swedes are usually smart and capable; but their inability to understand our language when they first come to us, makes their instruction difficult and tedious. . . . A good Welsh girl is one of the best,—usually neat, active, and quick to learn. . . .
>
> There are no better servants to be found than such as come from Canada and Nova Scotia, if one can secure such as bring from their own country a genuinely good character.[57]

The omission of African American servitors from this seemingly exhaustive survey is no small matter. Yet I would stress this passage's postsentimental proclivity to try to determine which groups, or populations, were capable of serving in a family-like manner, so as to clarify which other groups or populations would never attain that desired state. It probably goes without saying that nineteenth-century conceptualizations of "race" shaped the postsentimental quest. However, there was no uniformity about how the shaping worked. For instance, where this Beecher-by-marriage ignored African American attendants, Spofford enthused in one column about the service of freedpersons whom she denominated "our colored allies" and cautioned in another that the "employer of colored cooks and house-maids has as much complaint to make as the employer of white ones."[58] Since Spofford spent a great deal of time in Washington, D.C., after 1865, the latter charge may have been intended as a corrective to disparaging commentary emanating from the South. "My heart is pained and sickened," a Georgia woman wrote, "with [freedpersons'] vileness and falsehood in every way. I long to be delivered from the race."[59] Yet whatever Spofford hoped to accomplish, her wavering and contradictory counsel cannot have provided clear direction to homemakers or servants. Neither could the work of her friend, the popular humorist Gail Hamilton. "Oh for one hour of tyranny," the latter had a mistress-character sigh in 1871, "one hour of autocratic, irresponsible power, such as we knew in the halcyon days of slavery."[60]

Resisting this form of self-pity and the view of household government it implied, a male advisor told mistresses to loosen the reins. The unstated inference that privileged women created their own headaches may owe something to the fact that Robert Tomes's credentials as a domestic counselor rested on nothing more substantial than whatever could be derived from having written about the production of champagne in Rheims. There was nonetheless a progressive air to the passage in *The Bazar Book of the Household* (1875) that asked readers to contemplate a "family" life in which "servants shall not live in the houses of their employers, but merely resort there daily at those hours when their particular services may be required."[61] This was a brave gesture (though, Tomes acknowledged, one that "might not respond satisfactorily to all the requirements of employers") because the idea of "day service" repulsed homemakers who thought servant control the safeguard of their own domestic sanctities. "I should not be happy if people whose life and principal interests were elsewhere were coming into my house to work," a mistress commented, long after Tomes had broached this suggestion. "I want the love as well as respect of my help."[62] This "want" was denounced by self-styled "rationalists" who taught that "the colored servant's dislike to live in the house of the employer (and perhaps the employer's dislike to have her live there) are progressive forces; for with the destruction of this old custom, the strongest impetus is given to a normal regulation of the hours of labor." Yet homemakers were slow to agree. "When you said you wanted to work days, you left there," an ex-domestic named Dorothea Lewis recalled; the mistress "told you," she explained, "you'd not be able to come back."[63] It would be rather sweeping to blame writers such as Eunice Beecher and Harriet Spofford for such dictatorial conduct. The fact remains that no postsentimental advisor supported "day service" even to the limited extent of Tomes's en passant remark.

As if cognizant of how little "Reconstructive" advisors had done to ease tensions between the serving and the served, Helen Campbell stepped into the fray with a bold directive: "Dismiss sentiment," she advised. This fiat provides reason to pause for a moment before looking at *Prisoners of Poverty* to recap what had transpired in the years since the slaves had been freed. Most of a quarter-century had passed. During that time, "new humanitarians" had inveighed against individualized forms of charity and told homemakers to find new standards: "a capacity for routine is perhaps," the *Nation* advised, "on the whole, far more valuable in a household than intelligence." Simultaneously, the social chasm between the serving and the served enlarged markedly even as service workers (especially laundrywomen) tried to set prices or unionize. During this period, several communities expressed interest in the "Kitchen Garden" movement, a program that took "the little waifs and strays of humanity who crown the door-steps and alley-ways of the most squalid streets" to teach such castaways "how to do all the work of a house." A class-conscious revision of the kindergarten movement, this project had a practical aim: "A good situation is promised" to all kitchen gardeners "at twelve years of age if they have learned their lessons well."[64] More upsetting, and of course longer lived, was the shift to "day service" that evoked wistful portraits of service in days of yore. Some harked back to slavery—for example, Uncle Remus, whose stories started to appear in print in 1870—while others extolled native-born "help" of a certain age. "No girl of any species," *Lippincott's* taught in 1877, "can compare with an oldish American hired girl." Yet of course, looks to the past had ramifications for the present; for example, there was ominous import to the news that a Minnesotan in the South "had found out that only the harsh slaveholders made money in the old times."[65] Focused on the here and now, Campbell asked workers to tell their side of the story.

Investigation was on the curriculum when, following a divorce, Campbell trained as a home economist and taught for a time in a North Carolina cooking school. After writing *The Easiest Way in House-Keeping and Cooking* (1881)—a manual that judged the slackness of Southern domesticity a shameful legacy of slavery—Campbell wrote *The Housekeeper's Year-Book* (1882), a pocket-sized guide that assumes the assistance of a nonkin "girl." Her authority to advise on domestic matters was validated by a friend and housemate; Campbell, said Charlotte Perkins Stetson (later Gilman), was a mistress so competent that she was able to "take a green German damsel and train her—do all the managing—and glory in it."[66] More interested, though, in producing literature capable of advancing social justice, Campbell wrote a book-length report on the work of a waterfront mission in New York City. *The Problem of the Poor* (1882) led to a commission from the *New York Tribune* to interview working-class women. The book drawn from the resultant newspaper columns was not limited to service issues. Yet because waged attendance was a major job option for the poor, *Prisoners of Poverty* included two chapters on attendance. The first shared excerpts from interviews with women who had given up service to labor in factories and sewing rooms; the second outlined Campbell's vision of the way in which to make service more attractive to women with a choice of employment opportunities.

Historians of service have treated *Prisoners* as a breakthrough because Campbell was the first to collect reports of resentment about the imposition of livery, the social stigma of being known as a servant girl, and indeterminate working hours. What becomes apparent, though, when *Prisoners* is seen as yet another contribution to the literature of nineteenth-century U.S. service is how firm a hand Campbell kept on what kitchen witnesses were permitted to say in print. One of the first scholars to investigate *Prisoners* made the latter point in a footnote, finding it likely that Campbell "embellished the stories" printed in that collection "and possibly added dialogue."[67] More broadly significant, though, than editorial intervention reminiscent of the treatment of some ex-slaves' narratives is what looks like uncritical acceptance of testimony that uncaring mistress-ship drove willing workers from their posts. It is quite revealing, then, that one of Campbell's interviewees recalled her first mistress to have been "a smart, energetic woman" who provided "a good room and everything nice." But sentimental precepts lurk in the following comment: "she had no more thought for me than if I had been a machine." Similarly, another interviewee spoke favorably of an ex-mistress but criticized the bedroom given her and the kitchen in which she spent most of every working day. *Prisoners* quoted this woman's opinion that service was anything but family-like, in a manner befitting *Live and Let Live:* "It's hard to give up your whole life to somebody else's orders, and always feel as if you was looked at over a wall like, but so it is, and you won't get girls to try it, till somehow or other things are different." Still more pathetic is the observation that "except to give orders, they had nothing to do with me. It got to feel sort of crushing at last. I cried myself sick, and at last I gave it up, though I don't mind the work at all."[68]

It is easy to see why historians with a heart for laborers have found this material compelling. Campbell's work is nonetheless misprized if pondered without recognition of the weight of sentimentality that bore down on all participants as she interviewed, transcribed, and selected from among solicited remarks. The result was not identical to advice from Sedgwick or Gilman; rather, it was a *post*sentimentality that cast considerable doubt on affective relations between the serving and the served. "The lady just looked at me astonished," one of the women quoted in *Prisoners* recalled. "If you take a servant's place, you can't expect to be one of the family." Evidence that radical contemporaries saw sentimentality herein includes a faint-praise assessment from B. O. Flower; he recalled Campbell as a reformer who "possessed in a large degree the mother heart."[69]

Campbell might not have objected to this classification. But as if to prevent *Prisoners* from being dismissed as what she called "gush and maudlin melancholy," she concluded her thoughts on service with a set of guidelines intended to bring nonkin cooking, cleaning, and child-minding into line with other forms of "free" labor. Emphasizing set working hours and unvarying duties, a place in the employer's home in which to sit and entertain friends, and "[s]uch a manner of speaking to and of the server as shall show that there is no contempt for housework, and that it is actually as respectable as other occupations," her rules accorded with the precepts of those Amy Dru Stanley calls "ethical economists." Where Campbell diverged from that group was in choosing to "pitch" her rules with promises of nonkin affect. "Precisely such conditions as are here specified have been in practical operation for many years," *Prisoners* attested, and with success, for "The homes in which they have ruled have had the unfailing devotion of those who served, and the experiment has ceased to come under that head, and demonstrated that order and peace and quiet mastery of the day's work may still be American possessions."[70]

Promises of devoted attendance may have been intended to persuade mistresses who had been raised to govern sentimentally to give Campbell's rules a try. Taken, though, as expressive of the sort of service relations she espoused, they left *Prisoners* vulnerable to critique. The *Overland Monthly* did approve her book's capacity to "break through pretty parlor indifference"; *Prisoners*, it averred, was "far more adapted to catch attention and to make an abiding impression upon the careless or pre-occupied, than anything of the sort we remember to have seen before." *The Critic* concurred. "All of us have known that such conditions as Mrs. Campbell describes exist," this journal admitted, "but it is well to have the fact brought repeatedly before us, till we cannot ignore it or rest without trying to change it." Though these comments all but name *Prisoners* the *Uncle Tom's Cabin* of "free" women workers, that was its weakness for some. *Prisoners* was lacking, the *Overland Monthly* would decide, insofar as "a little more intellectual grasp, a little more learning would probably have made the book a really indispensable and abiding contribution to economic thought."[71]

These comments are well observed. Yet *Prisoners* deserved credit for a fairly pugnacious remark that turns out to have been farsighted.

"It's freedom we want when the day's work is done," one of her respondents was quoted as claiming. "You're never sure that your soul's your own except when you are out of the house, and I couldn't stand that a day." It is obvious to today's eyes that this statement of preference for "day service" indicates the direction in which cooks and maids (especially those of African descent) were reshaping the conditions of their labor; nor would it be long before the most high-minded approved. "Perhaps in the future the private kitchen will give way to cooperative cooking," *The Chautauquan* mused in 1901, "and in that event domestic service will enter upon a new phase. But meantime a practical improvement may be found in giving the servant more home life." This suggestion sounds like old-fashioned sentiment. But it isn't, since the passage continues: "There is no reason why she should not live outside, with her own family."[72] Had Campbell taken this line in 1887, she would have more claim to the status of an innovator, and indeed, six years later—after attending a Woman's Congress that formed a Domestic Science caucus dedicated to the proposition that nonkin attendance was labor, just as much as was millinery or coal mining—she scorned affect. "Till household service comes under the laws determining value, as well as hours and all other points involved in the wage for a working-day," charged *Women Wage-Earners: Their Past, Their Present, and Their Future* (1893), "it will remain in the disorganized and hopeless state which at present baffles the housekeeper, and deters self-respecting women and girls from undertaking it." Unfortunately, Campbell fell from this abstracted stance in a series of lectures published as a textbook that went into many classrooms declaring that "the constant presence in the family, the most intimate and incessant association of one who is and must be a stranger within our gates" comprised "an alien element."[73] Campbell's concern for working women makes this a call for revamping domesticity rather than a slight on servants. The same cannot be said of work Harland published in 1889.

Harland had produced several cookbooks dotted with "familiar talks" after her first sold so well; one, a revised edition of *Common Sense*, won praise for "humorous as well as sensible" counsel about servants from the *Catholic World*. After that, though, as if trying to drown out the sound of Campbell's interviews, she wrote *House and Home: A Complete Housewife's Guide* (1889). This publication was a startling departure since it ignored Sedgwick, praised Sarah Hale, and heaped abuse on "the illiterate despots of the kitchen," those "inferiors in birth, station and culture, whom we hire and wheedle to do such daily tasks as will leave us free to discharge aright duties which they are incapable of performing."[74] That Harland disliked Campbell's intervention became apparent ten years later: "the Prisoners of Poverty who make shirts for thirty-five cents a dozen," she told readers of the *Independent* in 1899, "and eke out the meager wages of a shop-girl by pleasing the floor-walker's fancy, would be better fed, better lodged and safer in soul as house servants." Yet when she wrote *House and Home*, it may have been just as salient that she had recently moved from Springfield, Massachusetts, to Brooklyn, New York. Not only would this move have influenced the kind of servants Harland could employ; just as important, urban living could have motivated the nation's preeminent advisor to augment her earnings by any means that came to hand. Pertinent, then, to the bile spewed in *House and Home* is the fact that this was not a Scribner's publication but an extended advertisement for a Philadelphia firm that specialized in baking goods. Harland may have been sincerely impressed, as she stated in the letter published in the first few pages of this guide, with the Clawson Brothers' triple extract of vanilla. That was, however, no reason for her to use the publishing opportunity offered (it is fair to assume) in return for her endorsement to excoriate most U.S. servants as "malcontent Arabs" while extolling the attendance of older black women. "Let it be noted," *House and Home* announced, "that the middle-aged mother or aunt of the smart colored damsel furnishes us with the best 'help' to be had in this, or any other country."[75] This "compliment" highlights the fact that no ex-servant interviewed in *Prisoners of Poverty* had been identified as of African descent. Deplorable, all the same, is Harland's willingness to tout cooking ingredients by lauding the attendance of black women who could remember slavery—in what amounts to an echo of Sedgwick's commendation of Elizabeth Freeman, the ex-slave whose comportment did so much to shape sentimental literature about servants who were waged. This echo recalls a long-favored rule: when "free" servants cause ructions, take refuge in evocations of the "family black and white" so tirelessly advanced by defenders of human bondage.

Campbell's decision to mute the topic of race in her *Prisoners* interviews may bespeak desire to foreclose hopes of reestablishing even a simulacrum of slavery. No nineteenth-century advisor did more, however, in that line than Lucy Maynard Salmon. It would be nice to report that concern for black servitors lay behind Professor Salmon's avowal that Northern homemakers should not try to "import" African American cooks and maids from the former slaveholding states. That, however, is unlikely since she justified her position by charging these workers with grave moral failings. This aspect of *Domestic Service*

(1897) is not shy. But neither is Salmon's determination to repudiate sentimental postulates. "[T]he problem," she charged, "is not so much how to improve the personal relationship between the employer and the employee as it is to decrease this relationship" and so bring service into line with other forms of labor.[76] The Epilogue examines this proposition with special interest in the literature—hence readers—Salmon chose to rebut, disdain, or ignore.

Epilogue

. . . substantial facts are supplanting sentimentality and
visionary theories. . . .

—Lucy Maynard Salmon, "Recent Progress in the Study
of Domestic Service" (1905)

Lucy Maynard Salmon holds an honored place in histories of
U.S. service because she wrote the first academic study of nonkin attendance. Her goal was not advisory, however; rather, she said, it was the
accumulation of objective information. "It is not expected," Salmon
announced, "that all, or even any one of the perplexing questions connected with domestic service will be even partially answered" by the
research she published in 1897, any more than it was "expected that any
individual housekeeper will have less trouble to-morrow than to-day in
adjusting the difficulties arising in her household." The idea was
instead "that the tabulation and presentation of the facts will afford a
broader basis for general discussion than has been possible without
them, that a knowledge of the conditions of domestic service beyond
their own localities and households will enable some housekeepers in
time to decide more easily the economic questions arising within every
home, [and] that [such knowledge] will do a little something to stimu-
late discussion of the subject on other bases than the purely personal
one."[1] Rejection of "purely personal" discussion, coupled with admiration for "knowledge . . . beyond" that cullable in one region or home
reflects Salmon's academic training. Perhaps use of the passive voice
sits awkwardly alongside the modesty of "a little something." But if so,
it is telling that hesitancy is nowhere to be found in the essays Salmon
published after *Domestic Service* was greeted with mixed reviews.

167

Quite to the contrary, pronouncements not unmixed with disdain characterized the pieces collected in *Progress in the Household* (1906). To date, *Progress* has not drawn scholarly attention. It is an era-ending document nevertheless in the literature of U.S. service insofar as it notices that body of print the better to make the case that belletrists were not the people to provide guidance about the up-to-date home and well-ordered "family" life.

A comparable attack appears in the section of *The Theory of the Leisure Class* (1899) that sarcastically avows, "The first requisite of a good servant is that he should conspicuously know his place." The imputation that servants were responsible for locating and occupying a suitable position was not aimed at workers; on the contrary, it was sly critique of conflict among purveyors of domestic sagacity. The reason Salmon—rather than Thorstein Veblen, W. E. B. Du Bois, or any other alert contemporary—dominates this epilogue is that she pronounced the existing literature of U.S. service silly, misdirected, or obsolete. This stand made sense to the college-educated "New Women" who tried to reform ideals of service and mistress-ship as the nineteenth century turned. Typical of this group's efforts is the prize-winning article that ridiculed counsel based on "a sentiment so inwrought with poetry, romance—religion even—that it successfully eludes detection."[2] Gestures toward religion were weighty in this context inasmuch as a specific understanding of Christian tenets underwrote the sentimental creed; at least as salient, though, was the stab at belles lettres. Salmon affirmed that stab by having *Progress in the Household* charge that "[t]he very absence of the figure of a domestic servant in the modern novel, and in current popular literature in every form," constituted evidence of a right-minded new attitude.[3]

It had, in fact, been some time since U.S. writers produced fiction as service-centered as Frances Hodgson Burnett's *Sara Crewe* (1888)—a novel better known today as *The Little Princess*—James Lane Allen's "Two Gentlemen of Kentucky" (1888), and Henry James Jr.'s "The Turn of the Screw" (1898). More recently though, and as Salmon ought to have known, Thomas Dixon Jr. had castigated "modern negro servants" in a novel called *The Leopard's Spots* (1902) as if responding to Charles W. Chesnutt's pointed comparison of freed and free servant-characters in *The Marrow of Tradition* (1901). Assertions of absence, in the face of such offerings, suggests that Salmon's real grievance lay less with modern novels than with writers who trivialized strife between those who managed households and those who cooked and cleaned. Strengthening this contention is the gratification with which *Progress in the House-*

hold reported that "flippancy is giving place to seriousness in considering the relations of mistress and maid."[4]

Flippancy was of interest again, a few years later, when two male researchers examined "The Depth and Breadth of the Servant Problem" in *McClure's Magazine*. Positing, as Salmon (and others) had before them that nonkin service comprised a "belated industry," I. M. Rubinow and Daniel Durant promoted the "startling possibilities of an eight-hour day" for servants as the single most forceful corrective to what they called "the medievalism of the home." Predicting, however, "the tremendous agitation that would be organized against" this innovation, this pair warned readers to expect to see conservative practices and attitudes "enforced by all the latent possibilities of wit and caricature centering around such a hyper-ludicrous notion as that the servant girl should quit work at a given hour, exactly like the butcher and baker and candlestick-maker. It would strike the national funny-bone as nothing in the history of crank legislation has yet struck it," Rubinow and Durant prophesied.[5] The article that made this claim never mentioned Salmon's research. Yet it revived her tactic of depreciating belletristic contributions to the literature of service while broaching recourses as visionary (at that time) as anything sentimentalists had avowed.

Did Salmon's work deserve to be forgotten so soon? Arts-and-letters periodicals did not create that impression when her first book was new. *Domestic Service* "deserves a hearty welcome," *The Critic* averred, "because it is truly helpful. In fact, it is one of the best studies of any phase of the labor problem that we have ever met with." *The Dial* concurred, finding *Domestic Service* "of the highest value." Other readers didn't, among them a reviewer for *The Bookman* who praised Campbell's *Home Economics* (1898) for its "delightful idealism" while deeming Salmon's work "stilted and sentimental" in parts.[6] This must have been a galling charge. Even more aggravating, though, may have been feedback from people who did not seem to have read the book; representing this contingent, *The Nation* dismissed Salmon's findings with a blithe assurance that "the problem of domestic service, from the point of view either of mistress or servant, has lost most of its terrors, and may be left to work itself out under the influence of mutual forbearance and good will."[7] This newsweekly would speak highly of "Miss Salmon's excellent book" in a review of the revised edition (which was identical to the first except for the addition of a chapter on service in Europe). But none could have foreseen that encomium when the first *Nation* review dismissed *Domestic Service* in a near-echo of advice that had been tired when *Godey's* trotted it out in 1857. "Time and uniform friendliness will," a good mistress-character had promised then, "in most cases, fashion 'one of those trusty family servants' you fancy so much."[8] Salmon did not agree, and neither did *The North American Review*; in 1898, it said that *Domestic Service* "has taken rank immediately as the most thorough and scientific treatise known on the subject." Use of the term "treatise"—long associated, in the literature of U.S. domesticity, with Catharine Beecher—may have been incidental here. Yet either way, this comparison added up to very little, considering the lack of competition for the rank mentioned, and it lost ground steadily as studies of service were commissioned by the Boston-based Women's Educational and Industrial Union, several different states' Departments of Labor, and the United States Commission on the Relations and Conditions of Capital and Labor. I. M. Rubinow would note in 1906 that *Domestic Service* provided a good history of servitude. Yet he added that Salmon had "signally failed" to ease in-house strife by advocating profit sharing as a way to give attendants incentive to work more faithfully. Her oversight lay, he explained, in thinking of homemaking as a profitable endeavor.[9]

Taking a longer view, two late twentieth-century commentators found Salmon guilty of arithmetic so wishful as to imply a defense of class privilege. Bettina Berch mounted this charge by finding *Domestic Service* "(deliberately?) biased and false" insofar as "less than casual errors seem to suggest that her whole 'study' . . . is actually a polemic against paying servants more," after Susan M. Strasser had deemed Salmon's book central to "an ideological movement to promote acceptance of the expansion of capitalist social relations."[10] Both arguments implicitly tackle David M. Katzman's assertion that Salmon was one of the turn-of-the-century "modernizers" who tried "to rationalize the organization of the home by introducing contemporary principles of science and management" and thus bring domesticity into the present day. Katzman was right to say, in *Seven Days a Week: Women and Domestic Service in Industrializing America* (1981), that this group encountered resistance from "housewives." He assumed a great deal nonetheless when he added that the latter "could not compete successfully with the rational, logical arguments of the reformers and simply withdrew from public discussion."[11] This account is not wholly wrong. But it *is* slanted in several ways, the most significant of which is the charge of withdrawal since, in fact, some were driven from the discussion quite purposefully— as Salmon would be, in turn.

A more nuanced sense of the clash between homemakers and servants, and the markedly different friction between homemakers and "New Women" reformers, can be found in Joanne J. Meyerowitz's *Women Adrift: Independent Wage Earners in Chicago, 1880–1930* (1988). Still more insightful, though, is Sarah Deutsch's explication of the three-way tension among waged attendants, "New Women," and homemakers resistant to change. "While middle-class/elite women often sincerely desired to protect . . . working-class women," Deutsch explains in *Women and the City: Gender, Space, and Power in Boston, 1870–1940* (2000), "they also needed both the presence of servants and their labor to retain middle-class status and their own freedom of movement." If, under these circumstances, "New Women" called for workers' "liberation" from the familial standard of attendance, that, Deutsch says, is because "their presence in the public sphere relied not on their moral authority as home-makers, but on their college degrees." This assessment of the situation is evenhanded. Yet it is gapped insofar as it fails to mention how hard Salmon worked to justify the authority shift. One of her disciples referenced human nature but then blasted mistresses specifically. "Women," she cried, "do not want intelligent equals to serve them: they want an inferior, a subordinate—*a servant, not an employee.*" In calmer tones, but with no less disdain, Salmon deplored the limits of female ratiocination: "Nothing to-day is so characteristic of women as a class," *Progress* alleged, "as their inability to assume an impersonal attitude toward any subject under discussion."[12] There *was* cause to query manners-mavens who said hateful things about cooks and maids. "Servants," a popular etiquette expert had announced in 1891, "are becoming a separate community; our enemies, rather than our humble friends; a lava-bed beneath our feet, full of danger and pitfalls and hidden honeycombing."[13] Yet Salmon did not distinguish between advice that was spiteful or compassionate, or even good or bad; instead, she mocked counsel per se. "The great improvement in the character of the general literature of the subject is seen," *Progress* opined, "in the gradual disappearance of the fault-finding, the sentimental, the goody-goody magazine article."[14]

As if feeling the barb, Marion Harland wrote an update of Gilman's *Recollections of a Housekeeper* titled *The Distractions of Martha* (1906) and was countered by *The Diary of Delia* (1907), a revival of the midcentury "servant's tale." The fact that the latter was written by Winnifred Eaton, the Chinese Canadian romancer who had published under the pseudonym "Onoto Watanna," has given it interest for some.[15] However, failure to interpret *The Diary of Delia* within the lineage of the literature of U.S. service can skew comprehension of a market-conscious writer's sense of intended audience. The same is true of

The Distractions of Martha but also of *The Whole Family* (1906), a multiperspectival novel that—while professing to provide a current and realistic view of middle-class U.S. domesticity—found no room for the thoughts of the three servant-characters who are named.[16] Perhaps the writers involved in this collaborative effort were tired of pieces such as those published in *The Independent* as "A Servant Girl's Letter" (1902) and "A Washerwoman" (1904). Yet another faction applauded this reportorial surge. "If Bridget herself were put upon the witness-stand," *The Outlook* enthused in 1904, "she could unfold a tale the variety and scope of whose subject matter would put to shame a veteran novel-writer."[17] That was, of course, the sticking point for people who wanted to keep servants' knowledge under wraps: "There appears to be too much deference to the criticisms and opinions of uneducated servants," one of this camp complained in 1906.[18] Lending support to this cohort, "one of the best known literary women of America" (Marion Harland?) sent the *Independent* a "Story of an Irish Cook" in 1905; it reiterated the precept that good service was family-like.[19] It hardly needs saying that this gospel had adherents long after it had come under attack. It was discredited, nonetheless, by every announcement in a local newspaper that "Aunt Jemima" would soon be exhibiting her renowned pancake-making skills. Scholarship on this white-sponsored huckster-figure has stressed racist nostalgia for the figure of the chattel "mammy." What was actually enacted, though, with each ad that hallooed "I'se in town honey!" was the kind of mobility allowed few if any slaves.[20]

Here, if Salmon had cared to look, was a contradiction capable of prying open the "unremarked elision between sentimental and domestic" that June Howard notes in *Publishing the Family* (2001). More interesting to her, though, were the formats in which service and mistress-ship were discussed and the authority that different formats deserved. Salmon did not say that advice crafted by belletrists could make very real tension seem like a minor irritation on which the best-trained minds could not be expected to dwell. That, however, is what she implied by having *Domestic Service* insist that "investigation and publication" of the right kind would move discussions of nonkin service "out of the domain of sentiment and transfer it to a realm where reason and judgment have the control."[21] This call to action made Salmon's work impressive to some. Yet her shaky grasp on economics and sociology left *Domestic Service* vulnerable to expert dismissal, and Salmon reacted badly to the brush-off. She did not vituperate servants, as Harland had in *House and Home*; substituted for that sort of bile, however, were expressions of contempt for the "fundamental ignorance . . . of the processes of reasoning" that *Progress in the Household* claimed to detect in "many housekeepers."[22] This attack marks a departure from the gender inclusivity of *Domestic Service*'s suggestion that "Men and women might better give to the study of domestic service as an occupation the time and energy that now are absorbed in considering the vices and virtues of individual employees."[23] Accompanying *Progress*'s contempt for "many housekeepers"—a phrase that really meant "most privileged women"—was ridicule of guidance offered on the basis of personal experience rather than long, lonely hours of research.

Twenty years younger than the advisors discussed in chapter 5, Salmon enrolled at the University of Michigan a year after *Common Sense in the Household* started its climb into best-sellerdom. Graduating with a BA in 1876, she returned to Ann Arbor in 1882 to work on a master's degree in history and then enjoyed a graduate fellowship at Bryn Mawr. Finding employment at Vassar College once her training was complete, Salmon was surprised by the expectation that she would teach economics as well as history. Trying to juggle classes, research, and an unexpected "prep," she chose to study tension about service as a case of labor strife rather than of feelings or personalities. This choice may seem obvious enough. Yet it marked so clear a departure from Salmon's previous research (on presidential appointments) that it is fair to infer an attempt to make her scholarship responsive to women's real-world needs. The result was *Domestic Service,* an aggregation of history, statistics, and tables but also comments about service excerpted from questionnaires sent to mistresses and attendants. The only previous advisor mentioned in all this was Melusina Peirce; her thoughts on "cooperative housekeeping" were disparaged, however, along with several other proposals for service reform. Today, *Domestic Service* looks a bit of a mishmash. But it was intended to have something Beecher had aimed at long before: scientific authority. "The popular magazine article is theoretical in character," Salmon avowed, but "often proposes remedies for existing evils without sufficient consideration of the causes of the difficulty. Household journals and the home departments of the secular and the religious press usually treat only of the personal relations existing between mistress and maid. The columns of the daily press given to 'occasional correspondents' contain narrations of personal experiences. The humorous columns of the daily and the illustrated weekly papers caricature, on the one side, the ignorance and helplessness of the housekeeper, and, on the other side, the insolence and presumption of the servant." Away with such fluff, *Domestic Service* proclaimed; a new literature of service had come to replace the old.

It was intended, however, not for homemakers but for experts with credentials like Salmon's. "The hope," she averred, was "that writers on economic theory and economic conditions will recognize the place of domestic service among other industries, and will give to the public the results of their scientific investigations of the subject, [so] that the great bureaus of labor . . . will recognize a demand for facts in this field of work."[24]

While this aim was laudable in certain ways, it enacted wholesale and deliberate departure from the position Sarah Josepha Hale had espoused when she suggested in 1834 that "political economy might be taught to the greatest advantage through the medium of romances." A few years later, in the midst of his "domestic & social experiments," Emerson said something comparable: "there must be a new Iliad written," he told Lidian, on the headaches of managing nonkin staff.[25] After emancipation, a satirist suggested that masters and mistresses record every instance of servile illogic. "The result would be a body of comedy which, if preserved, would not only be one of the most amusing pieces of literature in existence, but would throw more light on American civilization and manners in our day than anything the celebrated coming historian will find to his hand."[26] Missing the implied raillery, an essayist of 1872 rested a stale argument about mistress-ship on a survey of the way in which service had been depicted by Plautus, Richardson, Scott, Dickens, Thackeray, and de Tocqueville; shortly thereafter, Marion Harland's success as a novelist was woven into the review opining that "the Shakespeare of cook-books will yet be written by George Eliot." A high school principal in Indiana when this prophecy was made, Salmon could well have pondered this reviewer's observation that "it is almost entirely women who have acquired some reputation in the field of pure literature who have afterwards sought to set off domestic skill with literary charm."[27] But if so, she bucked the trend in 1893 when, as a junior history professor, she published an essay titled "Domestic Service from the Standpoint of the Employee" in *The Cosmopolitan*. This title may sound dull, yet it promised something excitingly different from *Prisoners of Poverty:* information about how service looked to those still laboring in nonkin homes. *Domestic Service* tried to follow up on that promise. But it failed to impress detractors who treated its findings like so much periodical pap.

Central to Salmon's methods was reliance on questionnaires mailed to Vassar alumnae, the replies to which she compared to "the expression at the polls of the wishes of the . . . inhabitants of a state." This method impressed arts-and-letters periodicals such as *The Critic*. *Domestic Ser-*

vice is "largely based," its reviewer explained, "on a series of inquiries sent out a few years since to employers and workers in domestic service, with the object of ascertaining the real condition of the service. Three circulars were prepared, specimens of which are given in the appendix to this volume—one for employers, one for employees, and a third asking for information about the teaching of housework and other phases of the general subject. Replies were received from 1025 employers and 719 employees; and, as they came from all parts of the country, they may be safely taken as fairly representing the condition of the service."[28] This was a bona fide breakthrough for commentators impressed by the "circular" for mistresses that asked, for example, how the respondent would evaluate the service in her own home and whether she had found it difficult to locate good servants and by the one for servants that asked (among other things) about years of service overall and with the present employer, whether other types of work had been pursued, the difference between wages received for service and other jobs, and if the respondent would give up housework if another job came along. Applauding this form of inquiry, *The Dial* hailed Salmon's attempt to debunk the doctrine that "amiability, kindness, and consideration, on the part of individual mistresses, would render the present method of employment tolerable." In contrast, naysayers responded as though nonkin service was a topic beneath serious consideration. "[I]t is far from improbable," *The Nation* scoffed, "that many a woman has made the 'servant problem' a subject of conversation a thousand times, and thus carries with her a wealth of wisdom as great as that attainable through the use of these statistics." Findings Salmon shared might "have some of the interest of gossip," then, "but we cannot assign them that of science."[29]

This was not well informed critique. Certainly Salmon had undertaken a large project for which she had insufficient training. Yet if competence or lack thereof had been the real snag, we would expect to find discussion of her methods among readers trained in data accumulation, analysis, and presentation. The fact that academic journals ignored *Domestic Service* shows that Salmon had failed, in Bruno Latour's terms, to "articulate" her project in such a way that the field of elite knowledge changed. All but mandating that failure, though, was resistance to the premise that nonkin service constituted a form of labor worth the attention given extradomestic employment. That resistance was weakening. But it remained sufficiently powerful that Rubinow and Durant still felt the need to combat it in 1910. Equally pertinent, resistance affected commentary on *The Philadelphia Negro* (1899) to the extent that even glowing reviews said little about Du Bois's trenchant analysis of the state of nonkin attendance, despite this topic's patent significance for a study of the life of African Americans at that time. Accentuating this situation for Salmon were two interrelated variables: the long tradition of advice based on what Rubinow and Durant would call "homiletic virtues," and die-hard notions of middle-class femininity that made the most admirable woman the most embracingly motherlike. A hint of that attitude is found in a posthumous biography that told the world of Salmon's forbearance with a manservant who went on drinking sprees and who could be difficult about what food to cook and who could be invited to dine. In *Apostle of Democracy: The Life of Lucy Maynard Salmon* (1943), Louise Fargo Brown hailed her subject's long and distinguished academic career.[30] Yet by suggesting that compassionate mistress-ship characterized her "private" life, she can be seen as exposing the failure of *Domestic Service*'s depersonalizing campaign.

The attacks on belletrists scattered throughout *Progress in the Household* highlight another sort of failure: *Domestic Service*'s indulgence in wordplay. When, for example, a question directed at employers asked for "Total number of domestic servants employed" over the course of the respondent's experience as a mistress, Salmon quoted one homemaker as replying "infinity-minus" and another as waxing poetic when she directed the professor to "read her answer in the stars." She may have included such things to show that mistresses liked to indulge in self-pity or to demonstrate that some preferred complaining about servants, with literary flourishes, to figuring out how to make things right. This interpretation is complicated, though, by realization that despite printing servants' responses within quotation marks, Salmon could not be sure—having relied on mail-in questionnaires—who had written what she presented as self-expression. Nor did she necessarily care, for one passage in *Domestic Service* bespeaks willingness to cater to those whose ribs were tickled by "darkey" humor. "A shrewd young colored woman gives her version, verbally, of the servant question," this passage begins. "She lays great stress on her own 'bringin' up,' as 'she wa'n't brung up by trash,' and thinks the average colored girl 'only a nigger.' She prefers to live 'at service,' but insists upon 'high-toned' employers, and 'can't abide common folks.'"[31] It may be coincidence that these lines recall "A True Story Repeated Word for Word As I Heard It" (1874), a well-known short story by Mark Twain. But even if coincidence *was* at work in this instance, Salmon's indulgence in such badinage reveals shared ground among an academic effort, Harland's "familiar talks," and the capers at a minstrel show.

This finding does not expose Salmon as an "Old" woman pretending to be "New." It reveals instead that, like most of the writers discussed in this study, she published advice with which her own practices did not always conform, the purpose of which was to guide readers toward new attitudes and ideals. More illuminating, then, than judgments about where and why Salmon clung to less-than-objective gestures is recognition that after claiming to be nonadvisory, *Domestic Service* concluded with suggestions about, for example, profit sharing in the household. There was more than one reason to ignore so radical a scheme. But condemnation of received axioms must have given some readers pause. "No system ever has been or ever will be found that will enable a housekeeper to conduct a household satisfactorily on the instinct or the inspiration theory," *Domestic Service* taught, or "to substitute sentiment for educated intelligence and . . . knowledge of economic conditions outside of the individual home." Whatever the truth of this claim, Salmon's use of it reveals how little she appreciated the fact that a leading strength of counsel from Sedgwick, Gilman, Hale, Beecher, Stowe, Harland, Spofford, and the rest is that these writers presented themselves as very much like their readers: more experienced at homemaking, perhaps, and possibly blessed with literary talent, but not more learned—on the contrary. Upholding this stance, Harland had the mistress-heroine of *The Distractions of Martha* seek guidance from a neighbor who considers servant management a skill learnable by all who devote themselves to making home life pleasant for kin. In stark contrast, a "New Woman" told privileged women to rely on print. "Let every mistress study the causes of her own difficulties and of her maid's incompetence: let her read—not to find fault, but to learn—the literature of the subject." Neighbors might be a help, Mary Roberts Smith admitted, if they could share knowledge of "the principles which should underlie the relations of employer and employed." That, however, was as far as the sharing should be allowed to range, for Smith deemed it imperative that homemakers "flee, as from an intellectual pestilence, the personal reminiscence—when women get together and have an 'experience' meeting, beginning with 'My last girl did so and so,' and ending by pitying themselves and learning nothing."[32]

Learning was paramount for W. E. B. Du Bois as well when he and a research assistant named Isabel Eaton investigated service in the Seventh Ward of Philadelphia. Door-to-door canvassing went well beyond Salmon's mailings to one college's alumnae; equally important, the scope of the Philadelphia project greatly exceeded her focus on servitude.

Above all else, though, the sociological approach mandated attention to race and race-based inequity to such an extent that the fault lines of Salmon's "color blind" questionnaires were fully exposed. "Probably over one-fourth of the domestic servants of Philadelphia are Negroes," Du Bois observed, "and conversely nearly one-third of the Negroes in the city are servants. This makes the Negro a central problem in any careful study of domestic service." The study that mounted this claim won laurels from the *American Journal of Sociology,* the *Yale Review,* and a leading voice in Salmon's field: "Such a study as this should be made in many cities and country districts for comparison," said the *American Historical Review.* Arts-and-letters periodicals were also impressed. "No one of the valuable social studies made by scientific investigators during the last few years equals in interest the study of 'The Philadelphia Negro,'" *The Outlook* announced soon after naming *Domestic Service* "a most valuable and scholarly contribution" to a much smaller discussion.[33]

These judgments must have been a blow to Salmon. Even she must have seen, however, the brilliance with which Du Bois dissected expectations that rested on a blend of memories and dreams. In the present day, he argued, Philadelphia's African American attendants were "principally young people who were using domestic service as a stepping-stone to something else; who worked as servants simply because they could get nothing else to do; [and] who had received no training in service because they never expected to make it their life-calling." Fighting off charges of inborn laziness and incompetence, he added that "to-day the ranks of Negro servants, and that means largely the ranks of domestic service in general in Philadelphia, have received all those whom the harsh competition of a great city has pushed down, all whom a relentless color proscription has turned back from other chosen vocations; half-trained teachers and poorly equipped students who have not succeeded; carpenters and masons who may not work at their trades; girls with common school training, eager for the hard work but respectable standing of shop girls and factory hands, and proscribed by their color." This was stirring prose but, more significantly among Salmon's peers, the product of data-collection methods more sophisticated than her own. If, as I have argued elsewhere, aspersions cast in *Domestic Service* drew a response from African American belletrists, then writers such as Charles Chesnutt and Pauline E. Hopkins were surely guided by the wisdom of *The Philadelphia Negro.*[34]

Less literary commentators competed with Salmon, too. In one such contribution, the daughter of a college president decided to find out who was to blame for the "growls and groans over servants" as the new century dawned. Literary antecedents to Inez Goodman's foray include a pair of servants' tales published before the Civil War. One was narrated by a fictive New Englander who had worked as "help" in her younger days. "I didn't go out 'cause 'twas necessary that I should," she explained, "for at my father's there was a house full of everything. We al'ays lived like the sweet cheeses, as the sayin' is." Three years later, the same periodical had a more refined heroine serve nonkin as a prank. "I insist upon it," the impish belle declares. "'Twill be good sport."[35] Almost fifty years after that, Goodman took up a comparable position in two articles published in the *Independent:* "Ten Weeks in a Kitchen" (1901) and "A Nine-Hour Day for Domestic Servants" (1902). The first recounted a stint of nonkin service to make the point that Goodman's strength was sapped by mistresses' unreasonable demands; the second talked about how easily the situation could be improved if employers would shorten their servants' working days. These summaries show that Goodman hoped to make a reformist contribution to what she called "the perplexing problem which threatens the very existence of our homes." Yet the way in which she chose to make her case had a sentimental sound. "How other women may look upon the subject I do not know," she averred, "but as for myself, I intend that the little domain over which I preside shall be a home, not only for my family, but for my maid. She shall find while under my roof, not only a lodging and a workhouse, but a comfortable home." Some may see diminution here from family-like to "comfortable home." Yet Goodman emphasized the idea that service reform was patriotic. "Norah's hours are from six to eleven a.m., and from four to seven p.m.," her second essay had a mistress-character report after reorganizing a servant's workload so that the live-in "girl" had time to decorate her room, visit kin, and relax with a book. "She read Hale's 'Man Without a Country' last week," this mistress adds proudly, "and came down singing the 'Star Spangled Banner' with great gusto. I feel as if I were manufacturing an American citizen to order."[36] The affective afterglow to Goodman's attempt to develop the ideal of family-like service into something like a civics class could have been cause for Salmon to trivialize her work. The more grievous shortfall, though, would have been her reliance on individual experience and anecdote.

College-educated reformers upheld Salmon's dictate that researchers abjure personalized reflection and affect-oriented opining: "we lose some possibly good housekeepers to make a lot of poor essay-writers," a commentator grumbled in 1900. The fact that Goodman flouted these strictures explains why Salmon slighted such work. "A number of young women have entered domestic service in disguise," *Progress in the Household* reported, "and from personal experience have narrated the life of a domestic employee. It may well be questioned whether the actual results reached are commensurate with the effort expended;—the experiment has meant months of unnatural life and strained relationships, and in the end we probably know little more in regard to the condition of domestic employees than could be known by turning the inner sight of our own consciousness on our own households and those of our acquaintances." Though Salmon softened this criticism slightly with a brisk head-pat—"the experiment has been interesting as indicative of a determined effort to look at the subject from every point of view"—she made it clear that she thought more highly of the efforts of historians, bibliographer-librarians, and statisticians.[37] This is all consistent enough. Yet considering how scrupulously Lillian Pettengill avoided Goodman's missteps, it seems odd that Salmon dismissed *Toilers of the Home: The Record of a College Woman's Experience as a Domestic Servant* (1903). Once it is recognized, however, that she disparaged Pettengill's work as cuttingly as she dismissed Goodman's—though these two writers' efforts were significantly different—it grows hard to think that anybody "simply withdrew" from conflict. More accurate is recognition that gatekeeping had powerful effects.

Pettengill must have been disappointed by Salmon's attitude toward her book since, as a Mt. Holyoke graduate, she had flown her "New Woman" colors high. "The patriarchal idea as a basis for domestic service," *Toilers* announced, "though very pretty in antique setting, is in this age and land of the industrially free a glaring anachronism cradled in snobbery."[38] Equally important, Pettengill had taken the trouble to do research that went well beyond Goodman's weeks of attendance and perusal of the newspaper; in addition, then, to reading *Domestic Service*, she spent two years serving in five different nonkin homes. After all that, she supported several of Salmon's conclusions. Agreement should have pleased Salmon, since *Progress* would complain of (both) plagiarism and neglect. Yet *Toilers* had a few opinions of its own, including advocacy of "day service" and support for servants' unions, that *Domestic Service* had rejected.[39] Equally repellent for Salmon may have been Pettengill's admission that despite holding a prestigious college's degree, she needed a job and took what she could get, only to find that she learned a great deal from her coworkers that could not be culled from books. An indefatigable proponent of women's higher education, Salmon cannot have appreciated that claim.

All the while, there were two specifically literary snags to *Toilers* that may have irked Salmon very much; one had to do with narrative style, the other with self-portraiture. Starting with self-portraiture, one of *Toilers'* recurring themes is how hard it was for Pettengill to transform herself into "the industrial me" when she set out to "look upon the ups and downs of this particular dog-life from the dog's end of the chain." Goodman had made little of her subterfuge, mentioning only the substitution of a shawl for her usual coat and hat. But Pettengill went to greater lengths, including use of an alias, "Eliza," and faked reference letters. Defending the ruse, *Toilers* asserts that the average servant could not tell inquiring mistresses what they ought to know, "and I am likely to wait long before one of her class pictures to the public the conditions of their industrial life. Neither pen nor brush, scrub-brush excepted, has so far been effective in their hands." A related decision had Pettengill recording a fellow immigrant worker's advice in a manner that recalls the Katzenjammer Kids and, later, performing the humble servant archly. "I, who deal only with pots and pans, dare not venture an opinion," this opinionated passage smirks; "Far be it from Eliza even to pretend to know anything about it," another comment preens.[40] If Salmon disapproved of such maneuvering, that may be because Pettengill "belletrized" information that the head of the Vassar History Department wanted to see tabulated and quantified.

Equally important to Salmon's attitude toward *Toilers of the Home* could have been impatience with a form of writing that brings kitchen testimony close to evangelical tracts that took their lead from *Pilgrim's Progress*. This may seem an odd mix. It *was* odd, though, for Pettengill to choose pseudonyms for her mistress-characters that spotlight character flaws. Thus, where the weepy "Mrs. Kinderlieber" expects her servant to supply emotional support, "Mrs. Scharff" lives in constant suspicion of being cheated by her cook and maid. Allegory is an intriguing choice in this context, because it could have been Pettengill's way of trying to turn individual experience into something with the weight of abstracted truth; if so, this strategy hints at hopes of adding to (or even rivaling) Salmon's work. This suggestion clashes, however, with Pettengill's insistence that her experiences be understood as less than representative of what might lie in wait for a recent immigrant, a poorly educated American, a worker whose job options were limited by such things as physical weakness or failure in other fields of endeavor, a person escaping a brutal father or indigent spouse, and so on. Indeed, though *Toilers* does not mention *The Philadelphia Negro*, Pettengill's emphasis on the limits of her investigation suggests acquaintance with Du Bois's arguments about the specific situation of younger African American attendants. That could have been a red flag for Salmon since, despite commending Isabel Eaton's neatly compiled statistics, *Progress in the Household* restricted mention of Du Bois to a bibliographic footnote.

Silence about Du Bois's arguments left a gaping hole in *Progress* even as it exposed the oddity of *Domestic Service*'s claim that it was "unnecessary" to consider "the question of slavery and its relation to the larger subject of service." Though this was not a position that a trained historian should have adopted, it was belied by the pages *Domestic Service* devoted to an account of service labor in the British North American colonies and the United States. One explanation of the oddity and belying is that postsentimentalists had emphasized the relationship between waged and chattel service, but not in the most thoughtful ways; it is hard to imagine many cooks or maids agreeing, for instance, with Harriet Spofford's claim that waged attendance "is far more honorable" in the United States than in other nations, because "here it has been seen in juxtaposition with actual slavery."[41] Even more important than laborers' opinions to the development of Salmon's arguments in *Domestic Service* could have been resistance to conflating waged and chattel forms of labor. It is possible too (though impossible now to verify) that *Progress* abandoned *Domestic Service*'s charge that African Americans from the South were prone to theft, dishonesty, and drink, because Salmon had come to see how much that opinion did to ratify the aspersions cast on the "shiftless sister in black."[42]

Substituted for such things, in Salmon's final contribution to the literature of U.S. service, were potshots at privileged women such as the mistress who declined—on Tiffany's stationery—to respond to a questionnaire on the grounds that such research was "impertinent" and the society matron who misunderstood the thesis of a lecture Salmon gave to her women's club. These cuts-and-thrusts may have elicited "ingroup" chuckles when aired at lectures for "New Women." Just as likely, though, they roused offense among others, especially when collected under the rubric of "progress." In 1902, Harland represented the offended against their college-educated counterparts: "Many . . . are at a loss," she told readers of the *Independent*, "to comprehend how any one who appreciates the difficulties already existing between mistress and maid should deliberately put up an acknowledged barrier" to harmonious service relations by suggesting that many employers treated servants unfairly. She would make a similar argument in the episode in *The Distractions of Martha* that pits a misused mistress against a self-righteous

"Women's Defensive League." This episode was, however, just a plotted-and-characterized retread of the *Independent* article that had portrayed the conflict as one between those who would uphold and those who would tear down valid social hierarchies. "There is," Harland concluded, "no class spirit among us" if privileged women have fallen to the depths of "fostering the idea in the minds of the more ignorant that they must band together for defense against wage-payers."[43] Salmon never responded to this charge; instead, she moved on to new research topics. A survey of U.S. newspapers gave her the authority to publish, from time to time, on historiographical methods.

Salmon's penchant for dispassion lived on in home economics textbooks such as the one that taught that "there is far too frequently an utter disregard of the actual condition of what may be termed the rolling stock of this business. It is economy to keep the machine well oiled, well repaired and well housed."[44] Judgments may differ as to whether "rolling stock" was a more respectful way to refer to servants than were Harland's postsentimental mutterings about "our over-hospitable wharves."[45] Quite obviously, though, both were far cries from the counsel of 1843 that taught that "until the housekeepers learn to look upon their domestics in a higher light than as mere machines intended to go through a certain round of labour, with but little regard either to their feelings or welfare, the present evils will continue to be experienced."[46] This discrepancy bothered some commentators very much, among them the author of *In His Steps* (1896), the best-selling sermon-novel that taught seekers to ask, "What would Jesus do?" "[I]f," Dr. Charles M. Sheldon advised, "the servant in the home, and the woman in the home, will honestly and in a spirit of love to each other sit down to confer together as to the best way in which they can serve each other, it will be a beginning toward better things. There can be no solution of a question as great and serious as the relation of servant to mistress without an appeal to the religious side of life."[47] W. E. B. Du Bois did not agree but did see the efficacy of extolling affect between the serving and served. "Nothing," he attested in 1901, "has come to replace that finer sympathy and love between some masters and house servants."[48] This was not the same as saying, as did a homemaker of his era, that "the family bond which does exist, in greater or lesser degree, between the two classes is worth maintaining."[49] Yet insofar as it was not wholly distinct either, Du Bois's claim suggests the enduring appeal of ideals worked out long ago.

A reform-minded "New Woman" probably meant to critique the soppy side of claims such as Du Bois's when she piled on the gore.

"After I had seen by the light of economic science the stress of the situation from which the servant problem arises," she shuddered in 1900, "all the comfort of our average American home appeared to me horribly stained with the blood of martyred Mary Anns."[50] As Judith Walzer Leavitt has demonstrated, an Irish-born cook *was* martyred to early twentieth-century thinking about nonkin service when journalists dubbed Mary Mallon a "Human Typhoid Germ." Print renderings of "Typhoid Mary" gave Mallon a "notoriety" that, in the words of Alan M. Kraut, "was and remains out of proportion to the sickness or death, or even popular fear, that she caused." Mallon's own behavior played a part in her fame. Overall, though, the materials journalists worked with had less to do with her acts or character than with perceptions of her job and the sort of people who did it. These perceptions had been guided for several previous generations by sentimentalists as different as Sedgwick, Cooper, Gilman, Emerson, and Fitzhugh; challenged by kitchen witnesses as distinctly situated as Jacobs, Garvin, Flowers, Wilson, and Keckley; and shaped again by antisentimentalists sure that U.S. servants were intrusive "foreign" bodies at the heart of home. *Post*-sentimentalists kept alive hopes of the household "gem" who would be family-like. Antisentimentality was definitely in the ascendant, though, when health authorities put "the germ woman" under hospital arrest for decades. Leavitt rightly points out that Mallon's case was handled differently from those of other "healthy carriers" who were food preparers but not cooks in private homes.[51] What I would add to her findings is recognition that immobilization was a return to the practices of the past, with one striking difference: Mallon was barred from pursuing her trade rather than fettered to a post.

Reactions to "Typhoid Mary" can seem a long way from affective literature. It is quite edifying, though, to link dis-ease about an "uppish" cook to inability to replace or counter what Rubinow and Durant called "copy-book maxims" with anything as responsive to the pressures that made nonkin service so baffling a fact of life. Some of those pressures were ideas about gender that splintered over variables of rank, class, and race; others were concepts of labor that hinged on the doctrine that domestic chores were not productive; and yet one more was the supposed (but extreme) sanctity of home and "family" life. Much seemed possible while these contingencies were in flux. Yet cynicism was never lacking. Jokes at sentimentalists' expense were one sign of change; another was postemancipation reference to servants as "children of a larger growth." Shoved offstage by such quips was the concern Sedgwick had shown for in-house workers when she had one servant-character tell another, *"home is home,* and we always hanker after it," even if family-like coresidence leaves the speaker "contented—yes—quite contented."[52]

Awareness of the influence of affective advice literature during the period in which "free" service was irruptively new has lagged for several reasons. Chief among the motivations not to see a body of literature that was neither obscure nor small has been the importance of coming to grips—after generations of neglect and miscomprehension—with the cruel reality of slavery. Vibrant scholarship on U.S. and comparative slavery, along with their various literatures, has begun to proliferate. Downplayed in this body of research, however, is recognition of the extent to which and the ways in which ideas about slavery shaped ideas about service of disparate kinds as well as of mastery and mistress-ship as such things related to home and "family" life. Work of this kind is now under way. Yet any number of good recent articles and books have neglected to consider the full context in which nineteenth-century discussions of nonkin attendance took place. Neglect of this sort makes it possible to examine Brook Farm's attitude toward labor without ever mentioning who swept the bedrooms, to discuss the foppish Adolph in *Uncle Tom's Cabin* (only) in terms of bondage rather than as an example of the manservant Emerson denigrated publicly, and to explore Christy Devon's stint of chambermaiding in *Work* (1873) without taking account of the post- and antisentimental advisors against whose counsel Louisa May Alcott reacted. Nor are literary historians the only offenders, since few accounts of U.S. labor give nonkin service anything like the attention it received in nineteenth-century print. Corrections to these misalignments will clarify the conflict between advisors such as Sedgwick and Beecher and between their writings and those of Robert Roberts, Sophia Ripley, and Eliza Potter as well as Harland, Peirce, Spofford, Campbell, and the rest. In addition, and perhaps more significantly for a greater number of scholars, corrections of this kind will create a richer sense of the milieu in which domestic reforms, rebuttals, and counterproposals were formulated by slave owners and employers but also waged, "bound," and chattel staff. In the process, a richer sense of nineteenth-century U.S. "family" life will be made available to those who strive to understand the past on its own terms. Last but not least, information will be accrued about turn-of-the-century assertions of authority that reprise gender roles in important ways, even as a new sense of the cultural importance of ex-slaves' narratives is made available to those who understand too narrowly the impact that this body of life-writing had in its day.

Comprehension of the uncertainty into which the "invention of free labor" threw discussions of service is the right place to start this project. It must be accompanied, though, by recognition of print influences on accounts such as the story in which a British traveler reported meeting a U.S. citizen who, despite having answered his knock at the door of an inn, rejected his assumption that she was a servitor. "I am no *sarvant*," she supposedly said. "Only *negers* are *sarvants*." This anecdote is rich. Yet it is best understood in terms of Alexander Saxton's notice that an identical opinion had been voiced in an early U.S. drama, Royall Tyler's *The Contrast* (1787).[53] The implication I derive from Saxton's discovery is that thoughts about service did not exist in a sphere unaffected by slavery, any more than the "servant problem" existed in a realm separate from its literature. An entry from a diary of 1851 supports this two-part claim, for it finds the police officer William Bell trying to persuade a teenager to give up prostitution by offering to find her "a good *situation* to *work* in *a respectable family*, where she would be well *provided* for."[54] If one shudders to think what a homemaker was apt to do when told that her new "girl" had been selling sexual favors to the coal-boat crews, the fact that Bell made such an offer measures belief in the affective creed or, at least, lack of compelling alternatives to it. Equally revealing (though of other belief systems and perceived lacks) is the young streetwalker's refusal of a nonkin home.

Refusal of that kind lay outside the ken of sentimental literature, except insofar as abolitionists queried the practicability of the family-like ideal. Salmon was, to some extent, these queriers' heir; unlike anti-slavery activists, however, she could offer no alternative to existing conditions except critiques of others' "visionary theories." This was more than the home economics textbook quoted earlier—"We wish we had some effective solutions to offer!" *Household Management* (1907) shrugged—and more again than Rubinow had come up with the year before: "no remedial scheme is here proposed," he was at pains to clarify.[55] He took a more advisorial stand after hooking up with Durant; by then, however, Salmon had found other interests and Harland had used up her last spurt of outrage. A few Transcendentalists may have smiled slightly in their last, long sleeps upon hearing that no recent experiment had managed to soothe the "uneasy relation of domestics." In contrast, fellow sleepers Catharine Sedgwick and Elizabeth Freeman are unlikely to have stirred, unless "Mumbet" nodded approvingly at the gains that African Americans had made. One era in the literature of U.S. service had come to an end; another was about to begin.

NOTES

Introduction

The epigraph is from Beth G. Crabtree and James W. Patton, eds., *Journal of a Secesh Lady* (Raleigh: North Carolina Division of Archives and History, 1979), 463. Though Catherine Anne Devereux Edmondston liked to congratulate herself (and other Southern mistresses) on training up servants so family-like as to refuse to work for wages or leave their posts, she recorded that a friend's house slaves had "plundered her shamefully . . . old servants, too, in whom she had every confidence" (ibid.).

1. For "none good," see the letter of 1836 quoted in Elisabeth Donaghy Garrett, *At Home: The American Family 1750–1870* (New York: Harry N. Abrams, 1990), 226; for the Alabama woman's comment, see Elizabeth Fox-Genovese's citation from the 1835 diary of slave-mistress Sarah Haynesworth Gayle in *Within the Plantation Household: Black and White Women of the Old South* (Chapel Hill: University of North Carolina Press, 1988), 23.

2. John F. Kasson, *Rudeness & Civility: Manners in Nineteenth-Century Urban America* (New York: Hill & Wang, 1990), 171; and Caroline Howard Gilman, *Recollections of a Southern Matron* (New York: Harper & Brothers, 1838), 81.

3. See Jeanne Boydston, "The Woman Who Wasn't There: Women's Market Labor and the Transition to Capitalism in the United States," in *Wages of Independence: Capitalism in the Early American Republic*, ed. Paul A. Gilje (Madison, Wisc.: Madison House, 1997), 37–39; and James W. Garnett, *Lectures on Female Education* (Richmond, Va.: Thomas W. White, 1825), 79. My thanks to Phil Gura for introducing me to Garnett and kindly making me a present of this book.

4. See the letter of 6 March 1847 in the Alexander-Hillhouse Correspondence in the Southern Historical Collection at the University of North Carolina at Chapel Hill.

5. Eugene Genovese, "'Our Family, White and Black': Family and Household in the Southern Slaveholders' World View," in *In Joy and In Sorrow: Women, Family, and Marriage in the Victorian South, 1830–1900*, ed. Carol Bleser (New York: Oxford University Press, 1991), 84, quotes the Reverend James Smylie's "Review of a Letter from the Presbytery of Chillicothe . . . " (1836).

6. See Helen Stuart Mackay-Smith Marlatt, ed., *Stuart Letters of Robert and Elizabeth Sullivan Stuart and Their Children, 1819–1864*, 2 vols. (Privately printed, 1961), 1:219; and the unsigned "Maids and Mistresses," *Scribner's Monthly Magazine* 6 (September 1873): 628.

7. See Robert J. Steinfeld, *The Invention of Free Labor: The Employment Relation in English and American Law and Culture, 1350–1870* (Chapel Hill: University of North Carolina Press, 1991); and, for adjustments made to English practice during the colonial period, Daniel Vickers, *Farmers and Fishermen: Two Centuries of Work in Essex County, Massachusetts, 1630–1850* (Chapel Hill: Institute of Early American History and Culture, 1994), 232ff. Sharon V. Salinger surveyed the urban side of this snarl in *"To Serve Well and Faithfully": Labor and Indentured Servitude, 1682–1800* (New York: Cambridge University Press, 1987), and Debra O'Neal followed in "Mistresses and Maids: The Transformation of Women's Domestic Labor and Household Relations in Late Eighteenth-Century Philadelphia" (PhD diss., University of California, Riverside, 1994).

8. Richard Parkinson, *A Tour in America, in 1798, 1799, and 1800*, 2 vols. (London: Printed for J. Harding and J. Murray, 1805), 2:422; for an eighteenth-century perspective, see Adolph B. Benson, ed., *Peter Kalm's Travels in North America: The English Version of 1770*, 2 vols. (New York: Wilson-Erickson, 1937), 1:204ff.

9. Though professing to dislike slavery, Anne MacVicar Grant defended the idea that a slaveholder's extended "family" was protective and even loving. See Grant's *Memoirs of an American Lady: With Sketches of Manners and Scenery in America, As They Existed Previous to the Revolution*, 2 vols. (London: Longman, Hurst, Rees, and Orme; and Mrs. H. Cook, 1808), 1:54. Grant's work was republished in Boston and New York in 1809 and then again in Philadelphia, Albany, and New York City in 1836, 1846, and 1876, respectively. *Memoirs* enjoyed such a resurgence at the turn of the century that it was reprinted three times in New York between 1901 and 1909.

10. See Eric Foner, ed., *Great Lives Observed: Nat Turner* (Englewood Cliffs, N.J.: Prentice-Hall, 1971), 95–96; and Mrs. A. J. [Margaret] Graves, *Woman in America: Being an Examination into the Moral and Intellectual Condition of American Female Society* (New York: Harper and Brothers, 1843), 34.

11. The prayer for deliverance was sent up in a letter Sarah Hicks Williams wrote to kin in New York after she married a Southerner and learned to mistress slaves. Williams's letters contrast the rural labor patterns of the North and South to conclude that slaves are less use, and more intrusive, than "help." Yet Williams did not see the antislavery furor as wholly right, for she commented in 1862: "The little folks & 'contrabands' are oppressing themselves with sugarcane." See James C. Bonner, ed., "Plantation Experiences of a New York Woman," *North Carolina Historical Review* 33 (July 1956): 406, and 33 (October 1956): 543.

12. See Harriet Beecher Stowe, "The Chimney-Corner for 1866: Being a Family-Talk on Reconstruction," *Atlantic Monthly* 17 (January 1866): 94.

13. Catharine Maria Sedgwick, *Live and Let Live; or, Domestic Service Illustrated* (New York: Harper & Brothers, 1837), 157; and "A Lady," *Susan Pike; or, A Few Years of Domestic Service* (New York: Chas. S. Francis, 1839), 13.

14. See Mary Louise Kete, *Sentimental Collaborations: Mourning and Middle-Class Identity in Nineteenth-Century America* (Durham, N.C.: Duke University Press, 2000), 105; Lora Romero, *Home Fronts: Domesticity and Its Critics in the Antebellum United States* (Durham, N.C.: Duke University Press, 1997), 6; and [Robert Tomes], "Your Humble Servant," *Harper's New Monthly Magazine* 169 (June 1864): 55.

15. Catherine Kelly, *In the New England Fashion: Reshaping Women's Lives in the Nineteenth Century* (Ithaca, N.Y.: Cornell University Press, 1999), 20.

16. Faye E. Dudden, *Serving Women: Household Service in Nineteenth-Century America* (Middletown, Conn.: Wesleyan University Press, 1983), 1–2; David E. Schob, *Hired Hands and Plowboys: Farm Labor in the Midwest, 1815–1860* (Urbana: University of Illinois Press, 1975), esp. 191–208; and Eugene Genovese, *Roll, Jordan, Roll: The World the Slaves Made* (New York: Pantheon, 1969), 328.

17. Jacqueline Jones provided information about the number of African American female servants laboring in Gilded Age U.S. homes in *Labor of Love, Labor of Sorrow: Black Women, Work and the Family, from Slavery to the Present* (New York: Vintage, 1985), 127–51, while Thomas Dublin reckoned the situation in the North in *Transforming Women's Work: New England Lives in the Industrial Revolution* (Ithaca, N.Y.: Cornell University Press, 1994), 22 and 24.

18. See Mrs. F. D. Gage, "The Housekeeper's Millenium," *Lippincott's Magazine* 4 (July 1869): 78; and Catharine Beecher, "An Appeal to American Women," a piece appended to *The American Woman's Home* (1869). I quote the "Appeal" from Jeanne Boydston, Mary Kelley, and Anne Margolis, eds., *The Limits of Sisterhood: The Beecher Sisters on Women's Rights and Woman's Sphere* (Chapel Hill: University of North Carolina Press, 1988), 250.

19. See Marlatt, *Stuart Letters*, 1:304.

20. Respectively, these are the theses of Carol Lasser's unpublished PhD dissertation, "Mistress, Maid and Market: The Transformation of Domestic Service in New England, 1790–1870" (Harvard, 1982); Dudden, *Serving Women*; and Amy Dru Stanley, *From Bondage to Contract: Wage Labor, Marriage, and the Market in the Age of Slave Emancipation* (New York: Cambridge University Press, 1998).

21. For Stowe's "Trials of a Housekeeper," see *Godey's Lady's Book* 18 (January 1839): 6; for Shammas's insight, see *A History of Household Government in America* (Charlottesville: University of Virginia Press, 2002), 20. Antebellum America's single most important guide to genteel domesticity, *Godey's Lady's Book*, is subsequently cited as *GLB*.

22. For "fad," see I. M. Rubinow, "The Problem of Domestic Service," *Journal of Political Economy* 114 (October 1906): 512; for Elizabeth Barnes's scholarship, see *States of Sympathy: Seduction and Democracy in the American Novel* (New York: Columbia University Press, 1997), 79.

23. For "could not *be* a lady," see Christine Stansell, *City of Women: Sex and Class in New York, 1789–1860* (New York: Alfred A. Knopf, 1986), 161.

24. See Gail Hamilton, *Woman's Worth and Worthlessness* (New York: Harper and Brothers, 1871), 75; Patience Price, "The Revolt in the Kitchen: A Lesson for Housekeepers," *GLB* 76 (February 1868): 142; [Parker Pillsbury], "Domestic Service," *The Revolution* 4 (12 August 1869): 89; and, for "strangers or enemies," Nicholas Wainwright, ed., *A Philadelphia Perspective: The Diary of Sidney George Fisher Covering the Years 1834–1871* (Philadelphia: Historical Society of Pennsylvania, 1967), 532. Fisher's harsh language is the more telling in that there had been a time when he had prided himself on the "good, attached old family servant" working in his home.

25. Harriet Prescott Spofford, "Between the Two Women," *Harper's Bazar* (5 December 1874): 790.

26. Virginia Cary, *Letters on Female Character Addressed to a Lady on the Death of Her Mother* (Richmond, Va.: Ariel Works; and Philadelphia: Towar, J. and D. M. Hogan, 1830), 185. This is where I found Cary's advice, but Sarah E. Newton lists an edition from 1828 attributed to "Mrs. Virginia Carey"; see *Learning to Behave: A Guide to American Conduct Books Before 1900* (Westport, Conn.: Greenwood, 1994), 174.

27. Penned in June 1838, the resonant image of an "uneasy relation" can be found in William H. Gilman et al., eds., *The Journals and Miscellaneous Notebooks of Ralph Waldo Emerson*, 16 vols. (Cambridge, Mass.: Harvard University Press, 1960–82), 7:6. Hereafter, this compendium will be cited as *JMN*.

28. Recent work in the "history of reading," which stresses readerly resistance, includes Scott E. Casper, *Constructing American Lives: Biography and Culture in Nineteenth-Century America* (1999); Elizabeth McHenry, *Forgotten Readers: Recovering the Lost History of African American Literary Societies* (2002); and Barbara Ryan and Amy M. Thomas, *Reading Acts: U.S. Readers' Interactions with Literature, 1800–1950* (2002).

29. Catharine Beecher, *A Treatise on Domestic Economy for the Use of Young Ladies at Home and at School*, 3rd ed. (New York: Harper & Brothers, 1843), 207; and *Letters to Persons Who Are Engaged in Domestic Service* (Leavitt & Trow, 1842), 56. I used the third edition of Beecher's *Treatise*, which was an overhauled version of the first, because it recommends *Letters to Persons* in a footnote on p. 213.

30. See Bruce Robbins, *The Servant's Hand: English Fiction from Below* (New York: Columbia University Press, 1986), xi.

31. Jeffrey Robert Young, *Domesticating Slavery: The Master Class in Georgia and South Carolina, 1670–1837* (Chapel Hill: University of North Carolina Press, 1999), 131. An earlier attempt to derive opinion from expression is Blaine Edward McKinley's PhD dissertation, "'The Stranger in the Gates': Employer Reactions toward Domestic Servants in America, 1825–1875" (Michigan State, 1969).

32. Elizabeth Fox-Genovese quotes Josey King feeling "something nearer" in *Within the Plantation Household*, 133.

33. Thomas had once mistressed staff; indeed, it was only after a stint as First Lady of Texas, followed by widowhood, that she became a servitor. The letter of 5 May 1883 is in her papers at the Perkins Library at Duke University.

34. See Farah Jasmine Griffin, ed., *Beloved Sisters and Loving Friends: Letters from Rebecca Primus of Royal Oak, Maryland, and Addie Brown of Hartford, Connecticut, 1854–1868* (New York: One World, 1999), e.g., 42 and 67; Karen V. Hansen, *A Very Social Time: Crafting Community in Antebellum New England* (Berkeley and Los Angeles: University of California Press, 1994), 44–45; and Anna Smith's letter in the Beecher-Stowe Collection at the Schlesinger Library. Stowe recalled Smith fondly but briefly in the Charles Edward Stowe, ed., *Life of Harriet Beecher Stowe Compiled from Her Letters and Journals* (Boston and New York: Houghton Mifflin, 1889), 200. See also Joan D. Hedrick's analysis of the Stowe-Smith relationship in *Harriet Beecher Stowe: A Life* (New York: Oxford University Press, 1994), 116ff.

35. David S. Reynolds is the scholar who first drew attention to "dark" reform literature; see *Beneath the American Renaissance: The Subversive Imagination in the Age of Emerson and Melville* (New York: Alfred A. Knopf, 1988), esp. 59–84. The most influential dark moralism in the literature of nineteenth-

century U.S. service was that found in abolitionist agitprop; I discuss certain antislavery activists' conflicted relationship to familial rhetoric in chapter 4. See also, however, Patricia Cline Cohen's examination of the legal ramifications of knowing whether a Northern servant had been seduced while working in a nonkin home in *The Murder of Helen Jewett: The Life and Death of a Prostitute in Nineteenth-Century New York* (New York: Alfred A. Knopf, 1998), 183–96.

36. "Mrs. Clarissa Packard" [Caroline Howard Gilman], *Recollections of a Housekeeper* (New York: Harper & Brothers, 1834), 151; and Sedgwick, *Live and Let Live*, 92. Regarding the latter, see also the note in a sketch Sedgwick wrote for kin: "Providence makes our homes Irish school-houses!" Mary Kelley published it in *The Power of Her Sympathy: The Autobiography and Journal of Catharine Maria Sedgwick* (Boston: Massachusetts Historical Society, 1993), 52.

37. Stephanie Coontz, *The Social Origins of Private Life: A History of American Families, 1600–1900* (New York: Verso, 1988), 13; Jeanne Boydston, *Home and Work: Housework, Wages, and the Ideology of Labor in the Early Republic* (New York: Oxford University Press, 1990), 99–100; and, for "affair," Drew Gilpin Faust's quotation from the writings of proslavery intellectual Nathaniel Beverley Tucker in *A Sacred Circle: The Dilemma of the Intellectual in the Old South, 1840–1860* (Baltimore: Johns Hopkins University Press, 1977), 121.

38. I am aware of Mary P. Ryan's assertion that Sedgwick wrote as a republican moralist rather than a sentimental didact. I agree that Sedgwick was a moralist. I think, though, that because *The Empire of the Mother: American Writing about Domesticity, 1830–1860* (1982) was written before scholars had scrutinized the politics of sentimental fiction, Ryan conceptualized this body of work primarily in terms of depreciated stylistic gestures; for example, she points to the use of "flowery prose" (30).

39. See Nell Irvin Painter, *Sojourner Truth: A Life, A Symbol* (New York: W. W. Norton, 1996), 59.

40. The inscription on Freeman's gravestone is slightly different; it was probably amended by Sedgwick's brother, Charles. I use the version in Catharine Sedgwick's handwriting that was saved among her papers; see Kelley, ed., *The Power of Her Sympathy*, 71; but also Sister Mary Michael Welsh, *Catharine Maria Sedgwick: Her Position in the Literature and Thought of Her Time up to 1860* (Washington, D.C.: Catholic University of America, 1937), 107.

41. For Du Bois's claim of kinship with the woman he called "Mom Bett," see *Dusk of Dawn* (Millwood, N.Y.: Kraus-Thompson, 1975), 111–13. This autobiography was first published in 1940. For a different remembrance of Freeman, see David Levering Lewis, *W. E. B. Du Bois: Biography of a Race, 1868–1919* (New York: Henry Holt, 1993), 14.

42. Preserved in a letter of 1836, Sedgwick's opinion is quoted in Bertha-Monica Stearns, "Miss Sedgwick Observes Harriet Martineau," *New England Quarterly* 7 (September 1934): 538. Child's opinion of Sedgwick is found in a letter, too; see Milton Meltzer and Patricia G. Holland, eds., *Lydia Maria Child: Selected Letters, 1817–1880* (Amherst: University of Massachusetts Press, 1982), 506.

43. See Mrs. Julia McNair Wright, *The Complete Home: An Encyclopaedia of Domestic Life and Affairs* (Philadelphia, Cincinnati, Chicago, and St. Louis: J. C. McCurdy, 1879), 447; and Oliver E. Lyman, "The Legal Status of Servant-Girls," *Popular Science Monthly* 22 (April 1883): 806–7.

44. See Harriet Prescott Spofford, "Help in Macedonia," *Harper's Bazar* (1 September 1877): 546. Garrette Brown was kind enough to explain to me the scriptural allusion in this essay's title; it recalls an angel who visited Paul (e.g., Acts 16:9).

45. Flora McDonald Thompson, "The Servant Question," *The Cosmopolitan* 28 (March 1900): 521.

46. Hasia R. Diner provides statistics to the effect that immediately before the Civil War, "Irish women cornered the domestic market in Milwaukee, Janesville, and Madison, Wisconsin. In that same decade a staggering 80 percent of all women engaged in paid household labor in New York City had come from Ireland." See Hasia R. Diner, *Erin's Daughters in America: Irish Immigrant Women in the Nineteenth Century* (Baltimore: Johns Hopkins University Press, 1983), 89. For the prevalence of African American female servants after the Civil War, see David M. Katzman, *Seven Days a Week: Women and Domestic Service in Industrializing America* (Urbana and Chicago: University of Illinois Press, 1981).

47. James L. Roark quotes the Rev. John Jones in *Masters without Slaves: Southern Planters in the Civil War and Reconstruction* (New York: W. W. Norton, 1977), 143.

48. See Thompson, "The Servant Question," 521.

49. Lucy M. Salmon, "Economics and Ethics in Domestic Service," as reprinted in *Progress in the Household* (Boston and New York: Houghton, Mifflin, 1906), 113–14. This essay first appeared in two installments, May and June 1898, of "Woman's Council Table," a section of *The Chautauquan.*

Chapter 1: The Family Work

Lucy Maynard Salmon quotes the original edition of *An American Dictionary of the English Language* in *Domestic Service* (New York: Macmillan, 1897), 71fn. I discuss Salmon's important contribution to the literature of U.S. service in the Epilogue.

1. The envious glance across the Mason-Dixon Line, from 1837, can be found in W. Emerson Wilson, ed. *The Mount Harmon Diaries of Sidney George Fisher, 1837–1850* (Wilmington: Historical Society of Delaware, 1976), 5. While waged, "bound," and chattel servants were all working in the slaveholding states in the 1830s, journal entries that Fisher wrote while in Maryland suggest that this praise was for slaves. On the fluidity of service arrangements in regions close to the border between slave and "free" states, see Stephanie Cole, "Servants and Slaves: Domestic Service in the Border Cities, 1800–1850" (PhD diss., University of Florida, 1994). Finally, for Sedgwick's recollection, see the remarks quoted in Mary Kelley, ed., *The Power of Her Sympathy: The Autobiography and Journal of Catharine Maria Sedgwick* (Boston: Massachusetts Historical Society, 1993), 51–52.

2. See Prof. E. A. Andrews, *Slavery and the Domestic Slave-Trade in the United States* (Boston: Light & Stearns, 1836), 34; William C. Taylor, *Cavalier and Yankee: The Old South and American National Character* (New York: Oxford University Press, 1957), 18; and, for an alert response to Taylor, Eric Foner, *Free Soil, Free Labor, Free Men: The Ideology of the Republican Party before the Civil War* (New York: Oxford University Press, 1970), 68–69.

3. See Henry Barnard's admiring comments on chattels' unintrusive service as collected in Bernard C. Steiner, ed., "The South Atlantic States in 1833, As Seen by a New Englander," *Maryland Historical Magazine* 13 (December 1918): 319.

4. [Catharine Maria Sedgwick], *A New-England Tale; or, Sketches of New-England Character and Manners* (New York: E. Bliss & E. White, 1822), 22.

5. This comment appeared first in an entry on Sedgwick that was published in volume 1 of the *National Portrait Gallery of Distinguished Americans* put out by James Barton Longacre and James Herring in 1834 and edited more recently by Robert G. Stewart (New York: Arno Press and the New York Times, 1970). The piece was republished but mistitled as "Caroline Maria Sedgwick" in *The American Ladies' Magazine* 8 (December 1835): 657–65. Twenty years later, it reappeared in Sarah Josepha Hale, *Woman's Record; or, Sketches of All Distinguished Women, from the Creation to A.D. 1854* (New York: Harper, 1855), 777. My thanks to Charlene Avallone for bringing this publishing history to my attention.

6. Though written in 1822, this diary entry was not published until the 1870s, a decade in which complaints about servants were much in vogue. See H. E. Scudder, ed., *Recollections of Samuel Breck* (Philadelphia: Porter & Coates, 1877), 299.

7. C. Dallet Hemphill, *Bowing to Necessities: A History of Manners in America, 1620–1860* (New York: Oxford University Press, 1999), 139.

8. See Catharine Maria Sedgwick, *Home* (Boston and Cambridge: James Munroe, 1835), 119.

9. [Jonas Hanway], *Advice from Farmer Trueman, to His Daughter Mary, upon Her Going to Service* (Boston: Munroe & Francis, 1810), 96. John Harold Hutchins explored Hanway's reform interests in *Jonas Hanway, 1712–1786* (New York: Macmillan, 1940).

10. See the unsigned *A Friendly Gift for Servants and Apprentices* (New York and Baltimore: Samuel Wood, 1821), 8. According to the authoritative electronic database WorldCat, the author of this little guide, first published in 1808, was Elizabeth Franks.

11. [Ann Martin Taylor], *The Present of a Mistress to a Young Servant* (Philadelphia: Carey, 1816), 3. Sarah Newton lists, with annotation, a few more titles in Taylor's corpus; like the *Present*, most were addressed to girls. However, Taylor's usual stance was that of a mother rather than a mistress. See Sarah E. Newton, *Learning to Behave: A Guide to American Conduct Books Before 1900* (Westport, Conn.: Greenwood, 1994), 138.

12. See [Taylor], *Present of a Mistress*, 15. Though published just once in the United States, this guide was republished in Great Britain in 1822 and 1835.

13. See Kelley, *The Power of Her Sympathy*, 126.

14. The Clements Library at the University of Michigan in Ann Arbor holds a fascicle made up of these two tracts sewed to a third called *Helps to Self-Examination*.

15. If William had been less of a solitaire, John Saillant might say, he would have been less erotically attractive to a white man. For a dazzling interpretation of *The African Servant* as an example of the literature of sexual slavery, see John Saillant, "The Black Body Erotic and the Republican Body Politic, 1790–1820," in *Sentimental Men: Masculinity and the Politics of Affect in American Culture*, ed. Mary Chapman and Glenn Hendler (Berkeley and Los Angeles: University of California Press, 1999), 89–111.

16. I quote William's story from a collection titled *The Dairyman's Daughter, the Young Cottager, and the African Servant* (New York: American Tract Society, n.d.), where this rumination appears on 17–18. It is worth noticing, though, that William's story was published under three different monikers. Printers in Great Britain usually called this tract "The Negro Servant," while publishers in New York and New England used "The Negro Servant" and "The African Servant" interchangeably. The third sobriquet, "The Officer's Servant," was the choice of the United States Christian Commission when it reprinted William's story in Philadelphia during the Civil War. So well liked was this tract that it was published in Welsh, German, and Spanish before being transposed into the syllabic characters of Cherokee.

17. One of Sedgwick's first stops, when she made a trip to England as an adult, was at Richmond's house. See Catharine Maria Sedgwick, *Letters from Abroad to Kindred at Home* (New York: Harper & Brothers, 1841), 1:22.

18. [James Fenimore Cooper], *The Spy: A Tale of the Neutral Ground*, 2 vols. (New York: Wiley & Halstead, 1821), 1:42.

19. Ibid., 1:14.

20. See [James Fenimore Cooper], *The Pioneers, or the Source of the Susquehanna*, 2 vols. (New York: Charles Wiley, 1823), 1:219.

21. The fan letter from Richard Henry Dana is collected in James Fenimore Cooper, ed., *Correspondence of James Fenimore-Cooper* (New Haven: Yale University Press, 1922), 1:93.

22. For an episode in which Cooper was irritated by the flight of teenaged human property, see Alan Taylor, *William Cooper's Town: Power and Persuasion on the Frontier of the Early American Republic* (New York: Alfred A. Knopf, 1995), 379. I am grateful to Dr. Taylor for sharing with me pieces of his research while it was in manuscript.

23. My knowledge of Stewart's life rests on Paul S. D'Ambrosio and Charlotte M. Evans, *Folk Art's Many Faces* (Cooperstown: New York State Historical Association, 1987), 84. That generous scholar, Elizabeth L. O'Leary, shared this essay with me.

24. [Catharine Maria Sedgwick], *Mary Hollis* (New York: Van Pelt and Spear, 1822), 21.

25. [Catharine Maria Sedgwick], *Redwood* (New York: E. Bliss and E. White, 1822), 1:183.

26. See J. H. Ingraham, *The Sunny South; or, The Southerner at Home, Embracing Five Years' Experience of a Northern Governess in the Land of the Sugar and the Cotton* (Philadelphia: G. G. Evans, 1860), 118.

27. I take the neologism "Vermontese" to be a witty riff on "Piedmontese," noted Swiss freedom fighters (e.g., William Tell).

28. See [Catharine Maria Sedgwick], "Slavery in New England," *Bentley's Miscellany* 34 (1853): 421–22; but also Richard E. Welch Jr., "Mumbet and Judge Sedgwick: A Footnote to the Early History of Massachusetts Justice," *Boston Bar Journal* 8 (January 1964): 13–19.

29. This finding is the work of P. A. M. Taylor, "A Beacon Hill Domestic: The Diary of Lorenza Stevens Berbineau," *Proceedings of the Massachusetts Historical Society* 98 (1986): 90–115. Though I have seen nothing that clarifies Berbineau's racial heritage, I take her to have been (or to have passed for) white,

since antebellum employers often noted the race and ethnicity of any worker who was not obviously Anglo.

30. See [Catharine Maria Sedgwick], *Clarence; or, A Tale of Our Own Times*, 2 vols. (Philadelphia: Carey & Lea, 1830), 1:120; and Mary E. Dewey, *The Life and Letters of Catharine M. Sedgwick* (New York: Harper, 1871), 40.

31. [Sarah Savage], *Advice to a Young Woman at Service in a Letter from a Friend* (Boston: John B. Russell, 1823), 25–26, 28–29, 8, 12, and 14. *Advice* was reprinted in New York in 1823 and again in Boston in 1825. Margaret Moore provides information about Savage's biography and literary output in "Sarah Savage of Salem: A Forgotten Writer," *Essex Institute Historical Collections* 127 (1991): 240–59.

32. For a good account of the holdings at the Charleston Library Society, see Jay B. Hubbell, *The South in American Literature, 1607–1900* (Durham, N.C.: Duke University Press, 1954), 183–84. For a more recent examination of circulation records that reveal what residents of two Southern cities liked to read, see Emily B. Todd, "Antebellum Libraries in Richmond and New Orleans and the Search for the Practices and Preferences of 'Real' Readers," *American Studies* 42 (Fall 2001): 195–209, noticing especially the reference to Sedgwick on p. 203.

33. Arthur Singleton, Esq. [Henry Cogswell Knight], *Letters from the South and West* (Boston: Richardson and Lord, 1824), 73.

34. See Virginia Cary, *Letters on Female Character Addressed to a Lady on the Death of Her Mother* (Richmond, Va.: Ariel Works; and Philadelphia: Towar, J. and D. M. Hogan, 1830), 203.

35. See Sarah Josepha Hale, *Northwood: A Tale of New England*, 2 vols. (Boston: Bowles & Dearborn, 1827), 1:211.

36. A white, sometimes sharp-tongued spinster said to exert a "most despotic rule over all the subordinates of the family," Barbara Winkle has much in common with Remarkable Pettibone of *The Pioneers*. Kennedy specifies, however, that as "a functionary of high rank in the family, and of great privileges," Winkle is granted "the civility of a place at table." In contrast, Heath depicts Katy Waddle as a form of property, a servant who "had fulfilled the office of pantry queen for so long a period, that she was now considered as a kind of freehold appendage, or heir-loom in the family." See John Pendleton Kennedy, *Swallow Barn; or, a Sojourn in the Old Dominion*, 2 vols. (Philadelphia: Carey & Lea, 1832), 2:225, 1:38–39, 1:76, and 1:78; and *Edge-Hill; or, The Family of the Fitzroyals* (Richmond, Va.: T. W. White, 1828), 7.

37. See John S. Hart, "Catherine [sic] M. Sedgwick," *Female Prose Writers of America* (Philadelphia: E. H. Butler, 1852), 18; and Hale, *Woman's Record*, 777.

38. See Edward Halsey Foster, *Catharine Maria Sedgwick* (New York: Twayne, 1974), 77. Foster does not comment on the several story fragments in Sedgwick's papers that describe episodes in which a vicious mistress wounds an old family slave (who is innocent, dignified, and female) in the upper arm.

39. See Catharine Maria Sedgwick, *Hope Leslie; or, Early Times in the Massachusetts*, 2 vols. (New York: White, Gallaher, and White, 1827), 1:58 and 1:105. A note on the character of Digby, an English manservant: though I initially understood his presence in the novel as a hint that it need not be unmanly to serve, I was edified by Philip Gould's argument that he signifies instead as a poor historian. This view makes him a sort of male Jennet: loose-lipped and danger-

ous when unmastered. See Philip Gould, *Covenant and Republic: Historical Romance and the Politics of Puritanism* (Cambridge: Cambridge University Press, 1996), 70–72.

40. Sedgwick, *Hope Leslie*, 1:233 and 232. A note of interest: as if some had queried the abuse heaped on Jennet, Sedgwick added a footnote to *The Linwoods* (a novel of 1835) to the effect that the name she gave this character did not mean "ass" but only "a small horse."

41. See "Mrs. Clarissa Packard" [Caroline Howard Gilman], *Recollections of a Housekeeper* (New York: Harper & Brothers, 1834), 151; the unsigned "filler" piece, "Hints about Help," *American Ladies' Magazine* 9 (November 1836): 621; and Sedgwick, *Hope Leslie*, 2:233.

42. Laura Wexler, "Tender Violence: Literary Eavesdropping, Domestic Fiction, and Educational Reform," in *The Culture of Sentiment: Race, Gender, and Sentimentality in Nineteenth-Century America*, ed. Shirley Samuels (New York: Oxford University Press, 1992), 17.

43. Charles A. Hammond notes that Roberts "invested in several houses and . . . lived a comfortable existence until his death in 1861." See the Foreword to Robert Roberts, *The House Servant's Directory* (Needham, Mass.: Q Marketing Limited for the Gore Place Society, 1977), iii.

44. See Robert Roberts, *The House Servant's Directory* (Boston: Munroe and Francis; New York: Charles S. Francis, 1827), 155 and ix.

45. Roberts, *The House Servant's Directory*, 155. The British guide, *The Cook's Oracle* by William Kitchiner, was reprinted in New York and Boston between 1822 and 1855.

46. Ibid., 69.

47. Marilyn Richardson, *Maria W. Stewart: America's First Black Woman Political Writer* (Bloomington: Indiana University Press, 1987), 45.

48. Ibid., 46. For a hint that another African American writer agreed, see Frank J. Webb's *The Garies and Their Friends* (1857), a novel in which a doddering black butler-character is named "Mr. Robberts."

49. On "free" servants' ability to save, see Faye E. Dudden, *Serving Women: Household Service in Nineteenth-Century America* (Middletown, Conn.: Wesleyan University Press, 1983), 222; and Hasia R. Diner, *Erin's Daughters in America: Irish Immigrant Women in the Nineteenth Century* (Baltimore: Johns Hopkins University Press, 1983), 90–94.

50. For the literary inclination of Southern schoolgirl Mary Early, see Kelley, "Reading Women/Women Reading: The Making of Learned Women in Antebellum America," *Journal of American History* 83 (September 1996): 401–24; and Marli F. Weiner, *Mistresses and Slaves: Plantation Women in South Carolina, 1830–1880* (Urbana: University of Illinois Press, 1998), 57.

51. Kathryn Kish Sklar discusses Beecher's knowledge of Sedgwick in *Catharine Beecher: A Study in American Domesticity* (New York: W. W. Norton, 1973), 44–46 and 176–77; whereas Caroline Howard Gilman pondered *The Linwoods* in "Editor's Boudoir," *Southern Rose* (31 October 1835): 38–39. Portions of *Recollections of a Southern Matron* (a novel by Gilman that will be examined presently) appeared in this edition of her juvenile periodical.

52. Foster quotes Hawthorne in *Catharine Maria Sedgwick*, 20.

53. See Thomas R. Dew's "Review of the Debate in the Virginia Legislature, 1831-'32," as reprinted in *The Pro-Slavery Argument*, ed. William Gilmore Simms (Charleston: Walker, Richards, 1852), 325–26. The letter dated 2 July

1833 is in the Sedgwick Papers at the Massachusetts Historical Society. Use of the term "blight" appears in a letter Gladys Brooks quoted without attribution in *Three Wise Virgins* (New York: E. P. Dutton, 1957), 202.

54. Frances Trollope, *Domestic Manners of the Americans*, 2 vols. (London: Whittaker, Treacher, 1832), 2:50–51; and the review of *Means and Ends* in *Brownson's Quarterly Review* (July 1839): 389. For a contrasting opinion, see "American Women," *United States Magazine and Democratic Review* 6 (August 1839): 128; and for mockery of both views, see "Notices and Intelligence," *Christian Examiner* 27 (September 1839): 134–35.

55. See [Sedgwick], *Clarence*, 1:80.

56. The unsigned "French Servant Maids" was a reprint from the English *Tatler*; see *GLB* 6 (March 1833): 141.

57. On Sedgwick's probes of masculinist thinking, see, for instance, Mary Kelley's introduction to *Hope Leslie* (New Brunswick, N.J.: Rutgers University Press, 1987), xxi–xxvii; chapter 4 of Dana D. Nelson, *The Word in Black and White: Reading "Race" in American Literature, 1638–1867* (New York: Oxford University Press, 1992); and Gould, *Covenant and Republic*, 64–90.

58. Evidence that Sedgwick hoped to placate and thus perhaps win a hearing from slaveholders—or even, perhaps, that she accepted aspects of the sentimental proslavery platform—is Jupe, a slave-character in *The Linwoods* who has no interest in being freed. See Catharine Maria Sedgwick, *The Linwoods; or, "Sixty Years Since"* (New York: Harper & Brothers, 1835), 224.

59. See Kelley, *The Power of Her Sympathy*, 155.

60. A prominent man of letters (and short-term Brook Farmer), George William Curtis said that Sedgwick's didactic novellas marked "an era in our literature"; see "Editor's Easy Chair," *Harper's New Monthly Magazine* 35 (October 1867), 665. He could have added that *Home* was printed fifteen times in six years, while *Live and Let Live* managed twelve editions in less than twenty-four months; see Foster, *Catharine Maria Sedgwick*, 117.

61. The comment about *Home* appears in Sedgwick's journal; see Kelley, *The Power of Her Sympathy*, 150. She mentioned the man reading *Live and Let Live* in a letter dated 23 March 1854; see Dewey, *Life and Letters*, 352.

62. See Sedgwick, *Home*, 72.

63. For more information as to who was serving nonkin where, see Thomas Dublin, *Transforming Women's Work: New England Lives in the Industrial Revolution* (Ithaca, N.Y.: Cornell University Press, 1994), 160, 183, and 202.

64. Sedgwick made this notation in her journal in 1835; see Kelley, *The Power of Her Sympathy*, 150.

65. See Sedgwick, *Home*, 7–8. To complete this survey of Sedgwick's didactic novellas, I must mention that service relationships are peripheral to the plot of *The Poor Rich Man and the Rich Poor Man*. However, when they do appear, they show that good people are served well, while selfish people have unending trouble even if they are rich.

66. *Ann Connover* (Philadelphia: American Sunday-School Union, 1835), 83 and 14.

67. See [Savage], *Trial and Self-Discipline* (Boston and Cambridge: James Munroe, 1835), 19 and 27, noting that the portrait of Phillis is authenticated in the frontispiece. This servant-character, Savage affirmed, "has been drawn without exaggeration" from a real person, "intimately known to the writer through the long period of more than thirty years" (n.p.). *Trial and Self-*

Discipline was printed three times in Boston in 1835 and once in London two years later.

68. For Gilman's memory, see the autobiographical sketch she wrote for Hart's *Female Prose Writers*, 56; while for the brief but admiring review, see "Critical Notices," *The New England Magazine* 8 (February 1835): 156.

69. See [Gilman], *Recollections of a Housekeeper*, chap. 5 and p. 52.

70. Ibid., 80–83.

71. Ibid., 148; and Caroline Howard Gilman, *Recollections of a Southern Matron* (New York: Harper & Brothers, 1838), 40, 100 and 237.

72. Qtd. in Mary Scott Saint-Amand, *A Balcony in Charleston* (Richmond, Va.: Garrett and Massie, 1941), 3.

73. See Sedgwick, *Means and Ends; or, Self-Training* (Boston: Marsh, Capen, Lyon and Webb, 1839), 102 and 15. This jab could have been influential since, according to bibliographer Sarah Newton, *Means and Ends* was a "popular text, often referred to by other conduct writers." See Newton, *Learning to Behave*, 190.

74. See the unsigned notice in *North American Review* 47 (October 1838): 489–91.

75. As far as can be judged from print, Hale's admiration for Sedgwick was less fulsome but rested on similar evaluative standards. "Miss Sedgwick," she observed, "remains among the front rank of those earnest and sincere writers whose talents have been employed for the purpose of doing good." See Hale, *Woman's Record*, 670–71 and 778.

76. The pairing and retitling reappeared in editions of 1852, 1854, 1867, and 1889; intriguingly enough, after the Civil War the Matron's recollections preceded those of the New England Bride. Noteworthy in this context is Gilman's comment in the preface to the first edition of her second novel. "The 'Southern Matron' was penned," she wrote, "in the same spirit, and with the same object, as the 'New-England Housekeeper'" (n.p.).

77. Linking *Northwood*'s republication to Daniel Webster's death, William C. Taylor discussed Kennedy's and Hale's revisions in *Cavalier and Yankee*, 138–39 and 187–88.

78. See [Gilman], *Recollections of a Housekeeper*, 130; and, for Mary Kelley's thoughts on Sedgwick's and Gilman's reactions to the tensions associated with feminine authorship, *Private Woman, Public Stage: Literary Domesticity in Nineteenth-Century America* (New York: Oxford University Press, 1984), 126 and 129ff.

79. On Gilman's exposure to slavery before moving to South Carolina, see her autobiographical sketch in Hale, *Woman's Record*, 671; but also Elizabeth Moss, *Domestic Novelists of the Old South: Defenders of Southern Culture* (Baton Rouge: Louisiana State University Press, 1992), 37. For "home of my choice," see the letter of 8 July 1837 (?) in the Gilman Papers at the American Antiquarian Society.

80. See also Daniel Walker Howe's thoughts on Samuel Gilman—which include notice of his small salary and growing conservatism—in "A Massachusetts Yankee in Senator Calhoun's Court: Samuel Gilman in South Carolina," *New England Quarterly* 44 (June 1971): 197–220. Howe's work is complemented by the unpublished letter in which Caroline Gilman doubts the news that Sarah and Angelina Grimké had freed their slaves. "[E]very one says," she wrote, "they

parted with them by sale." This letter, dated 5 June 1838, is in the Gilman Papers at the American Antiquarian Society.

81. Mary Alice Wyman shows little interest in the probability that slaves hired by the Gilmans would have had to turn their earnings over to their owner or at least defray expenses for their "keep," while Mary Scott-Amand's portrait of philanthropic Northerners is countered by Jan Bakker's sense that this plan was only put into effect "occasionally." See Wyman, *Selections from the Autobiography of Elizabeth Oakes Smith* (Lewiston, Maine: Lewiston Journal Co., 1924; repr., New York: Arno, 1980), 77; Saint-Amand, *A Balcony in Charleston,* esp. 15–16 and 117–18; and Bakker, "Caroline Gilman and the Issue of Slavery in the Rose Magazines, 1832–1839," *Southern Studies* 24 (Fall 1985): 274.

82. See Harriet Martineau's *Autobiography,* ed. Maria Chapman, 2 vols. (London: Smith, Elder, & Co., 1877), 2:21. In the letter of 1838 cited just above, Gilman said that she itched to rebut Martineau's remarks about U.S. slaveholders but preferred to hold herself above controversy.

83. See the letter dated 28 April 1828 in Dewey, *Life and Letters,* 195.

84. Sedgwick, *Home,* 72.

85. Sedgwick, *Live and Let Live,* 80–81.

86. Alexis de Tocqueville, "How Democracy Affects the Relations of Masters and Servants," *Democracy in America,* 2 vols. (New York: Vintage, 1990): vol. 2, book 3, chap. 5. This section of de Tocqueville's ruminations was first published in 1840.

87. See Sedgwick, *Live and Let Live,* 21–22.

88. Ibid., 141; and Dewey, *Life and Letters,* 256.

89. Channing's letter of 19 August 1837 is quoted in Dewey, *Life and Letters,* 270; while *Godey's* made its thoughts known in "Editor's Table," *GLB* 15 (September 1837): 140. A comparable review opined: "Such works as this of Miss Sedgwick must do good. She has spoken, we doubt not, to the conscience of many a householder." See *American Monthly Magazine* (July 1837): 395–96.

90. See "Literary Notices," *Knickerbocker or New York Monthly Magazine* 10 (July 1837): 86; realizing, too, that when A. Potter, DD, wrote a preface to *Wales and Other Poems* (1839), a collection of verse by a "free" serving-woman named Maria James, he mentioned Sedgwick rather than Gilman, Savage, or Cooper as the authority on nonkin attendance whom his readers would most likely recognize with respect.

91. "Miscellaneous Notices," *American Quarterly Notice* 22 (September 1837): 254; "Art. 5. *Live and Let Live,*" *New-York Review* 1 (October 1837): 457; and *JMN,* 5:503.

92. See W. A. Alcott, *The Young Wife; or, Duties of Woman in the Marriage Relation* (Boston: George W. Light, 1837), 131 and 159; while for "rotten," see Alcott, *Ways of Living on Small Means* (Boston: Light & Stearns, 1837), 29.

Chapter 2: Domestic and Social Experiments

The epigraph is from "Home" in Robert E. Spiller and Wallace E. Williams, eds., *The Early Lectures of Ralph Waldo Emerson,* 3 vols. (Cambridge, Mass.: Harvard University Press, 1972), 3:33.

1. For "woes," see Ralph L. Rusk and Eleanor Tilton, eds., *The Letters of Ralph Waldo Emerson*, 9 vols. (New York: Columbia University Press, 1939–94), 3:154; while for "social position," and the stab at abolitionists—both from May 1838—see *JMN*, 5:502 and 5:505.

2. This passage, dated 28 September 1837, was used in two Emerson essays, "Doctrine of the Hands" and "Fortune of the Republic." See Merton M. Sealts Jr.'s editorial comments in *JMN*, 5:379.

3. See *JMN*, 7:6, an entry dated 8 June 1838.

4. *JMN*, 7:536; this entry, written in December 1840, was lifted almost verbatim into "Man the Reformer."

5. See Rusk and Tilton, *Letters*, 2:370.

6. Emerson delivered the lecture "Religion" in Boston on 22 January and in Concord on 24 April 1840. It is collected in Spiller and Willams, *Early Lectures*, 3:275.

7. Chapters 5 and 6 of Carole Shammas, *A History of Household Government in America* (Charlottesville: University of Virginia Press, 2002); chapters 4, 5, and 6 of Jeanne Boydston, *Home and Work: Housework, Wages, and the Ideology of Labor in the Early Republic* (New York: Oxford University Press, 1990); Roediger, The *Wages of Whiteness: Race and the Making of the American Working Class* (London and New York: Verso, 1991), 5off.

8. See Len Gougeon, *Virtue's Hero: Emerson, Antislavery, and Reform* (Athens: University of Georgia Press, 1990), 37–40; and Robert D. Richardson Jr., *Emerson: The Mind on Fire* (Berkeley and Los Angeles: University of California Press, 1995), 269.

9. See Sarah Josepha Hale, "Sketches of American Character: The Springs," *The Ladies' Magazine* 1 (August 1828), 348.

10. According to Spiller and Williams, "Reforms" was delivered in Boston on 15 January and in Concord on 22 April 1840; the idea's first appearance is in a journal entry dated 28 June 1839. See *Early Lectures*, 3:264, and *JMN*, 7:220; and, for "influenza," see Rusk and Tilton, *Letters*, 2:387.

11. William Alexander Caruthers, *The Kentuckian in New-York; or, The Adventures of Three Southerns*, 2 vols. (New York: Harper & Brothers, 1834), 1:116.

12. On domestic workers' recompense during the antebellum period, see Christine Stansell, *City of Women: Sex and Class in New York, 1789–1860* (New York: Alfred A. Knopf, 1986), 115ff. and 156; but see also Faye E. Dudden, *Serving Women: Household Service in Nineteenth-Century America* (Middletown, Conn.: Wesleyan University Press, 1983), 65–66, 84, 95–98, 101, 143, 182, 219–25, and 237.

13. *JMN*, 7:197.

14. See Achille Murat, *The United States of North America* (London: Effingham Wilson, 1833), 5; and Alexis de Tocqueville, "How Democracy Affects the Relations of Masters and Servants," *Democracy in America*, 2 vols. (New York: Vintage, 1990): 2:179.

15. See *JMN*, 7:229 and 7:420.

16. Charles Butler, Esq., *The American Lady* (Philadelphia: Hogan & Thompson, 1836), 219.

17. See *JMN*, 7:420 and 5:285.

18. Ellen Tucker Emerson, *The Life of Lidian Jackson Emerson*, ed. Delores Bird Carpenter (Boston: Twayne, 1980), 48. I have corrected an "of of" in the printed text.

19. See Lidian's unpublished letter of 22 September 1835 to her sister Lucy in the Emerson Family Papers at the Houghton Library; see also *JMN*, 5:479, a passage dated 24 April 1838.

20. Lidian may have been dilatory due to a fond hope that servants would run her home without supervision. "We have prayers in the morning," she told her sister,

> a little before 7—breakfast at 7—then I hold a consultation with Nancy about dinner and can go to my work reading or writing without further care. We dine exactly at one. Mr E & myself then set about writing letters if there are any to write or finish—for the mail at 3—then I take my nap—and then my walk with Mr E. or to see Aunt Mary—or she comes here—or I sit down alone to my occupations. . . . We drink tea at six—half an hour before which Mr E. issues forth from his sanctum to sit the blind-man's-holiday with me. In the evening he brings down his work and I take mine and after talking a bit we "make a mum" and keep it till 9 o'clock when we call the girls and have prayers.

See E. T. Emerson, *Life of Lidian Jackson Emerson*, 63; and Delores Bird Carpenter, ed., *The Selected Letters of Lidian Jackson Emerson* (Columbia: University of Missouri Press, 1987), 38.

21. Underlining of the word "love" may bespeak an attempt to reassure Waldo that all was well, despite upsets, between his cook and his wife; see Carpenter, *Selected Letters of Lidian Jackson Emerson*, 45, for the letter of April 1836.

22. Ibid., 34.

23. Ibid., 7.

24. See Catherine Kelly, *In the New England Fashion: Reshaping Women's Lives in the Nineteenth Century* (Ithaca, N.Y.: Cornell University Press, 1999), 35.

25. For Martha Coffin Wright's letter, see Jeanne Boydston, *Home and Work: Housework, Wages, and the Ideology of Labor in the Early Republic* (New York: Oxford University Press, 1990), 77.

26. Ralph Waldo Emerson, "Man the Reformer," *Works*, 14 vols. (Boston and New York: Houghton and Mifflin Riverside Editions, 1870–78), 1:228.

27. See *JMN*, 12:67.

28. Ibid., 7:242.

29. See "Home," Spiller and Williams, eds., *Early Lectures*, 3:32.

30. The undated letter from Louisa Snow Jacobs to Lidian Emerson is in the Emerson Family Papers at the Houghton Library. It was probably written in November 1853 as a thank-you for presents to the new mother that included a christening gown. Jacobs signs off, "My Love to Gran-ma and my children," in what is presumably a reference to the Emersons' offspring. "Gran-ma" is more ambiguous since, while it probably denoted Ruth Emerson (Waldo's mother), it could have been a tender joke for Jacobs's own mother, who also worked for the Emersons. It was Sarah Snow who requested permission for Jacobs to name her daughter after Lidian.

31. Catharine Maria Sedgwick, *Live and Let Live; or, Domestic Service Illustrated* (New York: Harper & Brothers, 1837), 17.

32. See *Ann Connover* (Philadelphia: American Sunday-School Union, 1835), 20–21; and William Alcott, *The Young Woman's Guide to Excellence* (Boston: Charles H. Pierce, 1847), 35–37. Note that Alcott, as if to keep social ranks in their proper places, adds an explanatory coda: "I will not, indeed, say that any thing like as much credit is due to her as to him; but I may say, and with truth, that she was an important auxiliary in producing the results that have been mentioned" (37).

33. See Emerson, *Life of Lidian Jackson Emerson*, 71–72.

34. Rusk and Tilton, *Letters*, 7:437, recognizing that the words "& failures" are an insertion to the line; see Tilton's "Editorial Treatment," ibid., 7:xiii. Though Tilton considers this letter an early draft of the one planned for George and Sophia Ripley and says that Rusk's letter for the same date is closer to the missive sent, her comments are conjectural. I have quoted statements from both letters, since each provides a slant on Emerson's refusal to join Brook Farm.

35. For "arithmetic," see the letter tentatively dated 21 October 1840, as reprinted in Rusk and Tilton, *Letters*, 2:350; while for "must do alone," see *Letters*, 2:369–70. Note that the "solidly do" sentence is repeated verbatim in *Letters*, 7:437, so that it appears in both drafts of the refusal.

36. David Leverenz, *Manhood and the American Renaissance* (Ithaca, N.Y.: Cornell University Press, 1989), 74.

37. The list appears in R. W. Emerson, *JMN*, 7:115. A passage that seems to derive from it can be found in "The Protest," a lecture delivered in Boston on 16 January and in Concord on 3 April 1839.

38. For Colesworthy's request, see *JMN*, 5:338.

39. "Tragedy" debuted in Boston in January 1839 and was read again in Concord in April of that year; see Spiller and Williams, *Early Lectures*, 3:109.

40. Horace Greeley, "Anti-Slavery and Courtesy," *Daily Tribune* (20 June 1845): n.p.

41. See *JMN*, 5:382 and 9:120; the latter is dated, with a query, 1844 or 1845.

42. Annie Russell Marble discusses this non-coresidence in *Thoreau: His Home, Friends and Books* (New York: Thomas Y. Crowell, 1902), 112; so does Madelon Bedell, *The Alcotts: Biography of a Family* (New York: Clarkson N. Potter, 1980), 160–61. See also Rusk and Tilton, *Letters*, 2:371 (noting that key phrases from Emerson's refusal to join Brook Farm reappear in the letter that announces plans to welcome the Alcotts to "Bush"); and Abby's letter, dated 4 April 1841, in the Alcott Family Papers at the Houghton Library. I use the name "Abby" because that is how she signed her letters; "Abba" was what Bronson called her.

43. See Carpenter, *Selected Letters of Lidian Jackson Emerson*, 62.

44. See, in this context, John Tosh, *A Man's Place: Masculinity and the Middle-Class Home in Victorian England* (New Haven, Conn.: Yale University Press, 1999), 60ff. Tosh's study of the domestic lives of Englishmen of Emerson's era describes the "stay-at-home husband" whose daily presence "could be positively destructive" of domestic, and even conjugal, harmony.

45. See Rusk and Tilton, *Letters*, 7:375; and Carpenter, *Selected Letters of Lidian Jackson Emerson*, 86.

46. "If one of the maids left to be married," a memoirist recalled of nineteenth-century Boston, "a sister or cousin usually turned up to take her place."

See Louisa Crowninshield Bacon, *Reminiscences* (Salem, Mass.: privately printed, 1922), 34; cf. W. Emerson Wilson, ed., *The Mount Harmon Diaries of Sidney George Fisher, 1837–1850* (Wilmington: Historical Society of Delaware, 1976), 304.

47. Rusk and Tilton, *Letters*, 2:279.

48. In *Letters*, 7:375, Emerson says that McCaffery's chores were to include yard work, carpentry, and care of poultry and horses but also the domestic job of child-minding. Later, he would direct that the boy be paid a cash settlement of thirty dollars for a year's work, though the same had already been spent to transport and outfit him; see Rusk and Tilton, *Letters*, 2:387.

49. Rusk and Tilton, *Letters*, 2:382. Cf. the Salem Female Charitable Society's willingness to ignore its charges' parents as administrators thought best, in Carol Lasser's unpublished PhD dissertation, "Mistress, Maid and Market: The Transformation of Domestic Service in New England, 1790–1870" (Harvard, 1982), 44ff.

50. See Sedgwick, *Live and Let Live*, 90–91; and E. B. Beecher, *All Around the House; or, How to Make Homes Happy* (New York: D. Appleton, 1878), 313. Note the latter's expression of pity for former servants who are unhappy in their married lives since husbands cannot support them in the genteel ways to which they became accustomed while serving in middle-class homes.

Information on the books in the Emerson family library in 1882 can be found in Walter Harding, *Emerson's Library* (Charlottesville: University Press of Virginia, 1967); this source reveals that "Lydian" acknowledged ownership of the 1851 edition of Beecher's *Treatise*.

51. The quotation actually has Waldo Jr. saying that "she eats at a table which is not painted," meaning a table that does not have the color and gleam of mahogany. The "which" in this sentence suggests the input of an adult scribe. See Emerson, *Life of Lidian Jackson Emerson*, 78–79.

52. See *JMN*, 7:541.

53. The servant willing to dine with the Emersons was Louisa Snow (later Jacobs); see Rusk and Tilton, *Letters*, 2:389.

54. See *JMN*, 7:421, and Abby's letter of 4 April 1841 in the Alcott Family Papers, Houghton Library, Harvard University, Cambridge, Massachusetts.

55. Catharine Maria Sedgwick, *Home* (Boston and Cambridge: James Munroe, 1835), 72; and William A. Alcott, *The Young House-keeper; or, Thoughts on Food and Cookery* (Boston: George W. Light, 1838), 43.

56. Theodore Parker, "Thoughts on Labor," *The Dial* (April 1841): 506.

57. These passages can be found in Bradford Torrey and Francis H. Allen, eds., *The Journal of Henry David Thoreau*, 14 vols. (Salt Lake City, Utah: Peregrine Smith, 1984), 1:253 and 1:299.

58. For the letter to Lucy Jackson Brown (Lidian's married sister), see Walter Harding and Carl Bode, eds., *The Correspondence of Henry David Thoreau* (New York: New York University Press, 1958), 76.

59. Rusk and Tilton, *Letters*, 2:402 and 3:158.

60. See Henry David Thoreau, "The Laws of Menu," *The Dial* (January 1843): 331–40. Sherman Paul believes that Thoreau had read Menu by December 1839, the period in which he was formulating an essay titled "The Service" but before he went to live at "Bush." See Sherman Paul, *The Shores of America: Thoreau's Inward Exploration* (Urbana: University of Illinois Press, 1958), 71.

61. The letter to Lucy Jackson Brown is in Harding and Bode, *Correspondence of Henry David Thoreau*, 47.

62. See Paul, *The Shores of America*, 95; Robert D. Richardson Jr., *Henry Thoreau: A Life of the Mind* (Berkeley and Los Angeles: University of California Press, 1986), 103; and Richardson, *Emerson: The Mind on Fire*, 346.

63. It may be relevant that Hawthorne thought himself rightly spared intrusion on his working life. Pausing one day in 1843 to notice that the house was quiet with his wife away, he remarked: "how Molly [the cook] employs herself, I know not. Once in a while," he added, "I hear a door slam like a thunder-clap; but she never shows her face, nor speaks a word, unless to announce a visiter [*sic*] or deliver a letter. This day, on my part," he concluded with apparent satisfaction, "will have been spent without exchanging a syllable with any human being." See the journal entry quoted in Randall Stewart, ed., *The American Notebooks of Nathaniel Hawthorne* (New Haven, Conn.: Yale University Press, 1932), 178–79. Hawthorne's evaluation of the situation at "Bush" is found on p. 176.

64. "To be of most service to my brother," Thoreau told his journal in one comment of this sort, "I must meet him on the most equal and even ground, the platform on which our lives are passing. But how often does politeness permit this?" See Paul, *The Shores of America*, 18; and, for the journal entry penned just before Thoreau moved into "Bush," Torrey and Allen, *Journal of Henry David Thoreau*, 1:206.

65. For "contingences," see Torrey and Allen, *Journal of Henry David Thoreau*, 1:190, recognizing that a similar passage, which includes the housekeeper, appears in "Wednesday," a chapter in Thoreau's *A Week on the Concord and Merrimack Rivers* (1849). For Thoreau's comments about serving in New York, see Harding and Bode, *Correspondence of Henry David Thoreau*, 114 and 112.

66. For Thoreau's remarks, see Harding and Bode, *Correspondence of Henry David Thoreau*, 78 and 84; and for Emerson's claim, see *JMN*, 8:165. Harding and Bode call the story of Apollo and Admetus "one of Thoreau's favorite symbols" but do not observe that he used it most frequently during his term as an unhired man. Cf. Emerson's use of similar imagery in 1836 (*JMN*, 5:208–9).

67. Noteworthy, in this context, are the different ways in which the Emerson children addressed various nonkin coresidents. Thoreau was hailed by his first name, accompanied by a courtesy title. "Uncle Henry takes care that Edie [i.e., Edith, the Emersons' second daughter] shall take as high flights in Papa's absence as ever," Lidian told Waldo while he was away on a trip; "she rides on his shoulders or is held high up in the air." In contrast, Sarah Snow (who served the Emersons as a child nurse and seamstress, and whose daughter Louisa was mentioned earlier) seems to have been called "Aunt Snow." The relative ages of Thoreau and Snow would have been a factor here. See Lidian's letter to her husband dated 1 February 1843 and the letter of 16 April 1865 to Lidian from Snow. Both are in the Emerson Family Papers at the Houghton Library.

68. According to Wendell Glick, Thoreau reviewed Etzler's book at Emerson's request, intending his work as a piece for *The Dial*. Glick provides more information in "Paradise (To Be) Regained: Textual Introduction," *Reform Papers* (Princeton, N.J.: Princeton University Press, 1973), 275.

69. Fourierists looked on Etzler more favorably. Carl Guarneri notes that after reading Etzler, Associationist Albert Brisbane "harbored the dream of a huge

mechanized farm for the rest of his life." See Guarneri, *The Utopian Alternative: Fourierism in Nineteenth-Century America* (Ithaca, N.Y.: Cornell University Press, 1991), 125; and Thoreau, "Paradise (To Be) Regained," 26 and 40.

70. See *JMN*, 9:127.

71. Henry David Thoreau, "The Landlord," in *The Writings of Henry David Thoreau*, 20 vols. (Boston and New York: Houghton and Mifflin, 1906): 5:153–54. Subsequent quotations from this essay are found on p. 156.

72. Steven Fink, *Prophet in the Marketplace: Thoreau's Development as a Professional Writer* (Princeton, N.J.: Princeton University Press, 1992), 111.

73. See Amy Schrager Lang, *The Syntax of Class: Writing Inequality in Nineteenth-Century America* (Princeton, N.J.: Princeton University Press, 2003), 10; and Rusk and Tilton, *Letters*, 3:124, 3:155, and 3:190. So family-like was Louisa Snow that, in a letter written in 1842, she notified Lidian of the likelihood of another servant leaving to give her mistress a chance to ask around about a replacement before returning to Concord. This letter is in the Emerson Family Papers at the Houghton Library.

74. See *JMN*, 9:127.

75. Ralph Waldo Emerson, "Emancipation in the British West Indies," *Works*, 11:133; but see also Lydia Maria Child's judgment that a lecture Emerson delivered in 1843 was "not *satisfactory*" since it painted "such a glowing and graceful picture of Southern manners and character, that I might have supposed he considered arbitrary power one of the most beneficial influences on man. I should not have quarreled with this," she concluded, "had he made the least allusion to any *bad* effects." The opinion of 21 February is reprinted in Milton Meltzer and Patricia G. Holland, eds., *Lydia Maria Child: Selected Letters, 1817–1880* (Amherst: University of Massachusetts Press, 1982), 189.

76. Emerson, "Emancipation in the British West Indies," 11:133.

77. Unsigned "Hints about Help," *American Ladies' Magazine* 9 (November 1836): 621.

78. See Sedgwick, *Live and Let Live*, 41.

79. Mrs. A. J. [Margaret] Graves, *Woman in America: Being an Examination into the Moral and Intellectual Condition of American Female Society* (New York: Harper and Brothers, 1843), 135.

80. This argument was not peculiar to publications such as *Godey's*; on the contrary, cf. James Dawson Burns, *Three Years among the Working-Classes in the United States during the War* (London: Smith, Elder, 1865), 7 and 80; Thomas Butler Gunn, *The Physiology of New York Boarding-Houses* (New York: Mason Brothers, 1857), 168; and Graves, *Woman in America*, 133.

81. See Sarah Josepha Hale, *"Boarding Out": A Tale of Domestic Life* (New York: Harper & Brothers, 1846), 43; Eliza Leslie, "Annetta Haverstraw," *GLB* 26 (February 1843): 84; Graves, *Woman in America*, 24; and Gunn, *Physiology*, 298.

82. Daniel T. Rodgers reviewed the nineteenth-century taste for attacks on privileged women in *The Work Ethic in Industrial America, 1850–1920* (Chicago: University Chicago Press, 1974), 182–209.

83. For the "hungry hawk," see Anon., "Mrs. Mapletoft's Lodger," *GLB* 14 (March 1837): 128–33.

84. This harpy goes on to smirk, in the next installment, that "Bad men are often very good boarders" in that "they pay well, and with such I have made

money." See [Marie Turner], "The Boarding-House," *GLB* 16 (June 1838): 260, and *GLB* 17 (September 1838): 100.

85. Sarah Josepha Hale, *Keeping House and Housekeeping: A Tale of Domestic Life* (New York: Harper & Brothers, 1845), 39.

86. See ibid., 45; and [Hale], *"Boarding Out,"* 113.

87. For statistics on boardinghouses, see Mark Peel, "On the Margins: Lodgers and Boarders in Boston, 1860–1900," *Journal of American History* 72 (March 1986): 818. Looking at boardinghouses along with lodging houses (only the former provided meals), Peel finds that 927 were recorded in Boston alone in 1860, while more than 2,700 were in operation by 1900. This means that during the period in which pundits inveighed against these supposedly unhomely homes, "hotels and boardinghouses made up 69 percent of tenant housing" in just one city.

88. For Hale's living arrangements, see Ruth E. Finley's finding that Oliver Wendell Holmes's "Lady in Black Bombazine" was Hale. The "Lady" was a regular in his sketches about boardinghouse life; these were collected as *The Autocrat of the Breakfast-Table* (1859). Finley, *The Lady of Godey's: Sarah Josepha Hale* (Philadelphia: J. B. Lippincott, 1931), 97.

89. Stowe's impatience may have grown with recognition that she and her husband had intended to cut the household budget rather than institute labor reform. "Our first idea," she recollected, "was merely you know to take in one family of agreeable people with whom we were acquainted to lessen expenses & now it turns out that I have my house full of entire strangers . . . what a home to return to." Stowe's letter of July 1844 is in the Beecher Family Papers at the Schlesinger Library. The passage about "all sorts of company" can be found in T. S. Arthur, "Tired of Housekeeping," *GLB* 20 (March 1840): 139; while the story by Hale is "Mrs Morey," *The Ladies' Magazine* 7 (January 1834): 1–12.

90. See Emerson, *Life of Lidian Jackson Emerson*, 106–7; Rusk and Tilton, *Letters*, 3:331, for Waldo's sense of this last experiment; and, for the headcount of servants at "Bush," Richardson, *Emerson: The Mind on Fire*, 466 and 507.

91. See R. W. Emerson, "Domestic Life," *Works*, 7:113. Notes on this text, which include conjecture as to its dates and provenance, can be found on pp. 374ff.

92. See Harding and Bode, *Correspondence of Henry David Thoreau*, 119–21 and 189.

93. John Angell James, *The Family Monitor; or, A Help to Domestic Happiness* (Boston: Crocker and Brewster; New York: Jonathan Leavitt, 1833), 190–91; the *Liberator* of 8 October 1858 as quoted in Ronald G. Walters, "The Erotic South: Civilization and Sexuality in American Abolitionism," *American Quarterly* 25 (May 1973): 183; and William B. English's *Rosina Meadows, the Village Maid; or, Temptations Unveiled* (1843). The last is the story of a country girl who is nearly decoyed into prostitution by the employment agency that sends her to a brothel although she had been seeking service work. She is rescued by a kindly old gentleman but eventually ends up in a boardinghouse that is even worse; there, Rosina dies after being seduced.

94. Carpenter prints the teasing letter to Emerson, dated tentatively January 1863, in *Selected Letters of Lidian Jackson Emerson*, 220.

95. Ibid., 139–40. This letter is dated 29 February 1848.

96. See the letter of 3 March 1844 in George Willis Cooke, ed., *Early Letters of*

George Wm. Curtis to John S. Dwight: Brook Farm and Concord (New York and London: Harper & Brothers, 1898), 154.

97. Parke Godwin, *A Popular View of the Doctrines of Charles Fourier* (New York: J. S. Redfield, 1844), 58.

Chapter 3: *Educated Friends, Working*

This chapter's epigraph is from Theodore Parker, "Thoughts on Labor," *Dial* (April 1841): 506.

1. For the opinion of "A Gentleman," see *The Laws of Etiquette; or, Short Rules and Reflections for Conduct in Society* (Philadelphia: Carey, Lea and Blanchard, 1836), 185; while for "boot, perhaps," see William Gilmore Simms, "Morals of Slavery," as reprinted in Simms, ed., *The Pro-Slavery Argument* (Charleston: Walker, Richards, 1852), 214.

2. The mockery of "would-be democrats" is from Parke Godwin, *A Popular View of the Doctrines of Charles Fourier* (New York: J. S. Redfield, 1844), 58; while the description of Brook Farm appears in the letter of 9 November 1840 reprinted in O. B. Frothingham, *George Ripley* (Boston: Houghton Mifflin, 1883), 310. Emerson indicated recognition that the Ripleys shared his concern about "free" attendance, for, in his refusal letter, he made certain they realized that "The institution of domestic hired service is to me very disagreeable." See Ralph L. Rusk and Eleanor Tilton, eds., *The Letters of Ralph Waldo Emerson*, 9 vols. (New York: Columbia University Press, 1939–94), 7:436.

3. For "collision of caste," see J. Homer Doucet, "Reminiscences of the Brook Farm Association," as reprinted in Joel Myerson, ed., *The Brook Farm Book: A Collection of First-Hand Accounts of the Community* (New York and London: Garland Publishing, 1987), 226; while for Ripley's "true church," see the stepping-down letter in Frothingham, *George Ripley*, 81.

4. Frederick Pratt recalled "no *hired help*" in an account first published in the *New England Quarterly* in 1975; Joel Myerson republished Pratt's memories as "Two Unpublished Reminiscences of Brook Farm," *The Brook Farm Book*, 330–31. Pratt's parents were founding members of the Brook Farm community; his brother John would marry Anna Alcott.

5. Don C. Seitz quoted the comments of Charles A. Dana in *Horace Greeley: Founder of the New York Times* (Indianapolis: Bobbs-Merrill,1926), 120.

6. For "odious," see [Albert Brisbane,] "The Question of Slavery," *Harbinger* 1 (21 June 1845): 30.

7. John Thomas Codman, *Brook Farm: Historic and Personal Memoirs* (Boston: Arena Publishing Company, 1894), 10.

8. A later memoirist remembered things differently, for he suggested that the hired cook did not leave but died. First published in *The Atlantic Monthly* in 1878, Amelia Russell's memories were reprinted in book form as *Home Life of the Brook Farm Association* (Boston: Little, Brown, 1900), 60–61; see also Arthur Sumner, "A Boy's Recollections of Brook Farm," *New England Magazine* 10 (May 1894): 313.

9. See Georgianna Bruce Kirby's "Reminiscences of Brook Farm" in Myerson, *The Brook Farm Book*, 142. Kirby's recollections were first published in 1871 and 1872 in the magazine *Old and New*.

10. See Ralph Waldo Emerson, "Historic Notes of Life and Letters in Massachusetts," *Atlantic Monthly* 52 (October 1883): 534 and esp. 540; but see also "A Member of the Community" [George P. Bradford], "Reminiscences of Brook Farm," *Century* 45 (November 1892): 141.

11. For example, despite spending much time and thought distinguishing between what Charles Lane and Bronson Alcott hoped for from Fruitlands, Richard Francis overlooks the possibility that George and Sophia Ripley had dreams even slightly disparate for Brook Farm. See Francis, *Transcendental Utopias: Individual and Community at Brook Farm, Fruitlands, and Walden* (Ithaca, N.Y.: Cornell University Press, 1997), chaps. 5 and 6; but see also Robert Hardy, "'Housekeeping hereafter': The Preservation of Domesticity in Technological Utopia," *Journal of Utopian Studies* 13 (Spring 2002): 53–67.

12. Codman, *Brook Farm*, relates canine Carlo's death on p. 245 before defending four unnamed Brook Farmers' conversion to Catholicism on the next two pages. For Jenny Franchot's arguments, see *Roads to Rome: The Antebellum Protestant Encounter with Catholicism* (Berkeley and Los Angeles: University of California Press, 1994), esp. chap. 15; while for Carole Shammas's thoughts, see *A History of Household Government in America* (Charlottesville: University of Virginia Press, 2002), 178.

13. Henrietta Dana Raymond quotes this letter in *Sophia Willard Dana Ripley: Co-Founder of Brook Farm* (Portsmouth, N.H.: Peter E. Randall, 1994), 48.

14. Jeanie Attie discusses the *Treatise*'s civic agenda in *Patriotic Toil: Northern Women and the American Civil War* (Ithaca, N.Y.: Cornell University Press, 1998), 9–12; while "resolute unsentimentality" appears in Barbara Ehrenreich and Deirdre English, *For Her Own Good: 150 Years of the Experts' Advice to Women* (Garden City, N.Y.: Anchor Books, 1979), 168. Catharine Beecher's advice was published in her *A Treatise on Domestic Economy for the Use of Young Ladies at Home and at School*, 3rd ed. (New York: Harper & Brothers, 1843), 50 and 207.

15. The studies of sentimentality named range from chapter 2 of Fisher, *Hard Facts: Setting and Form in the American Novel* (1985), to Noble, *The Masochistic Pleasures of Sentimental Literature* (2002), and Brodhead, *Cultures of Letters: Scenes of Reading and Writing in Nineteenth-Century America* (1993). Meanwhile, the report of molasses spills can be located in Stephen Garrison and Joel Myerson, eds., "Elizabeth Curson's Letters from Brook Farm," *Resources for American Literary Study* 12 (Spring 1982): 4.

16. The comment about Minerva and Venus can be found in Frothingham, *George Ripley*, 312; while Sedgwick's references to Chesterfield appear in *Live and Let Live; or, Domestic Service Illustrated* (New York: Harper & Brothers, 1837), 72 and 120. For one of nineteenth-century advice literature's most egregious looks to the past, see "Masters and Servants," a *Godey's* piece of August 1856 that reprinted counsel from 1743. Here, an anonymous pundit (Sarah Josepha Hale?) claimed to see "excellent . . . advice . . . as applicable to-day as in the hour in which it was first published." The advice was that servants owed gratitude to those who provided them with homes.

17. "The Brook Farmers did not interpret the words 'the poor ye have always with ye' to mean 'ye must always keep some of your poor,'" George William Curtis explained in 1869. "They found the practical Christian," he added, "in him who said to his neighbor, 'Friend, come up higher.'" Emerson affirmed this

rendering years later. "It was a noble and generous movement in the projectors to try an experiment of better living," he avowed. "At the same time, it was an attempt to lift others with themselves, and to share the advantages they should attain with others now deprived of them." See Curtis, "Editor's Easy Chair," *Harper's New Monthly Magazine* 38 (January 1869): 271; and Emerson, "Historic Notes of Life and Letters in Massachusetts," 540.

18. Albert Brisbane, *A Concise Exposition of the Doctrine of Association* (New York: J. S. Redfield, 1843), 53; and Catharine Beecher, *Letters to Persons Who Are Engaged in Domestic Service* (Leavitt & Trow, 1842), 168–69.

19. See Nicole Tonkovich, *Domesticity with a Difference: The Nonfiction of Catharine Beecher, Sarah J. Hale, Fanny Fern, and Margaret Fuller* (Jackson: University of Mississippi Press, 1997), 128ff; and Beecher, *Letters to Persons*, 94.

20. Beecher, *Letters to Persons*, 68 and 34.

21. See George Willis Cooke, ed., *Early Letters of George Wm. Curtis to John S. Dwight: Brook Farm and Concord* (New York and London: Harper & Brothers, 1898), 45–46; Nathaniel Hawthorne's letter of 18 July 1841 is reprinted in Henry W. Sams, ed., *Autobiography of Brook Farm* (Gloucester, Mass.: Peter Smith, 1974), 22; and Frothingham, *George Ripley*, 71.

22. Raymond quotes the letter to John Dwight, dated 9 February 1840, in *Sophia Willard Dana Ripley*, 23.

23. Kate Sloan Gaskill discussed nicknames for Sophia and Marianne Ripley in "A Girl's Recollections of Brook Farm School," a piece first published in 1918; see Myerson, *The Brook Farm Book*, 306; while Codman recalls Sophia's dignity (he gestures toward the word "haughtiness") in *Brook Farm*, 17.

24. For resentment of kitchens, see Cooke, *Early Letters*, 157; and for the charge of dilettantism, see Lindsay Swift, *Brook Farm: Its Members, Scholars, and Visitors* (New York: Corinth Books, 1961; originally published in 1900), 86–87.

25. See, for instance, Nora Schelter Blair, "Two Unpublished Reminiscences," in Myerson, *The Brook Farm Book*, 337; and Ora Gannett Sedgwick, "A Girl of Sixteen at Brook Farm," *Atlantic Monthly* 85 (March 1900): 399–400.

26. For Emerson's remark see *JMN*, 8:393, noting that he thought the Ripleys were entitled to the "moral consideration" earned by the fact that they had staked their all on the reform community others could abandon summarily. "They have married it & they are it," he opined.

27. Raymond excerpted this letter in *Sophia Willard Dana Ripley*, 46–48.

28. Though quite possibly apocryphal, this anecdote corroborates reports that Sophia was temperamentally unsuited to a maternal role. See George William Curtis, "The Editor's Easy Chair," *Harper's New Monthly Magazine* 61 (September 1880): 634; but see also Kirby, "Reminiscences of Brook Farm," in Myerson, *The Brook Farm Book*, 155.

29. For "idol," see Raymond, *Sophia Willard Dana Ripley*, 8; while for "Woman," see *The Dial* (January 1841): 365–66.

30. Beecher, *A Treatise on Domestic Economy*, 61–62.

31. S. Ripley, "Woman," 363.

32. For Fuller's remark to W. H. Channing, which is part of a missive dated 25 and 28 October 1840, see Robert N. Hudspeth, ed., *The Letters of Margaret Fuller*, 6 vols. (Ithaca, N.Y., and London: Cornell University Press, 1983), 2:174; meanwhile, Edith Roelker Curtis quoted the letter that mentions Barker in *A Season in Utopia* (New York: Thomas Nelson & Sons, 1961), 54.

33. Though published anonymously, the "Letter" about Zoar has long been attributed to Sophia; see *The Dial* (July 1841): 122–29. Raymond excerpts the letter to Emerson in *Sophia Willard Dana Ripley*, 49.

34. Though accustomed during her father's lifetime to live-in service, Russell became a stockholding member of Brook Farm in her midforties. As if recognizing the criticisms that decision might arouse decades later, she represented herself as understanding little about the group's theories or goals and said nothing about the nieces she accompanied to Brook Farm. Russell added, however, that she grew to esteem Brook Farm's vision of friend-service, over time, and made a point of recalling life at the farm as "really very monotonous" rather than a scene of constant horseplay. See Russell, *Home Life*, 21–22, recognizing that praise of Sophia and remembrances of monotony were probably intended to rebut sniping put into print by Georgianna Kirby.

35. For "common parlance," see the refusal to allow a woman to work at the Boston Athenaeum that Carol Lasser quotes in her unpublished PhD dissertation, "Mistress, Maid and Market: The Transformation of Domestic Service in New England, 1790–1870" (Harvard, 1982), 114; while for Sophia's letter of 6 May 1841 to John Dwight, see Raymond, *Sophia Willard Dana Ripley*, 31.

36. This paragraph's quotations can be found in Beecher, *Letters to Persons*, 12–14 and 34.

37. Ibid., 72, 93, 100, 48, and 55; note also the reference to white slaves on p. 94. This last is particularly intriguing in light of Carol Lasser's discovery that an "old maid who had worked as a domestic in the home of Dr. Lyman Beecher found herself shunted aside in her old age." See Lasser, "Mistress, Maid and Market," 197; see also Kathryn Kish Sklar's discussion of Beecher's upbringing amidst "bound" attendants as well as white and black household "help" in *Catharine Beecher: A Study in American Domesticity* (New York: W. W. Norton, 1973), part 1.

38. Amy Kaplan, "Manifest Domesticity," *American Literature* 70 (September 1998): 581–606; for the unsigned review of *Live and Let Live*, see *GLB* 15 (September 1837): 140.

39. I interpret this sketch as a coded allegory of U.S. slavery because Irving sighs that poor Bull is badgered by a hotheaded son who, for want of better things to do, jumps on ridiculous bandwagons that "are rare food for scandal in John's neighbourhood." This poke at antislavery activists is followed by a tribute to slavery's romantic qualities. "There is something," the sketch concludes, "in the appearance of [John's] mouldering old mansion, that is extremely poetical and picturesque; and as long as it can be rendered comfortably habitable, I should grieve to see it brought to the ground." See Washington Irving, *The Sketch Book of Geoffrey Crayon, Gent.*, 7 vols. (New York: C. S. Van Winkle, 1820), 7:13.

40. Caroline Gilman, *The Poetry of Travelling in the United States* (New York: Samuel Colman, 1838), 60–61.

41. See Elizabeth Palmer Peabody, "Plan of the West Roxbury Community," *The Dial* (January 1842): 363; and Anne C. Rose, *Transcendentalism as a Social Movement, 1830–1850* (New Haven, Conn.: Yale University Press, 1981), 187 and 195–96.

42. Clara Endicott Sears quotes Lane's loose description in *Bronson Alcott's Fruitlands with Transcendental Wild Oats* (Boston and New York: Houghton Mifflin, 1915), 15.

43. The letter of August 1843 is quoted in Sears, *Bronson Alcott's Fruitlands*, 45. Martha Saxton points out that a principal at the Alcott House in England "had preached . . . that human ties were all to be voluntary and impersonal, not familial and close as Abba and her girls knew them." See Saxton, *Louisa May: A Modern Biography of Louisa May Alcott* (Boston: Houghton Mifflin, 1977), 131.

44. See Odell Shepard, ed., *The Journals of A. Bronson Alcott*, 2 vols. (Boston: Little, Brown, 1938), 1:147–48.

45. I am aware of Sarah Elbert's contention that Abby "was willing to be her own mistress and maid, but would not be maid to Master Lane." This description of the situation is useful. Yet Elbert, following Bedell, leans heavily toward Abby's preferred self-portraiture. Then too, representations of Abby as a feisty and clear-sighted social critic tend to ignore the times when she promoted her place in the middling class, at servants' expense. See Madelon Bedell, *The Alcotts: Biography of a Family* (New York: Clarkson N. Potter, 1980), 200; and Sarah Elbert, *A Hunger for Home: Louisa May Alcott's Place in American Culture* (New Brunswick, N.J.: Rutgers University Press, 1987), 58.

46. Rose quotes Abby's letter of 4 November 1843 in *Transcendentalism as a Social Movement*, 205.

47. For Abby's letter to her father dated 6 October 1834, see Elbert, *A Hunger for Home*, 50; while for "galley slave," see Frederick Llewellyn Hovey Willis, *Alcott Memoirs*, ed. Edith Willis (Boston: Richard G. Badger; Toronto: The Copp, Clark Company, 1915), 82. Frederick Willis lived with the Alcotts when he was a boy to become Abby's "little comforter."

48. Sears quotes Isaac Hecker's quip in *Bronson Alcott's Fruitlands*, 84.

49. The letter of 24 January 1841 illuminates Sarah Elbert's view of the reason Abby took in adult boarders and homeless children from time to time. The ability to play a version of hostess/Lady Bountiful helped Bronson's wife feel in charge, Elbert suggests, of a domesticity that was well off the norm. See Elbert, *A Hunger for Home*, 58; but see also Mary P. Ryan, *Cradle of the Middle Class: The Family in Oneida County, New York, 1790–1865* (Cambridge, Mass.: Cambridge University Press, 1981), 172ff., for a sense of the development of new female roles related to domesticity, especially child care.

50. For Lane's grievance, see Sears, *Bronson Alcott's Fruitlands*, 120.

51. "Transcendental Wild Oats" first appeared in *The Independent* on 18 December 1873. The source of the "strings" anecdote provides a comparable judgment; in this case, on being asked about the use of "beasts of burden" at Fruitlands, Louisa May is supposed to have responded that "There was but one, and she a woman." See Willis, *Alcott Memoirs*, 41 and 82.

52. See Rusk and Tilton, *Letters*, 3:230.

53. Martha Saxton discusses Bronson's chortle that he would follow suit by "furnish[ing] gentlemen with grooms, coachmen, and general domestic male help" in *Louisa May*, 186 and 189.

54. David M. Katzman explains how intelligence offices worked and reports nineteenth-century comments about them in *Seven Days a Week: Women and Domestic Service in Industrializing America* (Urbana and Chicago: University of Illinois Press, 1981), 101ff; see also Lasser, "Mistress, Maid and Market," 137ff.

55. For "*bosh*," see "A Gentleman," *Laws of Etiquette*, 187; while for "slave market," see the letter of 12 June 1848 in the Henry Watson Jr. Papers in the Perkins Library at Duke University. Similar comments were published by a

Southerner who thought that intelligence offices worked "just upon the same principle as purchasing negroes. . . . Their offices remind me," he wrote, "of the jails in Richmond, where the negroes are put for safe keeping till disposed of; only the 'negro jails' are not so filthy, nor have they that peculiarly disagreeable smell about them, at least not so infernally bad." William M. Bobo made these remarks in *Glimpses of New York City, by a South Carolinian (who had nothing better to do)*. This book was published in 1852 in Charleston, S.C., by J. J. McCarter, where the cited lines appear on p. 191.

56. See Bedell, *The Alcotts*, 282–85.

57. Sumner, "A Boy's Recollections of Brook Farm," 311 and 310; and Rebecca Codman Butterfield, "Brook Farm: Founded in 1841," a text first printed in its entirety in Myerson, *The Brook Farm Book*, 286–98. Several of the anecdotes and phrases in Butterfield's manuscript reappear in an interview published as Gertrude Cutter, "Brook Farm Reminiscences," *Good Health* 45 (September 1910): 751–60.

58. See Kirby as quoted in Myerson, *The Brook Farm Book*, 166.

59. For a memory of Cheever's refusal of the social equality on offer in the "New Household," see, for example, [Bradford], "Reminiscences of Brook Farm," 142; pertinent to this inquiry is speculation that Cheever was the natural son of a British lord. Regarding the Celtic women, see Ora Gannett Sedgwick, "A Girl of Sixteen at Brook Farm," 396, noting that one of the reluctant Celts was the "no Minerva" George Ripley had invited to live and labor at Brook Farm. A niece of the clergyman who had employed Georgianna Bruce as a child's nurse, Deborah "Ora" Gannett later married Charles B. Sedgwick of Syracuse, New York; he is said to have been the first congressman to espouse abolition on the floor of Congress. See Swift, *Brook Farm: Its Members, Scholars, and Visitors*, 75.

60. This comment is culled from an extended version of the essays Kirby had published in the early 1870s; see Georgianna Kirby, *Years of Experience: An Autobiographical Narrative* (New York: G. P. Putnam, 1887), 179.

61. See Shepard, *Journals*, 155.

62. See Unsigned, "Cassius M. Clay.—Slavery," *Harbinger* 1 (6 September 1845): 205; and Zoe Gatti de Gamond, *The Phalanstery; or, Attractive Industry and Moral Harmony* (London: Whittaker, 1841), 78. As Charles Crowe claims that nearly three-fourths of what appeared in *The Harbinger* was the product of Brook Farmers' pens, with George Ripley leading the contributors, the male cofounder of Brook Farm may have mounted the "monstrous family" charge; alternately, it may have been a specimen of Sophia's prose. See Crowe, *George Ripley: Transcendentalist and Utopian Socialist* (Athens: University of Georgia Press, 1967), 183; and Raymond, *Sophia Dana Willard Ripley*, 58–59.

63. *JMN*, 8:221–22. This line recurred, saliently enough, in Emerson, "Historic Notes of Life and Letters in Massachusetts," 543.

64. For "no more servants," see Godwin, *A Popular View*, 58; while the judgment of general corruption was the opinion of Gatti de Gamond, *The Phalanstery*, 75.

65. Thus Carl Guarneri, *The Utopian Alternative: Fourierism in Nineteenth-Century America* (Ithaca, N.Y.: Cornell University Press, 1991), 172–73; and Gatti de Gamond, *The Phalanstery*, 78.

66. Guarneri has found that a former "free" servant named Mary Paul enjoyed attending nonkin at the North American Phalanx even though women there

earned only two-thirds of male communitarians' daily rate. Laundry chores, such as Sophia and Amelia Russell undertook at Brook Farm, were the only domestic task that earned as much as farm labor. See Guarneri, *The Utopian Alternative,* 209; and Gatti de Gamond, *The Phalanstery,* 77.

67. See Raymond, *Sophia Willard Dana Ripley,* 28 and 42; while for the quotation from a letter to an also-converted niece, see Rose, *Transcendentalism as a Social Movement,* 185. For another view of Sophia at Brook Farm, see Crowe, *George Ripley,* 179.

68. Melusina Fay Peirce, "Cooperative Housekeeping III," *Atlantic Monthly* 23 (January 1869): 36.

69. For Ora Sedgwick's insistence that her memories of Sophia masquerading as a gypsy fortune-teller were correct, see "A Girl of Sixteen at Brook Farm," 402; while for Georgianna Kirby's fierce anti-Catholicism, see "Reminiscences of Brook Farm," in Myerson, *The Brook Farm Book,* e.g., 148ff.

70. See Raymond, *Sophia Willard Dana Ripley,* 53.

71. Once established at the North American Phalanx, Elizabeth Curson Hoxie welcomed the arrival of communitarians able to afford servitors: "I hope and pray," she told a correspondent, "Mrs Weld will be smart enough to get somebody here that can wash and iron." An experienced homemaker by this time, Angelina Grimké Weld *was* smart enough to come accompanied by a waged attendant whose labor she shared out with the reform group, as if to show that abolitionist convictions did not bar a mistress from relying on staff who were "free." For Hoxie's hope and prayer, see the letter of 5 September 1854 in the Curson Family Papers at the Houghton Library.

72. For "Pollyanna," see Curtis, *A Season in Utopia,* 296–97; while for Dwight's workload and commitment, see Amy L. Reed, ed., *Letters from Brook Farm, 1844–1847* (Norwood, Mass.: Norwood Press, 1928), 7–8 and 41. Grace Goddard's letter, dated 13 April 1848, is in the Goddard Family Papers at the American Antiquarian Society.

73. C. Vann Woodward, "George Fitzhugh, *Sui Generis,*" the introduction to his edition of *Cannibals All! Or, Slaves without Masters* (Cambridge, Mass.: Harvard University Press, 1960), x; and George Fitzhugh, *Slavery Justified, by a Southerner* (Fredericksburg, Va.: Recorder Printing Office, 1850), 10. For a survey of contemporary responses to the Virginian's arguments, see Harvey Wish, *George Fitzhugh: Propagandist of the Old South* (Gloucester, Mass.: Peter Smith, 1962), 113–28 and 194–213.

74. For alert commentary on Hale's novel, see Susan M. Ryan, "Errand into Africa: Colonization and Nation Building in Sarah J. Hale's *Liberia,*" *New England Quarterly* 68 (December 1995): 558–83; while for Fitzhugh's extravagance, see *Cannibals All!,* 72 and 198.

75. See T. S. Arthur, "Two Ways with Domestics," *GLB* 29 (August 1844): 61; a report on the census of 1845 that was published as "The Upper Ten Thousand," *GLB* 33 (October 1846): 188; and Fredrika Bremer, *The Homes of the New World: Impressions of America* (New York: Harper & Brothers, 1854), 111 and 171. In 1857, *Godey's* noted that respectable families routinely employed two servants, or more if there were children to be cared for; "Centre-Table Gossip: Maids of All Work," *GLB* 54 (March 1857): 286.

76. "A Sufferer," "Domestic Servitude," *The Knickerbocker Magazine* 19 (June 1842): 521 and 526. The initials "E. P." appear at the end of this essay.

77. See Grace A. Ellis, "Our Household Servants," *The Galaxy* 14 (September 1872): 352; and Ann Du Cille's research on William Wells Brown's reading in *The Coupling Convention: Sex, Text, and Tradition in Black Women's Fiction* (New York: Oxford University Press, 1993), 24ff.

78. "Mrs. Clarissa Packard" [Caroline Howard Gilman], *Recollections of a Housekeeper* (New York: Harper & Brothers, 1834), 151–52.

79. Reed, *Letters from Brook Farm, 1844–1847*, 32–33.

80. Ibid., 33.

81. Nora Schelter Blair recalled "infatuation" in "Two Unpublished Reminiscences," 335; while "mother-confessor" is the light in which George William Curtis is said to have regarded Sophia, in Cooke, *Early Letters of George Wm. Curtis to John S. Dwight*, 23. One can only guess how this claim relates to the fact that Curtis was the source of the anecdote mentioned earlier, in which George Ripley was thought to be the "mother of us all" at Brook Farm.

82. See Reed, *Letters from Brook Farm, 1844–1847*, 97.

83. See Russell, *Home Life*, 64, 88, and 81; and Sumner, "A Boy's Recollections of Brook Farm," 310.

84. For "Too much sentiment," see Ellis, "Our Household Servants," 353; while for "painful servant problem," see Morrison I. Swift's report on a communitarian experiment that was published as "Altruria in California" in *The Overland Monthly and Out West Magazine* 29 (June 1897): 644.

85. See Jane Sophia Appleton, "Sequel to the 'Vision of Bangor in the Twentieth Century,'" as reprinted in *American Utopias*, ed. Arthur O. Lewis Jr. (New York: Arno Press and the New York Times, 1971), 255–58; and George Melville Baker, *The Greatest Plague in Life: A Farce* (Boston: Chas. H. Spencer, 1868), n.p. This phrase was in such general use that a novel by the same name, written by Henry Mayhew, was published in London in 1847; it must have had long-lived appeal, since *Godey's* noticed it in 1861. Baker's farce has little in common with Mayhew's novel, the target of which is mistresses who are impossible to please rather than self-interested cooks and maids.

86. See Fitzhugh, *Cannibals All!* 220; and M. D. Conway, *Testimonies Concerning Slavery* (London: Chapman and Hall, 1864), 2.

87. Alice B. Neal's "Lydia's Wages" appeared in two parts, the first in *GLB* 49 (September 1854), and the second a month later; the climax of the story, quoted here, can be found in the second installment on p. 620. The later tale is Mrs. H. C. Gardner, "Labor; or, Striking for Higher Wages," *Ladies' Repository* 19 (January 1859): 84. A letter to the editor of *GLB*, printed in February 1855, called "Lydia's Wages" "the best story of the season."

88. See Catharine Sedgwick, "The Irish Girl," *Tales and Sketches, Second Series* (Philadelphia: Carey, Lea, and Blanchard, 1844), where the mistress's remarks appears on p. 201; and Mary Kelley, ed., *The Power of Her Sympathy: The Autobiography and Journal of Catharine Maria Sedgwick* (Boston: Massachusetts Historical Society, 1993), 51–52. My thanks to Jenifer Elmore for bringing "The Irish Girl" to my attention.

89. Helen Stuart Mackay-Smith Marlatt, ed., *Stuart Letters of Robert and Elizabeth Sullivan Stuart and Their Children, 1819–1864*, 2 vols. (Privately printed, 1961), 1:304 and 1:177; and Sarah Hale, *The Ladies' New Book of Cookery: A Practical System for Private Families in Town and Country* (New York: H. Long & Brother, 1852), 439.

90. Though asked to leave Brook Farm after an allegation of sexual misconduct, Abby Morton went on to earn fame as Abby Morton Diaz. See Diaz, *A Domestic Problem: Work and Culture in the Household* (Boston: J. R. Osgood, 1875), 7 and 9, noting that this book does not espouse de-privatized homemaking.

91. James Fenimore Cooper, *The Redskins; or, Indian and Injin*, 2 vols. (New York: Burgess and Stringer, 1846), 2:173; and Edward A. Pollard, *Black Diamonds Gathered in the Darkey Homes of the South* (New York: Pudney & Russell, 1859), 57–58.

92. See Catharine Beecher, "How to Redeem Women's Profession from Dishonor," *Harper's New Monthly Magazine* 31 (November 1865): 712; Basil Hall, *Travels in North America*, 3 vols. (Graz, Austria: Akademische Druck—u. Verlangsanstalt, 1965), 1:300; and W. Emerson Wilson, ed., *The Mount Harmon Diaries of Sidney George Fisher, 1837–1850* (Wilmington: Historical Society of Delaware, 1976), 287.

93. See Robert Tomes, "Your Humble Servant," *Harper's New Monthly Magazine* 169 (June 1864): 53; and Beecher, "How to Redeem Women's Profession from Dishonor," 713.

94. For "Farm House," see *GLB* 49 (July 1854): 64; while for the opinion of the "fastidious," see Margaret Hall, *The Aristocratic Journey: Being the Outspoken LETTERS OF MRS. BASIL HALL Written during a Fourteen Months' Sojourn in America, 1827–1828*, ed. Una Pope-Hennessy (New York: G. P. Putnam's Sons, 1931), 217.

95. On back stairways, see Daniel E. Sutherland, *Americans and Their Servants: Domestic Service in the United States from 1800 to 1920* (Baton Rouge: Louisiana State University Press, 1981), 33; for the line from the Bogert Account Book, see ibid., 67. The critique of architectural innovations can be found on the first page of New York's *Seneca County Courier* (4 August 1848). This issue reports on a Free Soil County Convention and the "Resolutions Passed at the Woman's Rights Convention held in this Village on the 19th and 20th Inst."

96. See Harriet Jacobs, *Linda; or, Incidents in the Life of a Slave Girl*, ed. L. Maria Child (Boston: published for the author, 1861), 15; and Elizabeth Fox-Genovese, *Within the Plantation Household: Black and White Women of the Old South* (Chapel Hill: University of North Carolina Press, 1988), 132. The specter of "testimony . . . from the kitchen" was raised quite purposefully by N. P. Willis in "The 'Forrest Testimony,'" *Home Journal* (6 April 1850): 2.

Chapter 4: Kitchen Testimony and Servants' Tales

The epigraph is from Anon., *Plain Talk and Friendly Advice to Domestics* (Boston: Phillips, Sampson, 1855), 43.

1. The note, dated 20 September 1862, is in the Nathaniel Parker Willis Papers in the New York Historical Society. It requested permission for Jacobs to revisit Idlewild, a former Willis home.

2. Anon., *Plain Talk and Friendly Advice to Domestics*, 188.

3. Jean Fagan Yellin quotes this letter in her 1987 edition of *Incidents in the Life of a Slave Girl* (Cambridge, Mass.: Harvard University Press, 1987), 232.

4. The gossipy novel that lampoons Willis as "Bazaleel Wagstaff Bayes" is *The Match-Girl; or, Life Scenes as They Are* (1855). According to Thomas Baker, the

leading authority on N. P. Willis and the Forrest trial, those who read the right periodicals would have known that the book's author, Julie de Marguerite (sometimes, "de Marguerittes"), had once been a member of Catherine Forrest's circle.

5. The discussion of Child's influence on *Linda* got under way with Bruce Mills, "Lydia Maria Child and the Endings to Harriet Jacobs's *Incidents in the Life of a Slave Girl*," *American Literature* 64 (June 1992): 255–72. More recently, Carla L. Peterson probed this topic in *"Doers of the Word": African-American Women Speakers and Writers in the North (1830–1880)* (New York: Oxford University Press, 1995), 154; to be followed by Holly Laird, *Women Coauthors* (Urbana: University of Illinois Press, 2000), see esp. chap. 2. Resistance to this line of thinking is found in, for example, Frances Smith Foster, *Written by Herself: Literary Production by African American Women, 1746–1892* (Bloomington: Indiana University Press, 1993), 106; and Donald B. Gibson, "Harriet Jacobs, Frederick Douglass, and the Slavery Debate: Bondage, Family, and the Discourses of Domesticity," in *Harriet Jacobs and Incidents in the Life of a Slave Girl: New Critical Essays*, ed. Deborah M. Garfield and Rafia Zafar (New York: Cambridge University Press, 1996), 176 fn23.

6. See Catharine Beecher, *An Essay on Slavery and Abolitionism, with reference to the Duty of American Females* (Philadelphia: Henry Perkins, 1837), 48; Angelina Grimké, *Letters to Catherine E. Beecher* (Boston: Isaac Knapp, 1838), 61–62; and Karen Sánchez-Eppler, "Bodily Bonds: The Intersecting Rhetoric of Feminism and Abolition," in Shirley Samuels, ed., *The Culture of Sentiment: Race, Gender, and Sentimentality in Nineteenth-Century America* (New York: Oxford University Press, 1992), 95.

7. See "The Forrest Case," Wilmington, North Carolina, *Daily Journal*, 2 February 1852.

8. Anna Cora Mowatt, *Fashion; or, Life in New York*, as reprinted in *Plays* (Boston: Ticknor and Fields, 1855), 45; and William Gilmore Simms, *Guy Rivers: A Tale of Georgia*, 2 vols. (New York: Harper & Brothers, 1834), 1:225–26.

9. See *Plain Talk*, 188.

10. The jibe appeared in a letter Willis wrote to the *New York Herald*; it was published in that periodical on 28 March 1850. Nine days later, Willis reprinted this letter in his own periodical, *The Home Journal*, after a lengthy piece titled "The 'Forest Testimony.'"

11. Though "An American" was probably linked to the Willis camp, his/her identity is unknown; see the cited remarks in the *New York Herald*, 1 April 1850, 4. For Mrs. Henry R. [Mary] Schoolcraft's sense of "monstronsities" [*sic*], see *The Black Gauntlet: A Tale of Plantation Life in South Carolina* (Philadelphia: J. B. Lippincott, 1860), 83.

12. See the unsigned *A Manual of Politeness, Comprising the Principles of Etiquette, and Rules of Behaviour in Genteel Society* (Philadelphia: W. Marshall, 1837), 140; and Caroline Lee Hentz, *The Planter's Northern Bride* (Philadclphia: T. B. Peterson, 1854), 119 and 174.

13. See Joyce Warren, ed., *Ruth Hall and Other Writings* (New Brunswick, N.J.: Rutgers University Press, 1986), 237; but see also, by way of contrast, "Bridget As She Was, and Bridget As She Is," a selection in Fanny Fern's *Folly As It Flies: Hit At* (New York: G. W. Carleton, 1868): 103–7.

.14. Lucien B. Chase, *English Serfdom and American Slavery: or, Ourselves—As Others See Us* (New York: H. Long, 1854), 248; and Maria Jane McIntosh, *The Lofty and the Lowly or Good in All and None All-Good*, 2 vols. (New York: D. Appleton, 1853), 2:39. A footnote to this last citation insists on its veracity: "Language actually used," it explains, "by a negro named Cato under like circumstances."

15. See Marion Wilson Starling, *The Slave Narrative: Its Place in American History* (Washington, D.C.: Howard University Press, 1988), 130–31; and Lewis Clarke, *Narrative of the Sufferings of Lewis Clarke, during a Captivity of More Than Twenty-Five Years among the Algerines of Kentucky* (Boston: D. H. Eli, 1845), 17.

16. See Douglass, *Narrative of the Life of Frederick Douglass, an American Slave* (New York: Penguin, 1986), 73; and William Wells Brown, *Narrative of William W. Brown, An American Slave* (London: Charles Gilpin, 1849), 64.

17. See Eric Gardner, "'This Attempt of Their Sister': Harriet Wilson's *Our Nig* from Printer to Readers," *New England Quarterly* 66 (June 1993): 226–46.

18. Pertinent, too, was the evidence that Kent had been employed by the Forrests before the trial; see Thomas Baker, *Sentiment and Celebrity: Nathaniel Parker Willis and the Trials of Literary Fame* (New York: Oxford University Press, 1999), 143ff.

19. The unsigned clipping is titled "A Sketch from Private Life." It is preserved in the Willis Scrapbook, 1846–1850, in the Nathaniel Parker Willis Collection at the Morristown and Morris County Free Public Library, Morristown, New Jersey. Here, as in many other places in this chapter, I am indebted to Tom Baker for knowledge of archival material about Willis and his household that has been scattered hither and yon.

20. Robert Garvin's testimony was transcribed by the law reporter of the *New York Herald* and republished as a pamphlet titled *The Forrest Divorce Suit: Report of the Trial of Catherine N. Forrest vs. Edwin Forrest for Divorce* (New York: Herald Book and Job Office, 1851). The passage cited appears on p. 40.

21. The chief justice tried to clarify Garvin's intent. "Do I understand the witness to say," he inquired,

> that he did not stop at the window at any time, but merely passed by.
> Witness—No sir; Mrs. Forrest came to the window and said to me not to clean them at that time. I did not remain at the window. I saw this and I returned. . . . When Mr. Willis went away, I went into the drawing room to see what I could see.

See *The Forrest Divorce Suit*, 43. I have corrected an obvious typographical error, inserting "not" in place of "dot."

22. Ibid., 39.

23. The *New York Herald*'s reporter did censor testimony at times. For instance, when Garvin testified to activities of Mrs. Forrest's sister and a male companion "on the carpet," the reporter breaks off with a bracketed notation that "here the witnesse's [*sic*] testimony is unfit for publication." He may have been required to shield people who were not themselves on trial; see p. 41.

24. Ibid., 48 and 59–60. According to Baker, who found evidence of some roughhousing and a bribe, Howard had been "handled" by Edwin Forrest to tes-

tify as the disgruntled husband thought best. See Baker, *Sentiment and Celebrity*, 149.

25. Susan P. Graber provides an account of Potter's career in "A Hairdresser's Experience in High Life," *Bulletin of the Cincinnati Historical Society* 25 (July 1967): 215–24. For Eliza M. Potter's words, see *A Hairdresser's Experience in High Life* (Cincinnati: published for the author, 1859), 68–69, 164, and 230; while for "code," see Sharon Dean, "Introduction" to the Schomburg edition of Potter's book (New York: Oxford University Press, 1991), xlvii.

26. See "A Servant of Servants," *The Greatest Blessing in Life; or, the Adventures of Catherine Sinclair, a Domestic, in Search of a Good Mistress* (Pawtucket, R.I.: Bliss, Potter, 1850), 45. WorldCat reports that this novel's "supposed author" was a Silas Little, of whom I have been able to learn nothing further. Catherine's good mistress, who is characterized as sisterly rather than motherlike, is described on pp. 106 and 158.

27. See Jane Tompkins, *Sensational Designs: The Cultural Work of American Fiction, 1790–1860* (New York: Oxford University Press, 1985), 145; Lora Romero, *Home Fronts: Domesticity and Its Critics in the Antebellum United States* (Durham, N.C.: Duke University Press, 1997), 82ff.; and Gillian Brown, *Domestic Individualism: Imagining Self in Nineteenth-Century America* (Berkeley: University of California Press, 1990), 41.

28. Martha Haines Butt, *Antifanaticism: A Tale of the South* (Philadelphia: Lippincott, Grambo, 1853), 89; and Mrs. R. M. Ruffin, "Julia Warren, or The North and South," *Tales and Sketches for the Fireside* (Marion, Ala.: Dennis Dykous, 1858), 40. *Antifanaticism* was dedicated to Caroline Lee Hentz, though it predated *The Planter's Northern Bride*.

29. See "Christopher Crowfield" in "House and Home Papers. IX," *Atlantic Monthly* 14 (October 1864): 434, 442, and 440.

30. Henry David Thoreau, *Walden* (New York: Modern Library, 1937), 193, 227, and 128; and Nicholas Wainwright, ed., *A Philadelphia Perspective: The Diary of Sidney George Fisher Covering the Years 1834–1871* (Philadelphia: Historical Society of Pennsylvania, 1967), 259.

31. See [Mattie Griffith], *Autobiography of a Female Slave* (New York: Negro Universities Press, 1969), 217, 128, 136, and 367. On the limited influence this novel had on readers of its own day, see Joe Lockard's thoughts in the "Afterword" to his edition of Griffith's novel (Jackson: University of Mississippi Press, 1998), 410.

32. "A Gentleman," *The Laws of Etiquette; or, Short Rules and Reflections for Conduct in Society* (Philadelphia: Carey, Lea and Blanchard, 1836), 185.

33. See *Plain Talk*, 21, 63–64, and 120–21; and Alice B. Neal, "The Servant Question," *GLB* 55 (October 1857): 327.

34. Angelina Grimké Weld is quoted in *The Patriarchal Institution, as Described by Members of Its Own Family*, ed. L. Maria Child (New York: American Anti-Slavery Society, 1860), 9 and 29.

35. See Barbara A. White, "*Our Nig* and the She-Devil: New Information about Harriet Wilson and the 'Bellmont' Family," *American Literature* 65 (March 1993): 19–52; Thomas B. Lovell, "By Dint of Economy and Labor: Harriet Jacobs, Harriet Wilson and the Salutary View of Wage Labor," *Arizona Quarterly* (Autumn 1996): 1–32; and Gretchen Short, "Harriet Wilson's *Our Nig* and the Labor of Citizenship," *Arizona Quarterly* 57 (Autumn 2001): 22.

36. Robert Reid-Pharr, *Conjugal Union: The Body, the House, and the Black American* (New York: Oxford University Press, 1999), 102.

37. A letter appended to *Our Nig* illuminates this point. "O," it has Wilson reporting, "I have at last found a home,—and not only a home, but a mother. My cup runneth over. What shall I render to the Lord for all his benefits?" See Harriet E. Wilson, *Our Nig; or, Sketches from the Life of a Free Black, in a Two-Story White House, North. Showing that Slavery's Shadows Fall Even There* (Boston: Geo. C. Rand & Avery, 1859), 133; but see also Claudia Tate's argument that Wilson casts no blame on "Mag," the mother-character who is forced to leave her child in a household she knows to be hard on nonkin staff. Tate's thoughts can be found in *Domestic Allegories of Political Desire: The Black Heroine's Text at the Turn of the Century* (New York: Oxford University Press, 1992), 32ff.

38. Most evidence about the treatment of nineteenth-century "bound" girls comes from homemakers' letters and diaries; indeed, this is one reason *Our Nig* is so important a literary recovery. There is nonetheless food for thought in the diary entries of Sarah J. Stoughton that refer to a "bound" worker. Writing in 1869, Stoughton found Flora "pleasant enough" except when the latter lost her temper and vented "gales" of ill will. Flora may have had reason to grow irritated, since she left the Stoughtons when they tried to curtail her social activities (specifically, her desire to make the acquaintance of men working on nearby farms). Stoughton's diary is in the American Antiquarian Society, Worcester, Massachusetts.

39. See Wilson, *Our Nig*, 71–72 and 74–75.

40. Elizabeth Breau, "Identifying Satire: *Our Nig*," *Callaloo* 16 (Spring 1993): 461; Jacobs, *Incidents in the Life of a Slave Girl*, 201; and P. Gabrielle Foreman, "Manifest in Signs: The Politics of Sex and Representation in *Incidents in the Life of a Slave Girl*," in *Harriet Jacobs and Incidents in the Life of a Slave Girl: New Critical Essays*, 87.

41. See Milton Meltzer and Patricia G. Holland, eds., *Lydia Maria Child: Selected Letters, 1817–1880* (Amherst: University of Massachusetts Press, 1982), 378; and Sánchez-Eppler, "Touching Liberty," 86.

42. See Meltzer and Holland, *Lydia Maria Child*, 91 and 522; and Harriet Beecher Stowe, *Dred: A Tale of the Great Dismal Swamp*, 2 vols. (Boston: Phillips, Sampson, 1856), 2:210. Nor was Stowe alone in thinking this way, for Emma Willard made the same suggestion in a congressional petition; see Faye E. Dudden, *Serving Women: Household Service in Nineteenth-Century America* (Middletown, Conn.: Wesleyan University Press, 1983), 222.

43. Thomas Dublin comments on the shift to "day service" as it took place in the Northeast in *Transforming Women's Work: New England Lives in the Industrial Revolution* (Ithaca, N.Y.: Cornell University Press, 1994), 160 and 202; while Dudden notices African American servants who "lived out" in Philadelphia before the Civil War in *Serving Women*, 64. Important too is Katzman's argument that African American women impelled the shift to "day service" once they had accrued enough leverage to negotiate arrangements that allowed them to spend more time with their own kin. See David M. Katzman, *Seven Days a Week: Women and Domestic Service in Industrializing America* (Urbana and Chicago: University of Illinois Press, 1981), 72, 88, 90, and 177ff.

44. This argument is complicated by the fact that Maher would end up serving not the employers who saved her letters but a family in Amherst, Massachusetts, where she lived and worked in such a family-like manner that she signed one letter "Miss Emily and Vinnie's Maggie." For "Who says I'se free?" see Leon F. Litwack, *Been in the Storm So Long: The Aftermath of Slavery* (New York: Alfred A. Knopf, 1979), 214; while for Maher's letters, see Jay Leyda, "Miss Emily's Maggie," *New World Writing* (New York: Third Mentor Selection, New American Library, 1953), 263 and 267.

45. Another questionable decision on Mary Lawton's part was that of calling her information source "Katy" rather than "Kate," the name that Leary used outside the Clemens home. For "they're my family," "wallpaper," and "serving them to the end," see Kate Leary, *A Lifetime with Mark Twain: The Memories of Katy Leary, for Thirty Years His Faithful and Devoted Servant* (New York: Harcourt, Brace, 1925), 127, xii, and 348–52.

46. My knowledge of Leary's relatives rests on a conversation I had with Warren and Katharine Leary Antenna after giving a paper on her great-aunt Leary at the Conference for Mark Twain Studies in Elmira, New York, in 1993. I thank the Antennas for their generous assistance with a junior scholar's quest.

47. According to Trudier Harris, only a few of Mildred's monologues are based on things that happened to Childress while she worked as a servant. I would still argue for the merits of comparing Mildred's stories to *Our Nig* insofar as both were the work of servant-writers who chose a fictive format. See Harris's introduction to Alice Childress, *Like One of the Family: Conversations from a Domestic's Life* (Boston: Beacon Press, 1986), xxvii. The "Mildred" sketches first appeared in Paul Robeson's newspaper, *Freedom*, after which they were picked up by the *Baltimore Afro-American*.

48. Childress, *Like One of the Family*, 2–3, 71, and 72.

49. In another story, Parker recounts the fun she and Rawlings had working on a cookbook together but notes the latter's failure to give her credit for several recipes, to mention her sweaty hours in a Florida kitchen dependent on a wood-stove, or to pass along any of the profits the cookbook made. "All I ever got," Parker reports, "was an autographed copy, but in those days I was grateful for any little crumb that white people let fall, so I kept my thoughts about the cookbook strictly to myself." See Idella Parker with Mary Keating, *Idella, Marjorie Rawlings' "Perfect Maid"* (Gainesville: University Press of Florida, 1992), ix, xiii, 83, and 69.

50. The fact that this query is repeated almost word for word thirty pages later (when Parker explains why and how she finally left the Rawlings's employment) should be noted. It may be a case of editorial intervention. But it could also show that this puzzle was a refrain in Parker's mind when she remembered Rawlings; ibid., 85 and 113.

51. See Elizabeth Young, *Disarming the Nation: Women's Writing and the American Civil War* (Chicago and London: University of Chicago Press, 1999), 22 and 125; and Michele Birnbaum, *Race, Work, and Desire in American Literature, 1860–1930* (Cambridge: Cambridge University Press, 2003), 29.

52. See Frances Smith Foster, *Written by Herself: Literary Production by African American Women, 1746–1892* (Bloomington and Indianapolis: Indiana University Press, 1993), 128–30.

53. See Elizabeth Keckley, *Behind the Scenes; or, Thirty Years a Slave, and Four Years in the White House* (New York: G. W. Carleton, 1868), 124 and 93–94; and Young, *Disarming the Nation*, 121.

54. See Keckley, *Behind the Scenes*, xiv.

55. Highlighting the injustice of this attack are stories in *Behind the Scenes* that recall Keckley's workrooms and the etiquette they entailed, accounts of her civic and charitable commitments, and memories of unstructured leisure time. Most directly refuting, however, of the idea that the freedwoman was a Lincoln servant is the story about trying to lodge on the same floor as Mary Lincoln and being denied. See Keckley, *Behind the Scenes*, 275–76. Rather different was the situation of Eliza Potter, the hairdresser who sometimes took a room in clients' homes. This aspect of Potter's memoirs was not fully addressed in a stellar recent essay, Xiomara Santamarina's "Black Hairdresser and Social Critic: Eliza Potter and the Labors of Femininity," *American Literature* (March 2005): 151–77. Quite possibly, Santamarina explores coresidence in *Belabored Professions: Narratives of African American Working Womanhood* (Chapel Hill: University of North Carolina Press, 2005). I look forward to reading this book, published while I was reading proofs.

56. Accusations of venal treachery include Justin G. Turner and Linda Levitt Turner, *Mary Todd Lincoln: Her Life and Letters* (New York: Alfred A. Knopf, 1972), 472; Ishbel Ross, *The President's Wife: Mary Todd Lincoln* (New York: G. P. Putnam, 1973), 267; and Jean H. Baker, *Mary Todd Lincoln: A Biography* (New York: W. W. Norton, 1987), 280.

57. For "revenge," see Young, *Disarming the Nation*, 138 (cf. Birnbaum, *Race, Work, and Desire*, 33); while for "unmasking," see Carolyn Sorisio, "Unmasking the Genteel Performer: Elizabeth Keckley's *Behind the Scenes* and the Politics of Public Wrath," *African American Review* 34 (Spring 2000): esp. 25.

58. See chapter 5 of Lori Merish, *Sentimental Materialism: Gender, Commodity Culture, and Nineteenth-Century American Literature* (Durham, N.C.: Duke University Press, 2000); and, for another way in which to desentimentalize probes of cross-race domestic affect, see my "Rubbed and Polished: Hurston's 'The Conscience of the Court,'" *American Literature* (forthcoming).

59. See Sorisio, "Unmasking the Genteel Performer," 20; and, for the quoted response to *Behind the Scenes*, see Jennifer Fleischner, *Mrs. Lincoln and Mrs. Keckly: The Remarkable Story of the Friendship between a First Lady and a Former Slave* (New York: Broadway Books, 2003), 317.

60. Qtd. in Litwack, *Been in the Storm So Long*, 155.

61. See "The Old Virginia Gentleman," *Selections from the Miscellaneous Writings of Dr. George W. Bagby*, 2 vols. (Richmond, Va.: Whittet & Shepperson, 1884), 1:7–8; and Geo. M. Cochran, "The Problem of Domestic Service," *Current* 1 (9 February 1884): 121. Cochran earned a response from Anna B. McMahan in the same magazine two weeks later.

62. This comment may have been the work of Harriet Prescott Spofford (a writer whose thoughts on service are discussed in chapter 5), since the *Bazar* was one of her favorite publication venues. She wrote domestic advice literature for it, and this article is laden with the sorts of things she said about attendants at other times. Yet because the piece was unsigned and, perhaps most significantly, not republished in the book Spofford made out of her *Bazar* essayettes, I

cannot be certain it was from her pen. See "Domestic Service," *Harper's Bazar* (2 May 1874): 284.

Chapter 5: Stupid Sentimentality

The epigraph is a citation from Helen Campbell's *Prisoners of Poverty: Women Wage-Workers, Their Trades and Their Lives* (Boston: Roberts Brothers, 1887), 237.

1. Helen Campbell, *Household Economics: A Course of Lectures in the School of Economics of the University of Wisconsin* (New York: G. P. Putnam's Sons, 1898), 221. For "stupid sentimentality," see Campbell, *Prisoners of Poverty*, 222.

2. For example, David M. Katzman quoted Campbell heavily but ignored Harland in *Seven Days a Week: Women and Domestic Service in Industrializing America* (Urbana and Chicago: University of Illinois Press, 1981), while Karen Manners Smith focused so narrowly on Harland that she failed to consider some of the contemporary opinions to which her subject must have been responding; see Smith's unpublished PhD dissertation, "Marion Harland: The Making of a Household Name" (University of Massachusetts, 1990). More recently, Sarah A. Leavitt noticed both advisors in *From Catharine Beecher to Martha Stewart: A Cultural History of Domestic Advice* (Chapel Hill: University of North Carolina Press, 2002) but did not see either as a labor theorist.

3. See p. 373 in the facsimile edition of *Common Sense in the Household: A Manual of Practical Housewifery* published by Oxmoor House of Birmingham, Alabama, in 1985; and [Spofford], "The Stranger in the Gates," *Harper's Bazar* (19 July 1873): 450.

4. Melusina Fay Peirce, "Cooperative Housekeeping I," *Atlantic Monthly* 22 (November 1868): 523, and "Cooperative Housekeeping III," *Atlantic Monthly* 23 (January 1869): 34; see also Campbell's "Preface" to *Prisoners of Poverty*, ii.

5. See the unsigned "Treatment of Servants," *GLB* 51 (November 1855): 424.

6. Peirce, "Cooperative Housekeeping III," 35; Harland, *Common Sense in the Household*, 380; Harriet Prescott Spofford, "What's In a Name?" *Harper's Bazar* (2 March 1878): 138; Spofford, "Between the Two Women," *Harper's Bazar* (5 December 1874): 790; and Campbell, *Prisoners of Poverty*, 241.

7. See Amy Dru Stanley, *From Bondage to Contract: Wage Labor, Marriage, and the Market in the Age of Slave Emancipation* (New York: Cambridge University Press, 1998), 21; and S. B. H., "Servants and Household Economy," *Century* 24 (October 1882): 955.

8. See the unsigned "Domestic Service," *Old and New* 6 (September 1872): 361.

9. Lori D. Ginzberg, *Women and the Work of Benevolence: Morality, Politics and Class in the Nineteenth-Century United States* (New Haven, Conn.: Yale University Press, 1990), particularly chap. 4; Gregory Eiselein, *Literature and Humanitarianism Reform in the Civil War Era* (Bloomington: Indiana University Press, 1996), 4; George Fredrickson, *The Inner Civil War: Northern Intellectuals and the Crisis of the Union* (New York: Harper & Row, 1965), e.g., 188; and Catharine Maria Sedgwick, *Home* (Boston and Cambridge: James Munroe, 1835), 127.

10. See Mary Louise Kete, *Sentimental Collaborations: Mourning and Middle-Class Identity in Nineteenth-Century America* (Durham, N.C.: Duke University Press, 2000), 31–32; and "South Carolina Society," *Atlantic Monthly* 39

(June 1877): 675. The latter, which was part of a series, is signed "A South Carolinian," an earlier piece having stated that anonymity was mandated by the candor of the reportage.

11. Though Stowe would write fondly of black servants she employed while living in Ohio, she was not as generous in private communications. See, in this context, the letter of 17 April 1867 in which she compared a new servant to a "humpbacked chimpanzee," finding the woman "inexpressibly *nigging*." It is in the Beecher-Stowe Collection at Radcliffe College, Schlesinger Library, Cambridge, Massachusetts. For Stowe's use of the word "American" to connote "white," see "The Chimney-Corner. XI. The Woman Question: or, What Will You Do With Her?" *Atlantic Monthly* 16 (December 1865): 677–78; and "The Chimney-Corner. X. The Woman Question: or, What Will You Do With Her?" *Atlantic Monthly* 16 (November 1865): 571.

12. See Augusta H. Worthen, "Servants," *GLB* 68 (March 1864): 286; and for the passage from Beecher's "True Remedy," see Jeanne Boydston, Mary Kelley, and Anne Margolis, eds., *The Limits of Sisterhood: The Beecher Sisters on Women's Rights and Woman's Sphere* (Chapel Hill: University of North Carolina Press, 1988), 138–39.

13. Hamilton's comic twist on this topic was to blame old-time housekeepers for expending so much energy on household chores that their descendants' vitality was permanently sapped; see Gail Hamilton, *Woman's Worth and Worthlessness* (New York: Harper and Brothers, 1871), 55.

14. See Stowe's letter of 5 October 1863 in the Beecher-Stowe Collection at Radcliffe College, Schlesinger Library, Cambridge, Massachusetts; and for Catharine Beecher's counsel, see "How to Redeem Women's Profession from Dishonor," *Harper's New Monthly Magazine* 31 (November 1865): 711. Useful too is Joan Hedrick's discussion of the younger sister's advice columns in *Harriet Beecher Stowe: A Life* (New York: Oxford University Press, 1994), 312ff.

15. See "The Girl That Stays," *Harper's Bazar* 24 (16 May 1891): 374–75.

16. Harland, *Common Sense in the Household*, 382.

17. The unsigned essay titled "Domestic Service" appeared on the first page of the *Seneca County Courier* (4 August 1848) with a superscription: "From the Massachusetts Quarterly Review."

18. See Charles Loring Brace, "The Servant Question," *The Nation* 1 (26 October 1865): 528; Parker Pillsbury's horror-mongering in "Co-operative Housekeeping," *The Revolution* 4 (29 July 1869): 57; and Abby Sage Richardson, "A Plea for Chinese Labor," *Scribner's Monthly Magazine* 2 (July 1871): 287.

19. For "incompetent," see Joel Williamson, *After Slavery: The Negro in South Carolina during Reconstruction, 1861–1877* (Chapel Hill: University of North Carolina Press, 1965), 35; while for the drawling gentleman, see "Richard B. Elder" [George W. Bagby], "Servantgalism in Virginia," *Lippincott's Magazine* 7 (June 1871): 633–34.

20. As Wilson's mood in this diary is generally cheerier, it is pertinent that she wrote this entry on her twenty-second birthday. Almost forty years later, Wilson's daughter would go out to service, too. Both women's papers are held under the mother's married name, Goodenough, at the American Antiquarian Society, Worcester, Massachusetts. Faye Dudden provides biographical information on Wilson in *Serving Women: Household Service in Nineteenth-Century America* (Middletown, Conn.: Wesleyan University Press, 1983), 97–99.

21. Armstead L. Robinson quotes the still-enslaved woman's comment in "'Worser dan Jeff Davis': The Coming of Free Labor during the Civil War, 1861–1865," in *Essays on the Postbellum Southern Economy*, ed. Thavolia Glymph et al. (College Station: Texas A & M University Press, 1985), 37. The freedwoman's speech was "preserved," dialect and all, in a letter written by a white mistress on 27 August 1867. See Williamson, *After Slavery*, 51.

22. Marli F. Weiner quotes this evocative phrase in *Mistresses and Slaves: Plantation Women in South Carolina, 1830–80* (Urbana: University of Illinois Press, 1998), 192.

23. On freedpersons' use of their new bargaining power, see Tera M. Hunter, *To 'Joy My Freedom: Southern Black Women's Lives and Labors after the Civil War* (Cambridge, Mass.: Harvard University Press, 1997), 26–31; and Jacqueline Jones, *Labor of Love, Labor of Sorrow: Black Women, Work and the Family, from Slavery to the Present* (New York: Vintage, 1985), 127ff.

24. James L. Roark quotes the Alabama woman in *Masters without Slaves: Southern Planters in the Civil War and Reconstruction* (New York: W. W. Norton, 1977), 143; while Drew Gilpin Faust quotes the Texas woman in *Mothers of Invention: Women of the Slaveholding South in the American Civil War* (Chapel Hill: University of North Carolina Press, 1996), 78. Faust dates Amelia Barr's remark, with a query, to 1866.

25. See the Atlanta *Daily Intelligencer* of 25 October 1865 as quoted in Hunter, *To 'Joy My Freedom*, 28.

26. For "plague, vexation & expense," see the letter C. Chesnut dated 8 November 1863, as quoted in Roark, *Masters without Slaves*, 89. The slaves in question had been freed by Union troops. For "all hazards," see Cicero Adams's letter of 14 August 1867 in the Hughes Family Papers in the Southern Historical Collection at the University of North Carolina at Chapel Hill.

27. For the slap at Irish servants, see Louise P.'s letter of 11 December 1866 to Armistead Burt in the Octavius T. Porcher Letters in the Perkins Library at Duke University, Durham, North Carolina; while for the reference to "some young white persons," see Julius J. Fleming, *The Juhl Letters to the Charleston Courier: A View of the South, 1865–1871*, ed. John Hammond Moore (Athens: University of Georgia Press, 1974), 256. The South Carolina man who had trouble with white women workers is quoted in Leon F. Litwack, *Been in the Storm So Long: The Aftermath of Slavery* (New York: Alfred A. Knopf, 1979), 353.

28. For "*cuss talk*," see E. L. Eblen's letter, dated 20 June 1866, in the Campbell Family Papers, Perkins Library, Duke University, Durham, North Carolina; while for the comment about "feeling," see the letter John B. Cocke wrote to John Hartwell Cocke on 6 June 1865, which Roark quotes in *Masters without Slaves*, 145.

29. Peirce, "Cooperative Housekeeping III," 34 and 36. Historians who have probed Peirce's work include Dolores Hayden, *The Grand Domestic Revolution: A History of Feminist Designs for American Homes, Neighborhoods, and Cities* (Cambridge, Mass.: MIT Press, 1981), 67–89; and Susan Strasser, *Never Done: A History of American Housework* (New York: Pantheon Books, 1982), 112 and 195–201.

30. The most accessible information on Peirce's life is found in a biography of her husband, semiotician C. S. Peirce; see Joseph Brent, *Charles Sanders Peirce:*

A Life (Bloomington: Indiana University Press, 1998), 60ff. Brent's information is based, however, on "An Examination of the Life and Thought of Zina Fay Peirce, an American Reformer and Feminist," an unpublished PhD dissertation (Ball State University, 1984) by Norma Pereira Atkinson.

31. Though "association" had been a key Fourierist term, Stowe showed that she meant something more like service industries when she spoke of finding ways to "lessen the labors of individual families by having some of the present domestic tasks done out of the house." See "The Transition," *Atlantic Monthly* 17 (February 1866): 220.

32. See Peirce, "Cooperative Housekeeping II," *Atlantic Monthly* 22 (December 1868): 690.

33. See "Cooperative Housekeeping III," 34, 36 and 33; and for William Heyward's expression of satisfaction, see Litwack, *Been in the Storm So Long*, 355.

34. See the unsigned "Biddy Dethroned" in *Putnam's Magazine* 5 (January 1870): 116–17.

35. Significantly enough, the twitterer wears his sentimentality proudly: "I want nobody who shall serve me for pay of money alone. . . . [W]e want the hearts as well as the hands." In a later installment, a respondent expresses interest in the post but points out its crucial blind spot: "if I am to read and travel and study and visit, and to be in all respects treated as an equal in the family, I don't see who is to do the work." See the letter from the "Rev. Eli Harkness" in *Old and New* 4 (October 1871): 491–97; and the reply published as "Wanted, a Domestic III," *Old and New* 5 (June 1872): 759–61. A final installment, "Domestic Service," appeared in September.

36. See Louisa M. Alcott, "How I Went Out to Service," *The Independent* 26 (4 June 1874): 1–2.

37. Harriet Beecher Stowe made her views known in "House and Home Papers. IX," *Atlantic Monthly* 14 (October 1864): 442; while Wells shared her thoughts in "Loyalty and Liberality," *About People* (Boston: James R. Osgood, 1885), 115, and "The Servant Girl of the Future," *North American Review* 157 (December 1893): 719–20.

38. Ruth Schwartz Cowan dates the word "housework" to 1871 in *More Work for Mother: The Ironies of Household Technology from the Open Hearth to the Microwave* (New York: Basic Books, 1983), 18. For the medical view of "house diseases," see Nancy Tomes, "The Private Side of Public Health: Sanitary Science, Domestic Hygiene, and the Germ Theory, 1870–1900," *Bulletin of the History of Medicine* 64 (Winter 1990): 510; while for the transformation of insects into "germs with legs," see Naomi Rogers, "Germs with Legs: Flies, Disease, and the New Public Health," *Bulletin of the History of Medicine* 63 (Winter 1989): 603, 601, 612, and 605. Spofford's contribution is from "The Last Resort," *Harper's Bazar* (27 February 1875): 139.

39. See Elizabeth Stoddard, *The Morgesons* (New York: Penguin, 1984), 150; the anonymously authored "Social Distinctions from Bridget's Standpoint," *The Nation* 9 (5 August 1869), 107; Francis A. Walker, "Our Domestic Service," *Scribner's Monthly Magazine* 11 (December 1875): 273; and Amy Kaplan, "Manifest Domesticity," *American Literature* 70 (September 1998): 582.

40. "China in Our Kitchens," *Atlantic Monthly* 23 (June 1869): 747–52; and Walker, "Our Domestic Service," 273. Cf. Fanny Roper Feudge, "How I Kept

House by Proxy," *Scribner's Monthly Magazine* 22 (September 1881): 681–87, the story of a Chinese manservant who loves his American master and mistress tenderly.

41. See John Kuo Wei Tchen's discussion of "Curiosity" in *New York before Chinatown: Orientalism and the Shaping of American Culture, 1776–1882* (Baltimore: Johns Hopkins University Press, 1999), 275; and the unsigned "My Chinese Cook," *Ladies' Repository* 30 (April 1870): 303. See also, for an extensive survey of negative stereotypes of Chinese men after 1850, Stuart Creighton Miller, *The Unwelcome Immigrant: The American Image of the Chinese, 1785–1882* (Berkeley and Los Angeles: University of California Press, 1969), 145ff.

42. Sarah Henshaw, "California Housekeepers and Chinese Servants," *Scribner's Monthly Magazine* 12 (September 1876): 736–39; cf. Margaret Hosmer, "Mary Ann and Chyng Loo: Housekeeping in San Francisco," *Lippincott's Magazine* 6 (October 1870): 354–61.

43. See "My Chinese Cook," 302.

44. *The Nation's* unsigned "Waiters and Waitresses. I" ran on 26 November 1874, 347; see also Harland, *Common Sense in the Household*, 378.

45. Harland, *Common Sense in the Household*, 376–77; and p. 2 of Shirley Abbott's introduction to the 1985 edition of Harland's guide; this introduction is entitled "Dear Mother of Us All."

46. "The Arts," *Appleton's Journal* (12 June 1875): 760; and Kate Sanborn's entry "Mary Virginia Terhune" in *Our Famous Women: An Authorized Record of the Lives and Deeds of Distinguished American Women of Our Times* (Kansas City, Mo.: S. F. Junkin, 1887), 638. Cf. S. B. H., "Home and Society," *Scribner's Monthly Magazine* 21 (January 1881): 472, realizing that Scribner's was the firm that published Harland's household manuals.

47. See "The Arts," 760; and Mrs. E. J. Gurley, "Mistress Work and Maid Work. Which Is Mistress and Which Is Servant," *Good Housekeeping* 2 (17 April 1886): 339.

48. Qtd. from *Alone* (Richmond, Va.: A. Morris, 1854), 332.

49. Peirce, "Cooperative Housekeeping III," 3; and Harland, *Common Sense in the Household*, 382.

50. See Sanborn, "Mary Virginia Terhune," 637.

51. For "invisible wheels," see [Elizabeth Smith Miller], *In the Kitchen* (Boston: Lee & Shepard; New York: Lee, Shepard, and Dillingham, 1875), 22; while for information on Spofford's home life and career, see Elizabeth K. Halbeisen, *Harriet Prescott Spofford: A Romantic Survival* (Philadelphia: University of Pennsylvania Press, 1935), esp. 103ff. and 115.

52. See Spofford, "Between the Two Women," 790.

53. Harriet Prescott Spofford, "The Prose of the Kitchen," *Harper's Bazar* (23 January 1875): 58.

54. See the anonymous review of *The Servant Girl Question* in "New Publications," *The Catholic World* 33 (July 1881): 573. "Mrs. Spofford's book," the review announced, "contains nothing new, and its views do not differ materially from what has gone before." The reviewer concluded, nonetheless, by praising Spofford for the cited passage, which allows for the possibility that some Irish servants are good because family-like.

55. See Harriet Prescott Spofford, "The Nature of Service," *Harper's Bazar* (28 November 1874): 770; and "Help in Macedonia," *Harper's Bazar* (1 September 1877): 546.

56. See Harriet Prescott Spofford, "Some Remedy," *Harper's Bazar* (20 February 1875): 122, noting that this passage was altered slightly when republished on p. 146 of *The Servant Girl Question* (Boston: Houghton Mifflin, 1881). This attitude did not make Spofford a proponent of inclusive dining arrangements, for she argued that table conversations would be impaired by the "presence of one who is not inherently and indissolubly a part of that circle." For "how can we get," see Josephine E. Martin, "Concerning Servants. Some Fresh Thoughts on a Stale Subject," *Good Housekeeping* 15 (July 1892): 7–9.

57. Eunice Beecher's thoughts on servants and other domestic muddles were collected in *Motherly Talks with Young Housekeepers* (New York: J. B. Ford, 1873), 249–50.

58. Spofford, "Between the Two Women," 790; and "Some Remedy," 122.

59. Mary Jones's yearning is the more revealing in that she and her husband had been prominent boosters of the claim that parentlike slaveholders could do a great deal of good within their plantation "families." Weiner quotes Jones in *Mistresses and Slaves*, 226.

60. "I only look at things on the surface," this humorist explained to a correspondent who admired her cheeky style. "That is my weakness. My strength is that I see them as they are, and not as tradition, or prejudice, or popular opinion, represents them." See Hamilton, *Woman's Worth and Worthlessness*, 55; and H. Augusta Dodge, ed., *Gail Hamilton's Life in Letters*, 2 vols. (Boston: Lee and Shepard, 1901), 1:384.

61. Tomes was no radical—or even much of an advisor—since he would go on to "advance" his proposals by concluding that "As large a liberty, as is conformable with their household work, should be allowed to domestics in receiving and visiting their friends." Though this counsel suggests consideration and kindliness, it put no pressure on homemakers to rethink the largeness of the liberty they allowed. See Robert Tomes, *The Bazar Book of the Household* (New York: Harper & Brothers, 1875), 136 and 148. It may be pertinent that the only other articles Tomes ever published on service topics—two brief and unoriginal essays—had appeared while Stowe's "House and Home Papers" were running in *The Atlantic Monthly*.

62. David Katzman quotes this remark, which was a response to a questionnaire circulated by Boston's Domestic Reform League in 1901–2, in *Seven Days a Week*, 178. On the topic of "day service," Phyllis Palmer says that commuting servants were the norm in many middle-class U.S. homes by 1920 but emphasizes the "vanishing point" of another postwar era, 1945. See Palmer, *Domesticity and Dirt: Housewives and Domestic Servants in the United States, 1920–1945* (Philadelphia: Temple University Press, 1989), xiii.

63. See I. M. Rubinow, "The Problem of Domestic Service," *Journal of Political Economy* 114 (October 1906): 515; and Elizabeth Clark-Lewis, *Living In, Living Out: African American Domestics in Washington, D.C., 1910–1940* (Washington, D.C.: Smithsonian Institution Press, 1994), 158.

64. See Campbell, *Prisoners of Poverty*, 242; "Social Distinctions from Bridget's Standpoint," 107; and, for a description of the "Kitchen Garden" program, S. B. H., "Servants and Household Economy," 955–56.

65. The tribute to "an oldish American hired girl" is from the unsigned "The Doings and Goings-On of Hired Girls," *Lippincott's Magazine* 20 (November 1877): 590; while "harsh slaveholders" is from the unsigned "Studies in the

South," *Atlantic Monthly* 51 (January 1883): 93. Notice in the latter the depre-
cation of "mere sentiment."

66. For more on these friends' relationship, see Mary A. Hill, *Charlotte Perkins Gilman: The Making of a Radical Feminist, 1860–1896* (Philadelphia: Temple University Press, 1980), 238–41.

67. Katzman, *Seven Days a Week*, 316 fn32.

68. Interviewees' remarks are excerpted from Campbell, *Prisoners of Poverty*, 224–31.

69. "Mrs. Campbell skims over the surface of conditions," B. O. Flower charged in 1901, "and though often very helpfully suggestive, she fails to strike at the root of economic evils." It may have been an attempt to soften this cri-tique that led him to recall Campbell as motherlike in *Progressive Men, Women, and Movements of the Past Twenty-Five Years* (Boston: New Arena, 1914), 124–25. Rose E. Paulson notes the harsher comment in "Campbell, Helen Stuart," an entry in *Notable American Women, 1607–1950*, ed. Edward T. James et al., 3 vols. (Cambridge, Mass.: Belknap, 1971), 1:281.

70. For Campbell's list of rules, see *Prisoners of Poverty*, 239–40; and for "devotion," ibid., 243.

71. See the unsigned "Mrs. Campbell's 'Prisoners of Poverty,'" *Critic*, n.s. 10(7) (11 June 1887): 294; the unsigned review of *Prisoners* in the *Overland Monthly and Out West Magazine* 13 (March 1889): 327–30; and its unsigned predecessor, commentary on Campbell's novel *Mrs. Herndon's Income* (1886), in "Recent Fiction," *Overland Monthly and Out West Magazine* 7 (February 1996): 213.

72. See "The Domestic Service Problem," *Chautauquan* 34 (November 1901): 126.

73. Campbell's friend Charlotte Stetson did something similar in another book given to U.S. students. "Of all popular paradoxes," *Women and Economics* (1898) avowed, "none is more nakedly absurd than to hear us prate of privacy in a place where we cheerfully admit to our table-talk and to our door service—yes, and to the making of our beds and to the handling of our clothing—a complete stranger, a stranger not only by reason of new acquaintance and of the false view inevitable to new eyes let in upon our secrets, but a stranger by birth, almost always an alien in race, and, more hopeless still, a stranger by breeding, one who can never truly understand." See Helen Campbell, *Women Wage-Earners: Their Past, Their Present, and Their Future* (Boston: Roberts Brothers, 1893), 247; Campbell, *Household Economics*, 221; and Charlotte Stetson, *Women and Eco-nomics: A Study of the Economic Relation between Men and Women as a Fac-tor in Social Evolution* (Boston: Small, Maynard, 1898), 255–56. On the last, note a similar comment in Charlotte Perkins Gilman, *The Home: Its Work and Influ-ence* (New York: McClure, Phillips, 1903), 42–43. Gary Scharnhorst surveys con-temporary reception of *Women and Economics* and *The Home* in *Charlotte Perkins Gilman* (Boston: Twayne, 1985), 54–56 and 73–74.

74. See the unsigned "New Publications," *The Catholic World* 32 (December 1880): 43; and Marion Harland, *House and Home: A Complete Housewife's Guide* (Philadelphia: P. W. Zeigler, 1889), 102 and 92. Hale is mentioned in the latter on p. 116.

75. Marion Harland, "Why Not?" *The Independent* 51 (24 August 1899): 2291–92; and Harland, *House and Home*, 93.

76. See Lucy Maynard Salmon, *Domestic Service* (New York: Macmillan, 1897), 198.

Epilogue

The epigraph is from Lucy Maynard Salmon, "Recent Progress in the Study of Domestic Service," *Atlantic Monthly* 96 (November 1905): 629.

1. See Lucy Maynard Salmon, *Domestic Service* (New York: Macmillan, 1897), xii. This essay was collected in *Progress in the Household* (Boston and New York: Houghton, Mifflin, 1906).

2. See Thorstein Veblen, *The Theory of the Leisure Class* (New York: Macmillan, 1899), 60; and Flora McDonald Thompson, "The Servant Question," *The Cosmopolitan* 28 (March 1900): 522.

3. Salmon, "Recent Progress in the Study of Domestic Service," 630.

4. See Thomas Dixon Jr., *The Leopard's Spots* (Norborne, Mo.: Salon Publishing, n.d.), 261; and Salmon, "Recent Progress in the Study of Domestic Service," 629.

5. For "belated industry," see Jane Addams, "Social Control," *The American Journal of Sociology* 1 (March 1896): 513–50; and Mary Roberts Smith, "Domestic Service: The Responsibility of Employers," *The Forum* 27 (August 1899): 683. For the later view, see I. M. Rubinow and Daniel Durant, "The Depth and Breadth of the Servant Problem," *McClure's Magazine* (March 1910): 583.

6. See the anonymous reviews published as "Domestic Service," *The Critic* 30 (29 May 1897): 367; and C. R. Henderson, "Phases of the Social Question," *The Dial* 22 (1 May 1897): 285–87; but see also Katharine Pearson Woods, "The Art of Organised Living," *The Bookman* 5 (July 1897): 416.

7. See the untitled review in *The Nation* 64 (1 April 1897): 250.

8. See the untitled review of the revised edition of *Domestic Service* in *The Nation* 73 (11 July 1901): 39; see also Alice B. Neal, "The Servant Question," *GLB* 55 (October 1857): 329.

9. See Mary Clark Barnes, "The Science of Home Management," *North American Review* 167 (November 1898): 638; and I. M. Rubinow, "The Problem of Domestic Service," *Journal of Political Economy* 114 (October 1906): 502.

10. Bettina Berch, "'The Sphinx in the Household': A New Look at the History of Household Workers," *Review of Radical Political Economics* 16 (Spring 1984): 105 and 112; and Susan M. Strasser, "Mistress & Maid, Employer and Employee: Domestic Service Reform in the United States, 1897–1920," *Marxist Perspectives* 1 (Winter 1978): 52–67. For an academic criticism from Salmon's day, see Mabel Hurd Willett, "Domestic Service," *Political Science Quarterly* 18 (September 1903): 548. This was a review of the revised edition of Salmon's book.

11. See David M. Katzman, *Seven Days a Week: Women and Domestic Service in Industrializing America* (Urbana and Chicago: University of Illinois Press, 1981), 260.

12. Sarah Deutsch, *Women and the City: Gender, Space, and Power in Boston, 1870–1940* (New York: Oxford University Press, 2000), 66 and 76; Smith, "Domestic Service: The Responsibility of Employers," 679; and Lucy M. Salmon, "Economics and Ethics in Domestic Service," as reprinted in *Progress in the Household*, 105.

13. Mrs. M. E. W. Sherwood, "The Lack of Good Servants," *North American Review* 113 (November 1891): 553.

14. See Salmon, "Recent Progress in the Study of Domestic Service," 629.

15. Dominika Ferens offers a suggestive analysis of *The Diary of Delia* by treating it as a peculiar kind of ethnographic exercise; see *Edith and Winnifred Eaton: Chinatown Missions and Japanese Romances* (Urbana and London: University of Illinois Press, 2002), esp. 173–80.

16. Elizabeth Jordan—the editor who gave authors involved in this collaborative novel their assignments—is quite likely to have read Salmon's essay in *The Atlantic Monthly*. For more on the genesis of *The Whole Family* and its critique of powerful domestic myths, see chapters 1 and 4 of June Howard's *Publishing the Family* (Durham, N.C.: Duke University Press, 2001). For the exclusion of servants as conducted at the turn of the century, see Clifford Edward Clark Jr.'s observation that a "main difference between Victorian and Progressive middle-class houses was the absence of a back staircase in the homes built after 1910." Clark adds that the Progressive home had fewer exits and entrances; see *The American Family Home, 1800–1960* (Chapel Hill: University of North Carolina Press, 1986), 167.

17. See Florence M. Kingsley's contribution to "The Maid and the Mistress" (295), a cache of three short pieces about service (one by Salmon) published in *The Outlook* 78 (1 October 1904).

18. Sarah Deutsch found this remark from 1906 in the papers of the Women's Educational and Industrial Union; see *Women and the City*, 67.

19. Quite different from the other *Independent* articles named, because it painted a demeaning portrait of its putative narrator, the unsigned "Story of an Irish Cook" renews opinions first seen in the 1830s. "Mrs. Carr's interests was my interests," this family-like attendant recalls. "I took better care of her things than she did herself, and I loved the childher [*sic*] as if they was my own." See *The Independent* 58 (30 March 1905): 716.

20. The scholarship that drew my attention to Aunt Jemima's mobility was chapter 3 of Michael D. Harris, *Colored Pictures: Race and Visual Representation* (Chapel Hill: University of North Carolina Press, 2003). Harris cites the best previous studies of this advertising icon on p. 265 fn1.

21. See Howard, *Publishing the Family*, 231; and Salmon, *Domestic Service*, 261.

22. See Salmon, "Economics and Ethics in Domestic Service," 97–98.

23. See Salmon, *Domestic Service*, 200.

24. Ibid., 1 and xii–xiii.

25. See the entry on Sedgwick in James Barton Longacre and James Herring, *National Portrait Gallery of Distinguished Americans*, ed. Robert G. Stewart (New York: Arno Press and the New York Times, 1970), 363; and Ralph L. Rusk and Eleanor Tilton, eds., *The Letters of Ralph Waldo Emerson*, 9 vols. (New York: Columbia University Press, 1939–94), 3:154.

26. This proposal was revived five years later in a discussion of male table waiters. "There would probably be no more amusing volume than a history of the experience of those who have long employed him" because "[t]here is, perhaps, hardly any form of human 'cussedness' which they have not encountered, and probably nobody has thoroughly explored the more obscure recesses of

human character who has not had the management of him." See the anonymously authored "Social Distinctions from Bridget's Standpoint," 107; and "Waiters and Waitresses II," *The Nation* 19 (10 December 1874): 379.

27. See Grace A. Ellis, "Our Household Servants," *The Galaxy* 14 (September 1872): esp. 349–51; and the unsigned "Recent Literature," *Atlantic Monthly* 43 (May 1879): 684.

28. See Salmon, *Domestic Service*, xi; and the anonymous review in *The Critic*, 367.

29. See Henderson, "Phases of the Social Question," 287; and the untitled review in *The Nation* of the first edition of *Domestic Service*, 250.

30. For Salmon's relationship with "William," see Louise Fargo Brown, *Apostle of Democracy: The Life of Lucy Maynard Salmon* (New York: Harper, 1943), 120–21 and 198ff. By way of comparison, see Caroline L. Hunt's description of the innovations that a trained home economist worked out in her own home in *The Life of Ellen H. Richards* (Washington, D.C.: American Home Economics Association, 1958), 62ff. and 169–70.

31. See Salmon, *Domestic Service*, 149.

32. Ibid., 170; and Smith, "Domestic Service: The Responsibility of Employers," 689.

33. See W. E. B. Du Bois, *The Philadelphia Negro: A Social Study* (Philadelphia: published for the University of Pennsylvania, 1899), 136; "Reviews of Books," *American Historical Review* 6 (October 1900): 164; "The Philadelphia Negro," *The Outlook* 63 (11 November 1899): 647; and "Books and Authors," *The Outlook* 56 (5 June 1897): 361.

34. See Du Bois, *The Philadelphia Negro*, 137–38; and Barbara Ryan, "Old and New Issue Servants: 'Race' Men and Women Weigh In," in *Post-Bellum, Pre-Harlem: Re-Thinking African American Literature and Culture, 1880–1915*, ed. Barbara McCaskill and Caroline Gebhard (New York University Press, 89–100).

35. Edith Woodley, "Aunt Tabitha's Fireside: No IX: The Misery Caused by Using the Wrong Pudding-Dish," *GLB* 48 (February 1854): 150; and Kate M. H. [sic], "Mrs. Appleton's Maid," *GLB* 54 (June 1857): 495.

36. Edward Everett Hale's "Man Without a Country" (1865) is the story of a brash youngster who learns too late to love his native land. It was popular with U.S. pedagogues well into the twentieth century. Though the name "Norah" usually indicated a Celt during the later nineteenth century, this particular Norah is shown to speak standard English and to act appropriately (from her mistress's point of view) when working-class friends come to call. The inference is that she is of Irish descent but U.S. birth. See Inez Goodman, "A Nine-Hour Day for Domestic Servants," *The Independent* 54 (13 February 1902): 397–400; and Goodman, "Ten Weeks in a Kitchen," *The Independent* 53 (17 October 1901): 2459–64.

37. See Thompson, "The Servant Question," 521; and Salmon, "Recent Progress in the Study of Domestic Service," 633.

38. Lillian Pettengill, *Toilers of the Home: The Record of a College Woman's Experience as a Domestic Servant* (New York: Doubleday, Page, 1903), 241.

39. In contrast, Goodman waffled on the topic of coresidential service after claiming to take pride in providing her live-in employees with something more

than lodging. "The maid who has at her disposal all of the day except nine definite hours, will prefer to live at her own home," she averred, "and go to her work as a man goes to his." This was a good system, she added, because it cut down on the traffic in and out of an employer's kitchen, especially from "followers" and "beaus." See Goodman, "A Nine-Hour Day for Domestic Servants," 399.

40. Pettengill, *Toilers of the Home*, viii, 80, and 397.

41. See Salmon, *Domestic Service*, 52; and Spofford, "The Nature of Service," 770.

42. See Walter Fleming, "The Servant Problem in a Black Belt Village," *The Sewanee Review* 13 (January 1905): 11; but see also—if only to understand how little rigor might be required when the topic was nonkin service, even by scholarly journals—Mrs. Orra Langhorne, "Domestic Service in the South," *Journal of Social Science* 39 (November 1901): 170–71.

43. See Marion Harland, "One Housewife's Protest," *The Independent* 54 (6 March 1902): 564.

44. See Bertha M. Terrill, *Household Management* (Chicago: American School of Home Economics, 1907), 85, noting this text's near-quotation from *Domestic Service* on p. 98.

45. Harland closed out her advisorial career beaming about Irish attendants. "After much experience in, and more observation of, the Domestic Service of these United States," she affirmed, "I incline to believe that, as a rule, we draw our best material from Celtic emigrant stock." See Marion Harland, "Why Not?" *The Independent* 51 (24 August 1899): 2292; and Harland, *Marion Harland's Autobiography: The Story of a Long Life* (New York and London: Harper & Brothers, 1910), 359.

46. Mrs. A. J. [Margaret] Graves, *Woman in America: Being an Examination into the Moral and Intellectual Condition of American Female Society* (New York: Harper and Brothers, 1843), 88.

47. See Charles M. Sheldon, "Servant and Mistress," *The Independent* 52 (20 December 1900): 3018–21; and Salmon, *Domestic Service*, 261.

48. This remark may, of course, reflect deliberate strategizing, both here and when reprinted in section 9 of *The Souls of Black Folk* (1903). See W. E. B. Du Bois, "The Relation of the Negroes to the Whites in the South," *Annals of the American Academy of Political and Social Science* 18 (July 1901): 138.

49. This comment was recorded in the *Annual Report 1906* published by the Massachusetts Bureau of Statistics of Labor; Katzman quotes it in *Seven Days a Week*, 178.

50. See Thompson, "The Servant Question," 525.

51. As part of an excellent probe of press coverage of Mary Mallon's case, which notices scare comments such as the idea that this Irish cook was "practically a human vehicle for typhoid fever germs," Judith Walzer Leavitt quotes the *New York American* in *Typhoid Mary: Captive to the Public's Health* (Boston: Beacon Press, 1996), 128–29; see also p. 71. Cf. Alan Kraut's thoughtful work in *Silent Travelers: Germs, Genes, and the "Immigrant Menace"* (New York: Basic Books, 1994); for the quotation cited, see p. 102.

52. See the unsigned "Domestic Service," *Old and New* 6 (September 1872): 363; and Catharine Maria Sedgwick, *Live and Let Live; or, Domestic Service Illustrated* (New York: Harper & Brothers, 1837), 191.

53. For "sarvant," see C. W. Janson in *The Stranger in America: Containing Observations Made during a Long Residence in That Country, on the Genius, Manners and Customs of the People of the United States* (London: Albion Press, 1807), 87; while for Alexander Saxton's observation, see *The Rise and Fall of the White Republic: Class Politics and Mass Culture in Nineteenth-Century America* (London and New York: Verso, 1990), 110ff.

54. Sean Wilentz discussed this episode in "Crime, Poverty and the Streets of New York City: The Diary of William H. Bell, 1850–51," *History Workshop* 7 (Spring 1979): 126–55.

55. See Rubinow, "The Problem of Domestic Service," 516; and Terrill, *Household Management,* 181.

INDEX

BARBARA RYAN teaches in the University Scholars Programme at the National University of Singapore. After winning two fellowships and a dissertation award from the University of North Carolina at Chapel Hill, she became a junior member of the Society of Fellows at the University of Michigan. Under the Society's auspices, she began to craft *Love, Wages, Slavery* while coediting an essay collection titled *Reading Acts: U.S. Readers' Interactions with Literature, 1800–1950* (University of Tennessee Press, 2002).

The University of Illinois Press
is a founding member of the
Association of American University Presses.

Composed in 9.5/12.5 Trump Mediaeval
by BookComp, Inc.
Manufactured by Thomson-Shore, Inc.

University of Illinois Press
1325 South Oak Street
Champaign, IL 61820-6903
www.press.uillinois.edu